GILBERT WHITE

Richard Mabey has been described by *The Times* as 'Britain's foremost nature writer'. He is the author of *Flora Britannica*, which was the winner of the British Book Awards Illustrated Book of the Year, and the Botanical Society of the British Isles' President's Award. His biography of Gilbert White won the Whitbread Biography Award in 1986, and his memoir *Nature Cure* was shortlisted for the same prize in 2005.

Richard Mabey's other books include *Food for Free, The Common Ground*, *Whistling in the Dark* (a personal study of the nightingale), *The Frampton Flora* and *Home Country*. He is a regular broadcaster and contributor to *The Times*, *Guardian* and *Granta*.

After spending most of his life in the Chilterns, he now lives in Norfolk, where he is President of the Norfolk and Norwich Naturalists' Society.

GILBERT WHITE

A Biography of the Author of
The Natural History of Selborne

———————

RICHARD MABEY

P

PROFILE BOOKS

This edition published in Great Britain in 2006 by
PROFILE BOOKS LTD
3A Exmouth House
Pine Street
London EC1R 0JH
www.profilebooks.com

First published in Great Britain in by
Century Hutchinson Ltd 1986
Pimlico edition 1999

1 3 5 7 9 10 8 6 4 2

Printed and bound in Great Britain by
Bookmarque Ltd, Croydon, Surrey

A CIP catalogue record for this book is available from the British Library.

ISBN-10: 1 86197 807 3
ISBN-13: 978 1 86197 807 3

To Ronald Blythe and Charles Clark

CONTENTS

ACKNOWLEDGEMENTS

My thanks for help in locating, viewing and interpreting source material to: the Bodleian Library, Oxford; June Chatfield and the Gilbert White Museum, Selborne; the Hampshire Record Office; the Hertfordshire County Library Service; Melanie Wisner and the Houghton Library, Harvard University; Oriel College Library, Oxford; Mrs Parry-Jones and Magdalen College Archives, Oxford; and Ian Lyle, Librarian of the Royal College of Surgeons, in whose keeping the working manuscript of the *Natural History* is currently resting.

Thanks also to those who helped with ideas, information and guidance during the preparation of the text: David Elliston Allen; Tara Heinemann; Chris Mead of the British Trust for Ornithology; Richard North; Max Nicholson; Philip Oswald; David Standing, curator of the Wakes' garden; and Dafydd Stephens. A special thank you to Anne Mallinson of the Selborne Bookshop, who was an unfailing source of support, contacts and local information.

I am grateful to the Leverhulme Trust for a research award that greatly facilitated my work in Oxford and Selborne, and to Wilfrid Knapp and the Fellows of St Catherine's College, Oxford, for their hospitality. Vicky and Ian Thomson were also generous with hospitality in Hampshire.

Sandra Raphael, Francesca Greenoak, Richard Simon and Isabella Forbes made valuable comments on various drafts. My assistant, Robin McIntosh, worked tirelessly, as usual, especially in the final stages.

Finally, I must express my warmest gratitude to Charles Clark, for suggesting that I write this biography in the first instance, and for his support and faith during its protracted progress; and to Ronald Blythe, whose advice, example and encouragement were a constant inspiration.

ILLUSTRATIONS

(Between pages 114 and 115)

The language of birds is very ancient, and, like other ancient modes of speech, very elliptical: little is said, but much is meant and understood.

Gilbert White, Letter XLIII to Daines Barrington, 9 September 1778

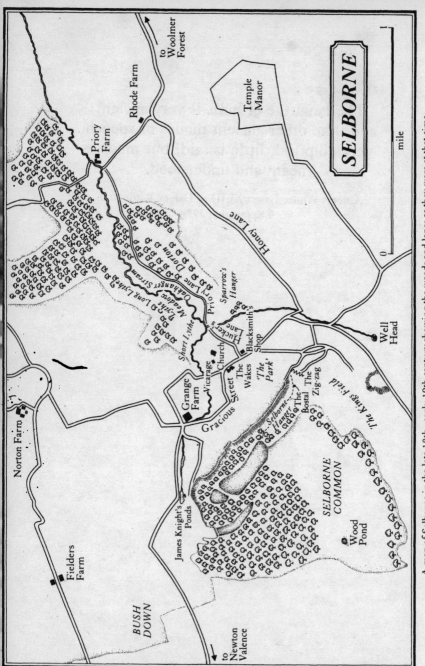

A map of Selborne in the late 18th – early 19th century showing the woods and lanes as they were at that time.

GILBERT WHITE

The British have for a long time regarded their relationship with the countryside as something quite distinctive, a badge of cultural identity. Despite having become a largely urban people, we continue to admire the rural village as the ideal form of community, and have an affection for the native that is probably without parallel in the industrialized world. It is a passion which has sometimes deteriorated into sentimentality, and which doesn't always have a very clear view of history, but it has left an indelible mark on our way of life. And standing as its principal text, as the first book to link the worlds of nature and the village, is Gilbert White's *The Natural History of Selborne*. This deceptively simple and unpretentious account of natural comings and goings in an eighteenth-century Hampshire parish has come to be regarded as one of the most perfectly realized celebrations of nature in the English language. The American writer J.R. Lowell once described it as 'the journal of Adam in Paradise'.[1] This was extravagant even by the generous standards of the tributes heaped upon this book, yet Lowell had succeeded in catching something essential about both the man and his writing. Selborne, the real English village that is the setting for the book, may fall a mite short as a model for paradise; but the dramas of courtship, birth, survival and migration that are played out in its woods and fields, have, as recounted by White, something almost sacramental about them, Although he lived at a time when the rule of reason and the supremacy of man were accepted almost as gospel, White contrived to portray the daily business of lesser creatures as a source not just of interest, but of delight and inspiration. To that extent the book is a glimpse of a place of sanctuary.

What is extraordinary, given the book's originality and importance, is how little is known about its author. To cast him as Adam, as Lowell did, is an example of the way his life and character have been repeatedly idealized, as if knowing too much about him might break the spell. This is a common enough process with national heroes, and is arguably a perfectly sufficient reason for a biography. Yet it is as well to make clear that I had an additional motive in beginning this study. Not long after discovering White, I began to be struck by what a modern figure he was; by the way that many of his attitudes and problems – for instance, how to reconcile a love for nature with an enjoyment of the stimulation of urban life – had recognizable parallels today; and most strongly, by how the facts of his protracted, compromised but ultimately triumphant resolution of these difficulties shone through the sentimental mists with which we shroud so much of our rural past, as a heartening and exemplary story.

But I must confess that, like many others, I did not come painlessly to the *Natural History*. For years I was put off by the aura of sanctity and bluffness which seemed to surround it. It was the kind of book presented on prize-giving days, and I saw it as a work, in all senses, of the old school. Even when I eventually came to read it, I cannot say my opinion changed dramatically. I could not cope at first with its rambling disorder, its sudden plunges into thickets of taxonomic Latin, and, for a while, I failed to notice the feeling behind the often dispassionate prose. Occasional, brilliant images floated up – scenes at night, when 'goat-suckers glance in the dusk over the tops of trees', and you could watch 'the proceedings and manoevres of rooks' – but not enough to dispel a certain coolness about the book as a whole.

It was seeing Selborne itself, the source of White's inspiration, that changed my view decisively, and helped me to understand what the book was truly about. I suspect this realization would have come eventually, but the village proved to be a powerful catalyst. It is not that it trumpets its associations with White. There are no elaborate monuments or commemorative street names. Even Gilbert's grave is hard to find and, stretched between two weatherbeaten stones, seems more like the resting-place of a small farmer, fallen on hard times, than a world-famous author.

But fortunately the landscape of the parish has changed very little since the eighteenth century. There is no need to view it through the glass of nostalgia or pastoral whimsy, because you can touch the actual stuff of White's writings. There might be little chance these days of seeing forty ravens playing over the Hanger, as there were one morning in the autumn of 1778; yet the beechwoods that cloak this steep hill behind the village are just as extensive as they were in the eighteenth century. So is the vast thousand-year-old yew tree, under which now lies the grave of a man who took part in the local farm labourers' uprising against the iniquities of the tithe system, thirty-five years after White's death. And the intricate network of sunken lanes still give a palpable sense of the kind of enclosed, intimate world that White lived in and immortalized. The fact that it is a living landscape prevents Selborne becoming some kind of sentimental museum piece; and it was precisely its sense of vitality and change inside an ancient framework that, for me, began to dissolve the veils of myth and remoteness from White, and show him as a real person in a real place.

Selborne, the village, also reveals White as a man whose active originality went some way beyond the writing of one considerable book. He helped dig the paths up the Hanger that are still the first port of call for modern pilgrims. He was an impassioned and progressive gardener, not just of conventional flowers and vegetables, but huge melon beds, home-made follies, and wild-flower patches. All this activity was recorded in a series of journals that developed, in Gilbert's middle years, into a continuous record of the natural year in Selborne that in its immediacy and sense of the continuity of life has no parallel in the eighteenth century. Two hundred years ago he wrote, on 4 June:

> Several halo's & mock suns this morning. Wheat looks black, & gross. Crickets sing much on the hearth this evening: they feel the influence of moist air, & sing against rain. As the great wall-nut tree has no foliage this year, we have hung the meat-safe on Miss White's Sycomore, which she planted as a nut.[2]

The journals lead one inevitably back to the *Natural History*,

4

the single reason why Gilbert White has been remembered. There is nothing whatever unusual in his earning a place in literary history on the strength of a single book. Exactly the same happened to two authors with whom he is often grouped, John Bunyan and Izaak Walton. What is remarkable is that he was able to produce something so wholly original and appealing out of such unpromising ingredients. For a writer, White's credentials hardly give one any expectation of what he was capable of: a country curate, never even a vicar, who spent the bulk of his life in the house where he was born. The book, at first sight, seems no more promising. On the surface the *Natural History* is nothing more than a casually edited collection of letters. Its tone is conversational and unprepossessing. By the somewhat self-satisfied intellectual standards of the time, it pays a quite disproportionate attention to trifling topics, like the singing of crickets, the subtleties of echoes and the way a pair of flycatchers kept their young cool in summer by fanning their wings above the nest.

Yet it was precisely this unorthodox focus that was the most radically original aspect of the book. The *Natural History* is a tribute to the detail and variety of life, a celebration of nature's 'minute particulars'. This is what makes it a unique breath of fresh air from a century that was still largely preoccupied with idealized notions of the power of reason, which had not yet realized that its expansive gestures and grand theories rested on the small, real facts of the world. Samuel Johnson, meditating among the echoing Celtic landscapes of the Inner Hebrides, caught the dilemma of the Age of Enlightenment perfectly:

> To abstract the mind from all local emotion would be impossible, if it were endeavoured, and would be foolish, if it were possible. Whatever withdraws us from the power of our senses, whatever makes the past, the distant, or the future predominate over the present, advances us in the dignity of thinking being.[3]

It was against this climate that White insisted that the

5

senses, far from suppressing local emotion, were the most powerful agents for summoning it up. Choosing as his arena the smallest and most intimate unit of human social life, a country village where he lived himself, he showed how watching the natural world at close quarters could generate not just understanding but respect, and an insight into the kindredness of living things. It was this blending of the scientific and emotional responses to nature that was White's greatest legacy, and its influence has been far-reaching. It helped foster the growth of ecology, and the realization that humans were also part of the natural scheme of things. It helped pioneer, too, that affectionate writing about place that has become part of the mainstream of English literature.

Yet the *Natural History* is not just a classic text in the development of our view of nature. For better or for worse, it has also become an institution, and a major consideration for any biographer is the fact that *The Natural History of Selborne* has become part of that curious concoction of ideas and artefacts which are seen as somehow defining 'the English way of life'. It is, apocryphally, the fourth most frequently published book in the language. When English settlers emigrated to the colonies in the last century, *Selborne* was packed alongside the family Bibles and sprigs of heather. It is hard to think of another book that could have brought together so many disparate voices to pay their respects. Coleridge jotted notes in the margin of his copy, and thought it 'a sweet delightful book'. Darwin praised it as one of the chief reasons for his interest in biology. W.H. Auden wrote an affectionate 'Posthumous Letter to Gilbert White'. And Virginia Woolf described the *Natural History* as 'one of those ambiguous books that seem to tell a plain story ... and yet by some apparently unconscious device of the author's has a door left open, through which we hear distant sounds'.[4]

The sheer depth of this affection becomes at once both an incentive for learning more about the man at its centre, and a major obstacle to succeeding. For it has helped to generate a formidable alternative life-story: the myth of Parson White. This figure is one of the long line of robust, guileless, instinctive and entirely fictitious countrymen with which we have peopled our rural past. His function is to safeguard the Selborne legend, and, though he appears in a number of guises, one assumption run through them all. This is that White was himself a figure from a pastoral, a kind of ruminant tranquil, simple, wholesome and unworldly. He wrote from his heart – his own nature – not from his head. And it was only because he had such qualities that he was able to write the book he did.

The myth has reached high places over the years. It is there in Lowell's 'Adam in Paradise' and Woolf's 'unconscious device' just as much as in the more blatant version of the modern editor who suggested that 'White rejoiced in his world, as a spaniel may rejoice to find new smells in the hedgerow.'[5] And few of those who have succumbed are as honest about their motives as Edward Thomas: 'In this present year, 1915, at least, it is hard to find a flaw in the life he led, which we may be excused for looking back upon dotingly as upon some inaccessible and imperturbable tract of our life.'[6]

The first versions of the myth began to appear during the period of rural unrest in the 1820s and 1830s, and have perceptible political undertones. The earliest I have been able to trace is from John Constable, writing at a time when he was having trouble in reconciling his love of Suffolk landscapes with his distaste for the cussedness and vulgarity of the labourers who inhabited them. In a letter to Archdeacon John Fisher in 1821 he applauded the example of the *Natural History*: 'It only shows what a real love for nature will do – surely the serene and blameless life of Mr White, so different from the folly and quackery of the world, must have fitted him for such a clear and intimate view of nature.'[7] But the official beginnings of Selborne mythology, the consecration of book and place as ingredients of an idyll, is usually credited to a journalist from the *New Monthly Magazine*. He visited the village only a couple of years after the 'Captain Swing' uprisings swept across the agricultural areas of southern England, Selborne included, in 1830, and this is what he chose to see:

> Chimneys reeking with evidence of clean hearths in full activity, walls neatly covered with vine and creepers in full bloom, and trim little gardens prank'd with flowers, seemed here to tell only of cheerful toil and decent competence, nor did it enter into the charmed fancy to enquire how often crime and wretchedness might disturb such a haven of rest. The whole landscape, indeed, so far surpassed expectation, as to seem almost too beauteous for reality.[8]

In wartime the *Natural History* has frequently been seen both as an escape from the realities of the war (see Thomas above) and as part of what was being fought for. Writing during the height of the Blitz in 1941, James Fisher found an explanation for White's appeal 'not in what he says so much as in the way he says it. His world is round and simple and complete; the British country; the perfect escape. No breath of the outside world enters in; no politics; no ambition; no care or cost.'[9]

But, from the late Victorian period onwards, White has most frequently been cast as a primitive, whose writing was not so much the product of intelligence and hard work as of a fortunate gift, as singing is to a bird. J.R. Lowell linked White with Izaak Walton as a folk-writer. 'Nature has endowed these men with the simple skill to make happiness out of the cheap material that is within the means of the poorest of us. The good fairy gave them to weave cloth of gold out of straw.'[10]

A short while later another American essayist, John Burroughs, plunged even deeper into organic metaphor:

> The privacy and preoccupation of the author are like those of the bird building her nest, or the bee gathering her sweets .... So many learned treatises have sunk beneath the waves upon which this little cockleshell of a book rides so safely and buoyantly. What is the secret of its longevity? One can

do little more than name its qualities without tracing them to their sources. It is simple and wholesome, like bread, or meat, or milk.[11]

This process of simplification has extended into White's private life. He has been presented as a recluse, an ascetic, even a village mystic. His relative and biographer Rashleigh Holt-White went so far as to pronounce: 'White had but one mistress: Selborne.' But nothing can quite prepare one for the daring invention of the bibliographer Edward Martin, who by joining together two separate rural stereotypes, succeeded in transforming Parson White into a Gentleman Jim:

> True manliness was in as much estimation in White's day as in our own, and we may be sure that he would not have received the boisterous welcome of the undergraduates of Oxford so often and apparently so gladly, were he of any type but that of a true, manly, and in sense, muscular, English gentleman.[12]

It is no surprise to find that he was eventually canonized as 'St' Gilbert by one of his eulogizers.[13]

*

To be fair, it is not just our obstinate desire to see the countryside and all things connected with it as refuges of peace and simplicity that has nurtured these caricatures of Gilbert White. There is also a great lack of direct evidence about the kind of person he was. Very little is known about his parents, or about the kind of upbringing he had. His correspondence with family and friends (much of it collected into Holt-White's *Life and Letters*, 1901) is fulsome about his home life and natural history activities, but reserved and circumspect when it comes to his emotional life. His remarkable journals also survive in manuscript in the British Library, but in forty years of almost continuous daily entries there is scarcely one that refers directly to his feelings. For these we have to turn, ironically, to a series of letters *to* him, from his close friend, John Mulso. Mulso's intimate, garrulous record of their long friendship is the best evidence there is about the texture of Gilbert's private life, and this biography is also, in part, the story of his life, as a very different – if entirely complementary – eighteenth-century character.

Circumstantial evidence about Gilbert's life is much more plentiful, particularly about conditions in Selborne itself, and about the larger intellectual and literary parish in which he moved. I must pay a debt here to those writers who have penetrated beyond the mythology, not only in suggesting interpretations of White's work and importance, but contributing new information about the parish and Gilbert's circle of friends; especially Edmund Blunden, Cecil Emden, H.J. Massingham, Max Nicholson and Anthony Rye.[14] Other valuable sources of parish evidence have been the Hampshire Record Office and the archives of Magdalen College, Oxford, which was the Lord of the Manor in the eighteenth century.

· A major aim of this biography is to explore these links between White and the eighteenth-century world of, and beyond, Selborne, and to avoid the usual assumption that the secret of his genius lay in a remoteness from outside influences. For instance, how much did his frequent mixing with literary society in Fleet Street shape his decision to write a book? Was his natural history truly original or merely an extension, or synthesis, of trends that were already in motion?

The study of natural history in the eighteenth century was breaking away from the closed superstitious world of medieval thinking. People were beginning to look about them, to ask what at times seemed like heretical questions, to put ideas to the test. Yet some of the old myths proved extraordinarily persistent, as did a belief that the natural world ought to conform to various moral orders. Gilbert White's major reference book on birds, Willughby's *Ornithology* (first published in 1678) had more on the distillation of swallows to produce a cure for the falling sickness than it did on the bird's nesting habits, and it devoted several pages to a detailed account of a group of nightingales discussing the European wars. Writers such as Robert Plot had begun to publish county studies but these were severe in style and indiscriminate in the way they mixed fact and fable. Before White, work on the natural history of a single parish would have been regarded as absurdly disproportionate, presupposing far too much in the way of local idiosyncrasy.

What was missing from the mainstream of natural history in the mid-eighteenth century was any sense of intimacy or wonder or respect – in short, of human engagement with nature. In some ways the contemporary belief in the power of reason was as great an obstruction to understanding as it was a means to knowledge. It tended to give humans an over-developed feeling of superiority over nature, to encourage the separation of observed facts from all the rich symbolism and associations that lay behind them.

This was perhaps less true of the school of thought which was the major influence on White's attitude to nature. 'Physico-theology' had been pioneered by John Ray, in *The Wisdom of God* (1691) and later by William Derham, and was, in Derham's words, 'a Demonstration of the Being and Attributes of God from his Works of Creation'.[15]. It was an exploration of design in nature, and a celebration of the miraculous way that the world fitted together and worked. To sceptical modern minds physico-theology is nothing more than a collection of truisms: creatures which were not properly 'designed' for their ways of life would simply cease to be. And combined with the persistent belief in the centrality of man, it threw up some ludicrous inverted arguments, like Ray's assertion that there was exactly the correct amount of gold and silver in the Earth's crust to regulate human trade; and Derham's that human beings were made the height that they were to enable them to ride horses. But it is too easy to poke fun at physico-theology. Its precepts meant a wholly new faith in and commitment to observation of Creation's *real* works, that made the earlier adherence to the divining of symbolism and pattern seem almost blasphemous. And in making clear the connections –

however obvious – between the way that organisms lived and the character of their surroundings, Ray and Derham were also pioneering the study of ecology.

*

This was the kind of intellectual background against which White's thinking and work must be seen. Yet there is an important sense in which his formal scientific discoveries (which have always been overplayed) were much less significant than the way in which he viewed the world and his place in it. Throughout his life he ignored orthodox demarcation lines, between art and science, fact and feeling. He discovered how a nightjar produced its song while he was picnicking in a Hermitage. He put up an extraordinary fake wooden statue not yards from the wild wood on the Hanger. His exact descriptions of weather sound, at times, like the pronouncements of a medieval soothsayer. In fact, the more he reveals his sensuous enjoyment of the natural world and his sympathy with the joys and sufferings of its inhabitants, the more he begins to resemble an early nineteenth-century romantic just as much as an eighteenth-century rationalist.

These questions of motive and purpose are central. Did Gilbert set out to make an original interpretation of the world? Was his commitment to Selborne carefully planned, part of an equally conscious decision to dedicate his life to writing a single book? White mythology often suggests a kind of earth-destiny to account for the conception of the *Natural History*: 'Selborne bore him, drew him, held him. Everything shaped and turned to the end that he should settle there and perfect work which could not be done elsewhere.'[16] The evidence, as it unfolds, tends to suggest an altogether more human mixture of accident, opportunity, natural talent and instinctive attachment.

It is this honest muddle of instinct and affection in White's superficially ordered life that joins him most closely with the creatures that he loved and studied. Gilbert was fascinated by instinct, and especially by the thought that it could guide small birds on vast journeys across the globe.

Migration was one of the most vexed questions in eighteenth-century science and philosophy, and many thinkers found it impossible – or just too humiliating – to believe that blind instinct could achieve feats of navigation that superior human intelligence was only just mastering.[17] No wonder many old superstitions about swallows hibernating, in ponds or caves, were revived as eighteenth-century 'modern myths': dumb sleep was so much less unsettling as an instinctual gift.

Yet as Gilbert returns to this question time and time again, it is clear that, for him, it was not just a scientific problem. He was intrigued and delighted by the annual return (or re-awakening) of his favourite parish birds, the swallows, swifts and martins; and increasingly their loyalty to the village seemed to echo his own not entirely rational attachment to Selborne. His book is, above all, an exploration of these links between humans and other creatures, a celebration of the life of a whole community. Gilbert White could perhaps have written the *Natural History* in some other village; but it would have had to have been his *own*.

Chapter Two

'A place of responses
or echoes'

Gilbert White made his home in Selborne for the last sixty-odd years of his life. He was also, by a curious stroke of fortune, born there, only a hundred yards from the house in which he died. Ancestors of the Selborne Whites had lived in the area at least as far back as the early sixteenth century. At different times branches of the family had settled in Farnham (Surrey), Basingstoke (Hampshire) and South Warnborough (also in Hampshire and just ten miles north of Selborne). Gilbert's great-grandfather, Sir Samson White, was born at Cogges, near Witney, Oxfordshire, and later became Lord Mayor of Oxford. So when his son, another Gilbert, accepted the living of Selborne in 1681, he was not venturing into completely foreign territory. He was 31 years old at the time, and a junior Fellow of Magdalen College, Oxford (Lords of the Manor of Selborne and patrons of the living of St Mary's Church). When the younger Gilbert came to reflect on his grandfather's appointment to a full vicarship at such a comparatively young age and low rank, he concluded it was because of the 'low estimation' in which the parish was held by Magdalen. The living, he discovered, had a long history of neglect. Fifty years previously the incumbent had been deprived of his income throughout the period of the Commonwealth, and had 'retired to a little tenement about a hundred and fifty yards from the church, where he earned a small pittance by the practice of physic'. He was restored in 1660, but was so impoverished that 'he left the vicarage-house and premises in a very abject and dilapidated state.' His successor had plans to start repairs but they were cut short by his death.

It was left to Gilbert's grandfather to make the vicarage a more agreeable place to live:

> At his first coming he ceiled the chancel, and also floored and wainscoted the parlour and hall, which before were paved with stone, and had naked walls; he enlarged the kitchen and brewhouse, and dug a cellar and well: he also built a large new barn in the lower yard, removed the hovels in the front court, which he laid out in walks and borders; and

entirely planned the back garden, before a rude field with a stone-pit in the midst of it.[1]

These sound like the actions of a man who had decided to put down roots in the village, and a few years later Gilbert confirmed this by marrying a local farmer's daughter. Rebekah Luckin was fourteen years his junior, but came from a family that had farmed in the nearby hamlet of Noar (or Nore) Hill for generations. 'Luckin's hedge' is listed as one of the traditional landmarks in the Selborne parish boundary.

Rebekah proved to be a strong and dependable partner and it may well have been her influence that persuaded the Whites to remain in Selborne, despite the village's comparative remoteness from the mainstream of rural society. It was an isolated, independent community in the eighteenth century, with no dominant local landowner and poor communications with the outside world. The nearest city, Winchester, was only fifteen miles to the west, but since the Romans had built a road between Winchester and Farnham that effectively bypassed the village, it had become a backwater, on the way to nowhere. Even William Cobbett, who had spent the first fourteen years of his life at Farnham, just ten miles to the north, seemed unfamiliar with it when he passed that way in 1822:

> I forgot to mention, that, in going from Hawkley to Greatham, the man, who went to show me the way, told me at a certain fork, 'That road goes to *Selborne*.' This put me in mind of a book, which was once recommended to me, but which I never saw, entitled '*The Natural History and Antiquities of Selborne*', (or something of that sort) written, I think, by a parson of the name of *White*.[2]

Selborne's inconspicuousness was largely the result of local geography. It lies on the western edge of the Hampshire Weald, a mass of steep, convoluted chalk hills covered, then as now, with woodland. The local roads kept largely to the low ground, and in many places had been worn deep into the soft chalk and sandstone rocks. In winter these hollow lanes filled with mud, water and sometimes snow and became inpassable to coach traffic. Even the chief way into the village, from Alton in the north, was little more than a sunken, rutted track, 18 feet below ground level in places and little more than 8 feet wide. It was not until 1847 that a properly surfaced road was built overland from Alton. Twelve years previously the writer James Mudie (who was preparing a topographical note for Edward Blyth's edition of the *Natural History*) had discovered what formidable obstacles to easy access these hollow lanes presented:

> all the way from Harteley, which is at least two miles, the traveller sees little, save a narrow stripe of sky, and steep banks, almost perpendicular, so near to each other that one carriage cannot pass another except at particular points, and presenting a mass of tangled roots interspersed with shivered rocks.[3]

Mudie had also begun to realize that this sense of being enclosed, wrapped-in, was an essential characteristic of the local landscape. Although he regarded Selborne as a beautiful spot, he saw 'no possibility of obtaining even a tolerable first or general view of it and at the same time enjoying the luxury of a carriage'.

*

Gilbert and Rebekah settled in at Selborne and produced six children. It was their eldest son John, born in 1688, who was to become the father of the Selborne naturalist. He qualified as a barrister, and eventually became a JP, but he never seems to have practised, and admitted later to a deep mistrust of the whole legal profession. When he was 31 he married Anne Holt, a rector's daughter from Streatham and an heiress in a small way, and retired to the country. Very little more is heard of him. He never worked and apparently did little at home except play the harpsichord and potter in the garden. Except for respectful and formal references, his family rarely mention him in their letters, and, by default, a picture of a rather inadequate and withdrawn personality emerges. In the little hard evidence available, he was hypochondriacal and found it hard to cope with his affairs. He may well have been a depressive.

John and Anne probably spent the first year after their marriage in September 1719 living with John's parents in Selborne, and it was there, ten months later, that Gilbert the younger was born, on 18 July 1720. Later that year John and Anne moved to a house of their own in the village of Compton near Guildford, and over the next seven years Anne gave birth regularly every September or October. Three children died in infancy. The next oldest to survive, Thomas (born in October 1724) went on to become a successful London merchant and amateur scholar. Benjamin (born in September 1725) was destined to become a distinguished bookseller and to publish Gilbert's *Natural History*. Rebecca (born in October 1726) married Mr Henry Woods and settled in Chilgrove, Sussex. John (born in September 1727) followed Gilbert to Oxford, and into the Church, but found himself in trouble in circumstances that were to cast a shadow over the rest of his life. Another son, Francis, was born in March 1728 or 1729 (the year is not recorded) while John and Anne were living briefly at East Harting, in Sussex. He died when he was little more than 21.

On 13 February 1728 or 1729, the Reverend Gilbert White died, and his widow, together with her two unmarried daughters, moved across the street to a house known as the Wakes,* which Gilbert had purchased and bequeathed to them for just this purpose. It was a smallish place then, with none of the rambling extensions it now sprouts. But when both daughters were married, on the same day in January 1729 or 1730 – Dorothea to her father's successor, the Reverend Basil Cane, and Elizabeth to a cousin, Charles White – it must have seemed little more than a lonely and echoing shell to Rebekah, 66 years old and used to having people around her all her life.

---

* The house is more properly known as Wakes', having once belonged to a family of the same name. But 'the Wakes' is the form now in common usage.

The obvious solution, now that John's swelling family had no permanent roots, was that they should come back to Selborne and move in with her at the Wakes. This they did, and the younger Gilbert thus returned to his birthplace at the age of about 9. Within three years he had acquired another brother and sister. Anne (born in April 1731) married Thomas Barker, of Lyndon Hall in Rutland, and some forty years later became one of Gilbert's favourite correspondents. Henry (born in June 1733) later went to Oxford and became rector of Fyfield, twenty-five miles north-west of Selborne.

By 1733 there were eleven people packed into a house which probably had no more than five bedrooms, two of them attics. It may have been a cheerful dormitory atmosphere for the six youngest Whites, who were then all under 8 years old; but Gilbert was a crucial five years older than his oldest brother, Thomas, and from the age of 10 must have become accustomed to being by himself. His father, with no work to do, acted as an occasional tutor, but, prone as he was to melancholy and withdrawal, can't have been much company for his son.

During these last and rather solitary childhood years Gilbert must have spent much of his time exploring the countryside round Selborne, and it would be surprising if he hadn't the same physical curiosity about natural history as most country boys of that age. But it does not seem to have been a formal interest, to the extent that he kept notes or a regular journal. (By contrast, his future brother-in-law, Thomas Barker of Lyndon, two years his junior, had begun a nature diary at the age of 10. A couple of austere notes penned in this diary in the spring of 1736 are the only surviving record of Gilbert's early interest in natural history. 'A flock of geese flew N' the first reads, adding – in acknowledgement to the observer – the initials G.W. Gilbert was 15 at the time and probably spending the Easter holidays with his aunt, Mary Isaac, at Whitwell rectory, a couple of miles away.) Whatever his childhood experiences of Selborne's countryside and wildlife, they did not seem to be the kind which may be recalled as precise memories, and Gilbert's writings are unusual for the lack of specific references to, or anecdotes from, his early years. But one aspect certainly made a lasting – though possibly unconscious – impression on him, and that was the character of the Selborne landscape. The parish, as we shall see, contains a great variety of scenery within a comparatively small compass, and the mere fact of being able to pass from water meadow to rocky lane to wooded hill-top in a five-minute walk would have been an education for young Gilbert. Long before he became detached enough to realize he was living in a geographically privileged parish, or self-consciously to contemplate 'the view', he would have been imprinted by the essential qualities of the local landscape.

What were these? For once, it's possible to hint at an answer from modern evidence, because the countryside in the vicinity of the village has changed very little. It's the kind of dense, luxuriant, muddled landscape which is still quite common in the hillier regions of southern England; but which in Selborne has been emphasized by a combination of local geology and social history. It is highly distinctive, a matter not just of particular features but of the relations between them. These are some notes which I took in November 1983, trying to capture these characteristics in the jumble of damp closes and copses that lies between the church and the Lythes, one of Gilbert's favourite walks:

> No real views or prospects – except momentarily glimpsed through the trees, and framed in a gap at the end of the valley. What you do see is much more a matter of close-up detail and texture: layered freestone; tree-roots contoured round the layers; fungus on the dying trees, saplings in the gaps left by fallen trunks, yet these textured too – bent, opportunist, twiggy, eaten, snapped, re-shooting. Beyond the trees, broken, tufty grass, surrounded by more woods; dips in the ground; tiny coppices in further dips just visible by the tops of their winter twigs; glimpses of water – in ruts, pools, winding drainage ditches, but mostly invisible until

you are close by, hidden by trees and tussocks; the water broken up, too – shelves of gravel in the streamlets, bays, cattle wallows, loops and islets, fallen trees bridging the water and entangled with the hedges.

The pattern is repeated, though without so much water, up on the common, and in the deep lanes that cut through the parish. It is a quirky, unexpected, intimate mixture, full of vitality and a sense of interdependence, that draws you down into its details, not into generalities beyond. It is also a landscape which could hardly fail to mould the outlook of any sensitive young person who spent a good deal of time inside it, and it is echoed not just in the contents of White's book, but in the rhythms and structure of much of the writing itself. White, I am sure, was conscious of this. The second of his letters to Thomas Pennant (Letter X in the *Natural History*) is typical of his rambling style. He chats enthusiastically about the eating habits of young owls, the ducks that visit the woodland ponds, and a house-martin glimpsed in Oxford in early winter. Then he breaks off, almost apologetically, and attempts to explain this torrent of discursive ornithology. 'The parish I live in,' he writes 'is a very abrupt, uneven country, full of hills and woods, and therefore full of birds.'[4] It is not hard to imagine him being struck by this thought, out, perhaps, on one of the network of paths that lead out of the Wakes' meadows and switch-back and criss-cross along the foot of the Hanger.

The landscape of the entire parish repeated this unpredictable, muddled mix, whether in deep woodland or out on the open heaths of Woolmer Forest. Only in the north-western quarter, in the flat 'champain' country of hop and arable fields was it conspicuously more ordered.

The danger here, of course, is of interpreting the lie of the land with tutored hindsight, of putting modern sensibilities into eighteenth-century heads. Yet in the earliest indigenous description of the local scenery, the highly functional 'Directory of the Bounds', the scenery sounds every bit as 'abrupt and uneven' as it does in White's descriptions.

Beating the Bounds, or Perambulation, was kept up in Selborne at sporadic intervals throughout the seventeenth and eighteenth centuries, becoming more frequent at times of uncertainty and dispute about land-rights. Traditionally the ceremony was carried out to check that the boundary landmarks were still in place, and to impress on each new generation of village children precisely where the ancient demarcation lines between parish and parish lay. The route was normally passed down through collective memory, but after the 1703 walk (in which Gilbert's grandfather took part) the details – 'Taken from the oldest records as they were constantly perambulated in ancient Times' – were inscribed in the Parish Register. This is an extract from the route taken during the afternoon of the first day:

> From thence inclining to the right hand towards Park Pond, the Bounds are through the middle of the said Pond: and then keeping straight on across the Park up the Hill, leave forked Pond a little on the left hand, thence over the next Hill into the Bottom, keeping near to the Edge of Grigg's Green, and over the moor that lyes on the left hand under Weaver's Down, from thence by a Slade up the Hill towards the east side of the Hill, and then passing over and leaving the top of the Hill a little to your right hand, keep down the side of the Hill to a green way, (where you see Foley Ponds on the left) and keeping all along that way on the east side of Iron Barrow or Iron Hill, down to dead man's Thorn, where is also a large stone, near to a road, and here a Gospel is to be read, a Psalm to be sung, and a Cross made X.[5]

The Perambulation took three whole days and covered close on eighteen miles (or nearer thirty, if you counted 'all its curves and indentings'). Selborne was a sizeable parish in the eighteenth century, embracing a great variety of soils, vegetation and farming styles. This variation has always been one of the sources of the district's pervading sense of unevenness and intimacy. But underlying everything are two more fundamental influences: geology and social history.

There is still no better description of local geology and geography than Gilbert's own account in the opening sections of the *Natural History*. Essentially the parish can be divided into two broad regions, along the line of the village street. To the south-west is a range of steep chalk-hills culminating in the wooded slope known as Selborne Hanger or, more usually, simply the Hanger. To the north-east is a flatter area on sandstone, where the soils become pro-gressively more acid until they merge with the Surrey heathlands. Where the two rocks meet, the water which has percolated down through the chalk emerges in a series of springs, and it was close to this source of water, and the fertile, loamy soils it encouraged, that the settlement of Selborne grew up.

The dominant feature of the village is the Hanger. It rises steeply about 300 feet above the level of the street, a louring whaleback that is rarely out of view. It was less wooded in White's day, but even without trees it would have reduced the amount of daylight for those living in its shadow by as much as three hours. In the eighteenth century the south-east end of the Hanger was chiefly open, scrubby sheep-down. On the top was Selborne Common, a tract of rough grazing, open enough for the village to hold its cricket matches, but studded with oak and beech pollards, and also known as the High Wood. Straighter, younger beeches grew on the slopes. Beeches were Gilbert's favourite trees, and he was deeply upset when Magdalen College felled large quantities during the middle decades of the century.

On the other side of the spring line was a belt of wet meadows, pastures, copses of ash, hazel and maple, and another wooded common known as Dorton. Then, out on the extreme eastern edge of the parish, the dark expanse of Woolmer Forest began. This was not a forest of trees, but a 'legal' forest, a large area of land, nearly 9000 acres, subject to forest laws designed to preserve game for royal hunting parties. What little woodland it did contain was largely decrepit and not regenerating. (White went so far as to say that it was 'without one standing tree in the whole extent', though he may well have been applying rather severe standards of uprightness.[6]) Woolmer was chiefly a sweep of undulating sandy heathland covered with heather and bracken, and broken here and there by patches of peat and bog in the hollows. It was a haunt of nightjars and snipe, and until the early years of the eighteenth century – to the delight and frequent downfall of the local poachers – of red deer and black grouse. On the western edge of the Forest were three large pools, Oakhanger, Bin's and Woolmer Ponds, the last having a circumference of nearly a mile and a half at the time White was writing, and attracting huge flocks of wild duck in the winter.

Other oddities were scattered throughout the parish: more ponds in the northern corner of the village, formed by the damming of one of the brooks, where Gilbert used to watch swallows feeding; a romantic, secret ravine, no more than a couple of hundred yards from the street, draped with moss and ferns and carrying one of the other local streams; miniature hangers, perched on the sides of the dry valleys that radiate at right angles from the streams; a chalk outcrop topped with downland and ancient quarry pits at Noar Hill. And passing between and through them, circulating around the village and occasionally tunnelling their way into the outside world, were the hollow lanes. There was scarcely a single lane in eighteenth-century Selborne that wasn't more or less underground. Centuries of wear from traffic and weather had worn them deep down into the soft sandstone and chalk rocks. As a consequence the lanes were more than just a system of by-ways. They were landmarks, physical records of the past history and everyday experience of the parish. Every extreme of weather – gale, snow, downpour – left lingering traces here long after its effects had vanished on the surface. Drifts and landslides were trapped like climatic fossils. And every horse or coach that succeeded in passing along them helped pummel the floor of the lane down again.

Yet there was a paradox about the lanes. Although their origins were entirely artificial, they had developed one of the wildest, most apparently natural countenances of any parish feature, and Gilbert was fascinated by them:

> In many places they are reduced sixteen or eighteen feet beneath the level of the fields; and after floods, and in frosts, exhibit very grotesque and wild appearances, from the tangled roots that are twisted among the strata, and from the torrents rushing down their broken sides; and especially when those cascades are frozen into icicles, hanging in all the fanciful shapes of frostwork. These rugged gloomy scenes affright the ladies when they peep down into them from the paths above, and make timid horsemen shudder while they ride along them; but delight the naturalist with their various botany.[7]

They could also, needless to say, become impossible to negotiate, and it was the precarious balance that they maintained between isolating the village and providing an escape route that was to become as important to Gilbert as any of their wild flowers or 'curious *filices*'.

*

The hollow lanes date back at least to the Saxon period, which is when most of the features of the Selborne landscape acquired their current names, as Gilbert worked out during his researches for the *Antiquities*. For instance, hanger is from OE *hangra*, a steep, and later a wooded, slope; lythe from OE *hlithe*, a steep pasture; Plestor, the open space near the church, from OE *plegstow*, a playground. Even Selborne itself is derived from OE *sealh* or *sele*, sallows, and *burne*, a stream.[8]

In late medieval times Selborne began to acquire a social independence that matched its physical quirkiness. It came about in the most roundabout way, in the wake of an extraordinary history of local ecclesiastical debauchery. There had once been an Augustinian Priory in Selborne, just beyond Dorton. It had been founded by the Bishop of Winchester in 1233, had marked time inconspicuously for a century or two, and then collapsed in scandal in 1484 from a surfeit of almost every indulgence forbidden to the monastic calling. When Gilbert wrote up the Priory saga in the *Antiquities* he spoke with grave disapproval of the monks' 'sensuality and ... general delinquency'.[9] He also quoted from that fiercely radical and populist attack upon church corruption, *The Vision of Piers Plowman:*

> Now is religion a rider, a romer by streate;
> A leader of love-days, and a loud begger;
> A pricker on a palfrey from maner to maner,
> A heape of hounds at his arse, as he a lord were.

Gilbert thought this poem 'a striking picture of monastic insolence and dissipation; and a specimen of one of the keenest pieces of satire now subsisting in any language, ancient or modern'; and this sympathetic reference is one of the few clues to his own feelings about the proper role and deportment of the clergy. But he did see the funny side of this tumble from grace, and while he was still fresh from disentangling the Latin text of William of Wykeham's commission of inquiry into the affair, he wrote an altogether more boisterous account to his nephew Sam Barker:

> They were become mighty hunters, and used to attend junketings, and feastings; had altered their mode of dress; and used to let *suspectae* come into their cloisters after it was dark; had suffered their buildings to dilapidate; had pawned their plate; administered the sacrament with such nasty cups, and musty, sour wine, that men abhorred the sight (*ut sit hominibus horrori*) ... they also were got into a method of laying naked in bed without their breeches, for which they are much reprimanded.[10]

What set off the decline isn't known for certain, but it's tempting to think that Selborne's wayward *genius loci* had some part in it. The Priory was actually situated within the boundaries of the Royal Forest of Woolmer, and under siege by the pleasures of the flesh. King Edward I frequently stayed at the Priory when he was on hunting trips, and expected his large retinue to be fed and entertained. If that was a drain on the monks' finances it was nothing compared to the testing their sacred vows received from the spectacle of the aristocracy at play, and from the ever-present temptation of other kinds of royal beast in the Selborne woods. The Brothers were regularly hauled up for poaching offences before itinerant magistrates, and on one occasion the Prior himself paid the then huge sum of £4 not to have his dog's feet mutilated (a frequent procedure in royal forests to discourage illegal hunting).[11]

Following William of Wykeham's inquiry in 1373 various attempts were made to reform the Priory, but without success, and in 1484 the formal process of dissolution was begun. William Waynflete, who was then Bishop of Winchester, decided to appropriate it, together with all its Selborne lands, to supplement the income of Magdalen College, Oxford, which he had personally founded in 1459. Magdalen, in effect, became the Lord of the Manor, and thus the patron of the local church of St Mary.

But the college's chief interest in the Selborne estates was a financial one, and by the middle of the sixteenth century its only direct representative in the parish was a priest (who doubled as woodman and bailiff) living in a house next to the already crumbling Priory buildings. Soon he was gone and by the eighteenth century Magdalen's influence extended not much further than appointing the vicar, and attending, usually in the persons of the College President and Bursar, the Manorial Court in the Grange tithe barn. This was normally held annually, except when there were special cases to be considered; and the college representatives must have been relieved that their trips to this inaccessible, upstart community were no more frequent. Between visits they relied for help and contact on the vicar and any other friends they could muster in the area. Now and then, there are revealing glimpses of just how distant and occasionally casual the relationship between Magdalen and the village was. In 1719, for example, the College wrote to the Vicar of East Worldham (three miles north of Selborne) giving him full authority to manage and cut the

coppice-wood in Selborne.[12] It was, on the surface, a
baffling exercise in delegation, since Gilbert's energetic and
able grandfather was still vicar, and had performed this
service thirty years before. But he may have fallen out with
Magdalen that very year, by taking the villagers' side in a
conflict over common rights. Magdalen had made an attempt to claim rights over the local woods and common, the
Selborne copyholders had resisted, and the case had gone to
court. The result was a clear defeat for the College, and a
Decree in Chancery affirming the villagers' common
rights.[13]

A few years later Magdalen's agent and rent-collector was
an elderly man called Jethro Longworth. In 1730 (when
Gilbert was 10 years old and about in the local lanes and
woods) Longworth wrote to the Bursar in a small and shaky
hand, asking if the monies could be exchanged 'in this
county for there is much Robing on the Road'. A letter the
following year, shakier still, has the postscript 'pray excuse
my scribble for I can scarce see what I write.'[14]

Absentee landlordism was the downfall of many rural
communities in the eighteenth century, but Selborne
flourished without the yoke of a squire. No single landowner
determined the pattern of farming locally, or was able to
institute widespread changes in the landscape. Instead there
were a large number of owner-occupiers, copyholders and
customary tenants, mostly with holdings of between ten and
twenty acres. The largest owner had seventy-five acres.
Gilbert, by the time of his death, had some forty acres
scattered around the parish in a number of closes and strips
in the common fields.[15] Selborne, consequently, was an
independent even if not particularly prosperous community,
and – a fact important for the work Gilbert would one day be
undertaking – a place where people could move about where
they wished and exercise rights over a considerable area of
common-land. Common rights are notoriously difficult to
describe with accuracy or certainty, but the Decree in
Chancery of 1719 had given a sound legal footing to at least
some of the traditional practices. The ancient tenements in

the village (there were forty-seven listed in 1793)[16] had three fundamental rights attached to them. The occupiers could graze all kinds of cattle on the Hanger, the High Wood and Dorton. They could cut and gather underwood, free, for repairing the fences between their land and the common. And on the payment of a small charge (one shilling and fourpence for most of the eighteenth century)[17] they could buy the firewood that was cut from the tops of the beech pollards scattered throughout the common. Beyond these three basic rights we are in the realm of 'customary practice' and handed-down tradition. Magdalen College almost certainly retained the right to cut the larger trees for timber, though there seems to have been an understanding that they would retain a beech 'presence' on the Hanger to guarantee a source of mast for grazing animals. Most of the citizens of Selborne, whether copyholders or not, had also 'since time immemorial' cut peat for fuel in Woolmer Forest, and gathered dead or fallen branches 'in proper season' for firewood.[18]

While all these rights were exercised and jealously guarded they helped protect the commons against 'reclamation' as farmland, and encouraged a diverse pattern of land use. But not everyone approved of such emancipated behaviour among the rural working class, especially the surveyors who, during the last decades of the eighteenth century, were engaged on a county by county assessment of the state of the nation's agriculture. The Board of Agriculture representatives have become notorious for their censorious attitude towards the standards and values of rural inhabitants, and they had stern, disapproving words for East Hampshire. They thought the workers over-paid and ill-disciplined, and were appalled at the state of the roads. Many failed to find Selborne at all. Arthur Young (1768) approached no closer than Alton, four miles to the north, and even there found most of the farms were less than a hundred acres in extent.[19] Abraham and William Driver (1794) mention the increase in hop-planting in the district but regarded much of the countryside as little better than a jungle:

30

We are sorry to observe such immense tracts of open heath, and uncultivated land, which strongly indicate the want of means, or inclination, to improve it, and often reminds the traveller of uncivilised nations, where nature pursues her own course, without the assistance of human art.[20]

For Charles Vancouver (1810) it was not just the heaths but the extensive woodlands (15 per cent, he estimated in the district) that were behind the deplorable lack of agricultural discipline. The local workers spent too much time in day-work, cutting wood and peat, when they should have been in the fields. They also spent too much time doing nothing at all, he complained in shocked tones, often going home at 4 pm in the summertime, when the 'correct' hour was 6.[21]

The only contemporary survey of Selborne village is a census carried out by Gilbert himself, in an official return to the Bishop of Winchester in 1788.[22] He found that the long village street, together with a few side-lanes and a scatter of outlying farms, supported a population of 676, divided among 136 tenements or families. Baptisms had risen from a yearly average of nearly thirteen in the 1720s to more than twenty in the 1770s. The number of deaths were more stable, at around ten a year. Men and women had the same life expectancy, and in general 'the inhabitants enjoy a good share of health and longevity: and the parish swarms with children.' It also, according to White, 'abounded' with poor, though it's clear from his description that these lived way above the standards usual for the eighteenth-century rural poor. Many were 'sober and industrious, and live comfortably in good stone or brick cottages, which are glazed, and have chambers above stairs: mud buildings we have none.'[23] The village was not prosperous enough to maintain a schoolmaster and the education of the village children was in the hands of 'two or three dames'. But there was a total of £10 a year in charitable endowments for the children of the poor. One of these had been made in 1719, by Gilbert's grandfather. It was provided by the income from a piece of land in Hawkley, usually about £3 a year, and was intended

'For teaching the poor children of Selborne to read, write, sew & knit, say their prayers & catechisms'. The Vestry Accounts show that comparatively few people were receiving Parish Relief. In 1789, for example, twenty villagers were receiving an average of about six shillings a month. In 1791 the number had risen to twenty-five, but only about half a dozen were receiving relief on a regular basis.[24]

In general the diversity of land-work available – picking hops, barking timber, as well as more orthodox farming tasks – and the marginal income from the commons kept most people above the real poverty line and maintained a spirit of enterprising self-sufficiency in the community.

Perhaps the last word on the pervading character and influence of the landscape should be left to Cobbett, one local witness who is unlikely ever to be accused of glamourization. The day he had his tantalizing glimpse of the road to Selborne he had been exploring the country just to the south-east of the parish. He'd been given anxious warnings against venturing into this interior. The terrain, he was told, was treacherous. He would either find himself careering down slippery chalk slopes, or wallowing through two-foot-deep mud in the tracks. Cobbett plunged in, and during the next few hours encountered some of the most dramatic scenery that even he, a seasoned tourist, had ever seen. He was astonished by the suddenness of the edge of Hawkley Hanger and the view over the plunging, wooded hills. It was 'like looking from the top of a castle into the sea' with the cross-hangers running into it 'like piers'. He slithered down muddy hanger sides ('like grey soap') by gripping onto the underwood, took to one of the deepest hollow lanes, whose towering sandstone walls terrified the horses, and rode off into the mud. 'Talk of *shows*, indeed! Take a piece of this road; just a cut across, and a rod long, and carry it up to London. That would be something like a *show*!' He ended the day in the company of a doltish local guide, getting hopelessly lost in the dark in Woolmer Forest. It was, he reckoned, 'the most interesting day, as far as I know, that I ever passed in my life'.[25]

Chapter Three
Widening Horizons

When he was 13 or 14 years old, Gilbert went off to school in Basingstoke, to study under the Reverend Thomas Warton. This almost certainly involved private tuition, not a spell at the local school, as has often been assumed. Dr Warton was the vicar of Basingstoke and appears to have had no connection with the Basingstoke Grammar School. He was something of a maverick, an ex-Professor of Poetry at Oxford, who had once been reported to the Vice-Chancellor for sedition. He had two sons, Joseph, two years younger than Gilbert, and Thomas, born in 1728, a precocious boy who had translated the epigrams of Martial at the age of 10 and who went on to become not only Professor of Poetry, like his father, but Poet Laureate. Joseph was reported by his biographers to have been 'educated under his father's eye', and it's likely that the three boys, Tom, Jo and Gilbert, formed an intimate and precocious tutorial group under Dr Warton's tutelage. A list made by Gilbert in one of his pocket books of 'Books that I carryed to Basingstoke, January 17, 1738/9' is chiefly a tally of classical texts, but also includes Wilkins' *Natural Religion* and James Thomson's epic landscape poem, *The Seasons*.[1]

Very little else is known about his school education, except that, with Selborne being fifteen miles away from Basingstoke, he probably boarded with the Wartons, at least during the week. But it would have been assumed early on that as an intelligent young man from a middle-class though not very prosperous family, he would go on to university, and then probably take holy orders. He chose Oxford, and was admitted as a commoner to Oriel College on 7 December 1739. The reason he chose Oriel rather than Magdalen, where his grandfather had been a Fellow, was almost certainly due to the influence of his Uncle Charles, who had been a student at Oriel between 1710 and 1714, and had taken a consistent interest in Gilbert's education. But the choice couldn't have been regarded as a matter of great importance at the time. At 19, Gilbert would hardly have been concerned about which college he attended, nor – having so far shown no hint of an exclusive attachment to his native village – that his place at Oriel meant that he could never be vicar of Selborne. In the event Gilbert did not take up residence at the usual time. By an unkind coincidence his mother Anne died on the same day (3 December) that he was formally admitted, and he had to postpone his entrance until April 1740.

What part did Oxford play in shaping Gilbert's outlook and interests? Perhaps not a great deal in a narrow academic sense. Mid-eighteenth-century Oxford had a notorious reputation as a den of indolence, degeneracy and corruption. Standards of scholarship were at one of their lowest ebbs, and Gilbert may have found more enlightenment (as many generations of students have) outside the formal framework, in his private reading and a circle of new friends. One cause of the University's malaise was that it had found itself, for involved historical reasons, on the losing side in the long-standing feud between the Jacobites and the reigning Hanoverians. It had lost influence, friends and money, and had seen a drastic reduction in the number of students wishing, or financially able, to enter. During the period Gilbert was an undergraduate the entire annual intake averaged less than 200.[2]

Yet equally one could see Oxford's lethargy developing as a kind of buffer between the gentleman's-club insularity of the colleges and the embryonic, untried academic structure of the university. The cultural and scientific debates of the age were not so much ignored as blunted. Some of the colleges were almost masonic in the way they awarded honours and favours. Lectures were rarities. The university library (the Bodleian) was open for only six hours a day. Some of the books were even chained to their shelves. Tutorials, and even examinations, were often little more than exchanges of stock questions and responses, or disputations upon a few standard problems in grammar or logic. Sometimes, if a tutor failed to turn up, debates were carried out with a blank stone wall.

The reaction of the students to this atmosphere – and the sanctimonious disapproval of it by outside commentators –

was affectionately satirized by Gilbert's school-friend Tom Warton in *The Companion to the Guide, and a Guide to the Companion*, published not long after he was appointed Professor of Poetry. This was part of his bawdy, irreverent, alternative syllabus:

> NAVIGATION is learned on the Isis, GUNNERY on the adjacent hills ... The Doctrin of the SCREW is practically explained most evenings in the private rooms, together with the motion of fluids ... Nine-pin and skittle alleys for the instruction of scholars in Geometrical Knowledge, and particularly, for proving the centripetal principle.[3]

In reality things were neither as cheerfully depraved as in Warton's skit, nor as awful as in Edward Gibbon's famous indictment, in which, casting his mind back forty years, he claimed that 'the greater part of the public professors have for these many years given up altogether even the pretence of teaching.' Lectures and tuition were available in a range of disciplines that went beyond classics and logic, into, for example, botany, Anglo-Saxon history, modern languages, mathematics and even astronomy. And if those lectures that were given were not always the most inspiring, they were at least voluntary. In fact, students were able to study pretty much what they wanted; and this gave the more assiduous ones the freedom to construct a very broad syllabus for themselves. Gilbert was lucky in having, as his tutor at Oriel, Dr Edward Bentham, a theologian then in his early thirties, who read three lectures every week without charging attendance fees. (He also published a moderately progressive account of moral philosophy in 1745, based on some of these lectures.) Gilbert would have been able to discuss 'natural religion' and physico-theology with Bentham, and its influence on the growing cult of naturalism in art and literature with his contemporaries at Oriel. They were a bright company, many with a taste for poetry: John Scrope, Bob Carter, Chardin Musgrave, Nathan Wells, Tom Mander, and a rich, stout and witty bishop's nephew from London called John Mulso, who was to become Gilbert's closest friend.[4]

Gilbert had no doubt been introduced to Mulso by his other old school-friend, Jo Warton, Tom's elder brother. Mulso, Warton and the poet William Collins, who had come up to Queen's College in 1749, had been the top three scholars of their year at Winchester School. Collins and Jo Warton had both begun to publish naturalistic poetry somewhat in the style of Thomson in the *Gentleman's Magazine*, before they ever came to Oxford. Gilbert had probably also dabbled with verse, to judge from his frequent forays into poetry later in life. Even Mulso proved to have an acute, if rather formal, critical sense. The four became close friends and shared a growing sympathy towards landscape and nature. Ten years later Jo Warton published a translation of the works of Virgil, and in his dedication praised the author's affection for nature in the most fancifully romantic terms. Virgil was to be thanked for giving 'life and feeling, love and hatred, hope and fear, wonder and ambition to plants and trees, and to the very earth itself: and for exalting his favourite insects, by endowing them with reason, passion, arts and civil government'.[5]

Gilbert was never a particularly well-to-do student, but it's clear from his account books that he lived a full and far from puritanical life. He went boating on the river and joined the Music Club. He kept a gun, and as Mulso reminded him much later (to Gilbert's great embarrassment) used to shoot small summer birds to keep his hand in for the winter. When it was available he indulged an undisguised taste for exotic food. As for drink, he enjoyed port, wine and cider, though never in the notorious quantities imbibed by Collins and the two Wartons. He frequented the coffee-houses that doubled as informal libraries and work-rooms, though never became an out-and-out 'lownger'. But to see him as a model of moderation would be to make him into altogether too passive a figure. One of the central features of Gilbert's personality was his ability – and, it seems, his need – to pursue, with equal gusto and commitment, ideas and habits which seem on the surface to be quite incongruous. It would have been absolutely in keeping with Gilbert's character to have found him ensconced in the coffee-house in New College Lane, drinking cider with Collins and earnestly discussing Derham's *Physico-theology* in an atmosphere which Tom Warton captured in his *Companion*:

> As there are here Books suited to every Taste, so there are Liquors adapted to every species of reading. Amorous Tales may be pursued over *Arrack Punch* and Jellies; *Insipid Odes over* Orgeat *or* Capillaire; *Politics over* Coffee; *Divinity over* Port ... In a word, in these Libraries Instruction and Pleasure go hand in hand; and we may pronounce in a literal sense, that Learning remains no longer a ... dry ... pursuit.[6]

It can be hard to keep hold of this image of Gilbert as a high-spirited young man. It is not just the formidable crusts of two centuries of history which get in the way, but the shadows of the clerical mantle and the book laboriously pieced together in later life. Together they conjure up the picture of a figure preserved in a state of permanent and studious middle age. He was still only 22 when he took his Bachelor of Arts examination on 17 June 1743, and not past celebrating with a night on the town later. His account for 28 June notes a total of eight shillings spent on 'Horse hire and Dinner' and wine. The Degree ceremony was two days later, and on this occasion Gilbert had the singular honour of being presented with a copy of Pope's six-volume translation of the *Iliad* by Pope himself. It isn't clear why Gilbert was favoured in this way, whether it was some kind of award, perhaps, or a surprise arranged by the family. The Whites and Pope did have a few mutual friends, notably Steven Hales (see p. 84), the non-resident Vicar of Farringdon near Selborne, and the poet's neighbour in Teddington, and it is possible that they had plotted this ceremonial presentation by one of Gilbert's favourite authors as a grand finale to graduation.

By his twenty-third birthday Gilbert was back in Selborne, to spend a summer free of any particular plans or responsibilities. Then it was Michaelmas again, and he returned to Oxford to attend 'Dr Bradley's first course of Mathematical Lectures'. On 30 March 1744 he sat a short examination, paid the necessary fees to the Vice-Chancellor's office, ordered a peal of bells at St Mary's in the High, and became a Fellow of Oriel College.

It was as simple as that. Fellowships then had nothing like the status they hold today, and, except in the case of exceptionally talented scholars, were chiefly intended to be temporary, short-term awards, to tide graduates (and clerics, especially) over until they came into a living or an inheritance. Certainly the appointment, at this stage, meant little more than a nominal change in Gilbert's way of life. He continued to spend the vacations in Selborne and term-time in not very demanding academic duties and study at Oxford. But there are glimpses, now and then, of a less gregarious existence than he had enjoyed as an undergraduate. Although some of his friends, including Tom Mander and John Scrope, were still in residence, the group was beginning to drift away, some to be tutors, some to take holy orders. Jo Warton had returned to Basingstoke to act as a temporary curate to his father. William Collins had gone straight to London to try his hand as a writer and man about town. John Mulso, who had graduated the year after Gilbert, was making a long round of visits with his well-to-do family. Mulso spent his first post-Oxford summer of 1744 at Leeds Abbey near Maidstone, and, when he wrote to Gilbert describing the place, he was already clearly aware of the direction in which his friend's interests were moving. The house was commodious and pleasant, with

> a large Garden well stock'd with Fruit and adorn'd with Fountains, Cascades, & Canals: a most romantic wood behind it with large Fish ponds.

But the library had been sold off and

> nothing remains but ye skeleton Cases. I really believe that my Brain will be moss'd over like our old walls, for here is very little Company, and those come so seldom that it is all

Form & Starch'dness ... I long to hear from You & to know
ye State of that poor College, which I do not expect to see
again these many months ... where is Jo: Warton now and
Tom? is that agreeable Toad Carter with you? All these
claim my Love, never forgetting dear Tomkyns of New
College: & Jack Rudge.[7]

So began, on 18 July 1744, the long correspondence
between the two men. Only Mulso's letters survive, but
they provide a frank and comprehensive insight into what
passed between the pair, and at times read almost as if they
were written with half an eye to recording Gilbert's fortunes
for posterity. On the evidence of his other surviving
correspondence it is hard to believe that Gilbert was as open
in return, and there is not much that he and Mulso obviously
had in common. Mulso, who was rather more than a year
younger than Gilbert, was the nephew of the Bishop of
Winchester, and slipped automatically into a life of privi-
lege, where comfortable livings were his virtually for the
asking. He was constitutionally lazy, and hypochondriacal
on an extravagant scale. The little interest he did have in
'natural knowledge' was largely vicarious, a reflection of –
and a compliment to – his friend's enthusiasms.

But at least Mulso was blessedly free of illusions about
himself, and was for ever lampooning his own shortcomings
and frailties. His wit, a kaleidoscope of extended puns,
convoluted literary allusions and affectionate but wickedly
accurate jibing, is one of the best things about his letters,
and, in the setting of his rather corpulent prose, gives them a
distinct Restoration flavour. He was always a *cleverer* writer
than Gilbert, the sparkling columnist as against the reflec-
tive essayist. He simply did not have very much to say.

What was crucial about their relationship was the un-
shakeable faith Mulso had, right from the outset, in the
originality and importance of Gilbert's vision. Even when he
was criticizing his style or chiding him for procrastination, it
was only because of his belief in what his friend had to offer
the world. He was a constant source of support and

confidence, and of wise counsel when the path Gilbert had chosen proved too lonely and single-minded. If, when his own spirits were low, admiration sometimes declined into obsequiousness, it was never badly meant. The worst that can be said – and it hardly amounts to a criticism – is that the envy which he so cheerfully confessed of Gilbert's energy and intellect occasionally made him dwell a little too fulsomely on his own blessings. Not long after they had left Oxford Mulso became engaged, and wrote to Gilbert from the security of his new relationship: 'Jenny [Young] intends to set apart a Room in ye Vicarage by the name of ye White Room; I could almost perswade Her to have a Child or two ye less, for Fear of excluding my friend.' It was a generous thought that Gilbert would have appreciated, but did Mulso realize the smart it would also have caused his bachelor friend?

*

Women had been on Gilbert's mind a good deal in those first months after the camaraderie of his undergraduate days began to fade. Jenny Croke – the daughter of Mrs Croke of Oxford, a family friend who ran a high-class haberdashery and collected rents from some of Grandmother White's tenants in the city – had taken his fancy enough for him to confide in his friends. They looked on the prospect of his ensnarement with consternation. Tom Mander reported that Gilbert was on 'the highroad to ye dreary and dolorous land of Matrimony', which prompted Mulso to issue a sonorous warning. 'Do you really find Celibacy hang heavy upon your Hands? . . . Upon my word I would not advise You to play so much as you do with ye Tangles of Neaera's Hair: those meshes will hold fast a Heart of stronger Wing for Flight than your's is.'[8] (Though Mulso himself was breathless about what he called 'those mysteries', and had been awestruck by the women of Canterbury during his stay in Kent: 'I never met in one place such an Assembly of Beauties. I believe I saved my Heart by ye beautiful Confusion.')

Early in 1745 Gilbert met Mulso's sister Hester, nick-named Hecky and then 18 years old. She was a bright and assertive young woman, but apparently no beauty. Fanny Burney's sister, who encountered her years later, remarked that she looked 'less forbidding than usual; but she is deadly ugly to be sure; such African nose and lips, and such a clunch figure'. Gilbert and Hecky hit it off from the start, no doubt recognizing in each other a similar independence of spirit. Gilbert had a great deal of respect for her intellect (as, in fact, he had for most of his female friends and relations) and he sent her some of his early attempts at poetry for comment. She proved to have a sharp critical eye, but also a light heart:

> Your Description of Selbourne has left nothing to '*the craving imagination of Miss Hecky,*' and it was kindly done to send me so lively a Picture, as I fear I am not to see the Original ... I hope your Father has not seen your more than Poetical Compliments, for if he has he must not see me, unless he has a Turn for Poetry, and knows that a Poet must give *the Perfections he does not* find.[9]

These mildly flirtatious blandishments and billets-doux passed frequently between them over the next few years. Gilbert paid her 'a very neat compliment' and she confessed to liking his hair. She wrote a sermon for him, and took to referring to him as 'Whit*ibus*', and 'Busser-White', nick-names he had acquired at Oxford when the use of the word buss, meaning to kiss, was more current.* Hecky reckoned him a great asset at parties, and was full of mock distress during a family visit to Oxford because her Gil would not be there. Without Busser, Mulso reported, 'She is apprehen-sive of a Dearth of Civilities ... and fears She shall not get her Degree, because She has not her favourite *Batchelour to answer under*'.[10] Mulso occasionally pretended not to under-stand the private jokes that passed between the pair. 'Whether there is any particular Hint of Improvement by ye

---

* This was a particularly complex pun, with its suggestion of the Latin possessive case in 'Whitibus'. But it was all beyond the wit of one nineteenth-century clerical descendant, who wrote to Oriel College for more information about his relative's spell as 'bursar' of the college.

Termination She is pleased to give to your Name,' he wrote, 'You best know: as to me, I never see those Things, because I do as I would be done by.'[11] But he knew better than most that there were no hidden intensities in the relationship, and certainly not the romantic attachment that some later writers have conjured up. It is quite clear that Gilbert and Hecky's relationship was no more and no less than the mutually teasing friendship between a young man and his best friend's sister.

Hecky's waspish brilliance soon carried her into more rarefied intellectual circles. By the time she was 23 she had acquired a measure of fame for a voluminous dispute with the novelist Samuel Richardson about parental authority, sparked off by his book *Clarissa* (he called her 'a little spitfire'). Her brother logged the exchange like a tennis match: 'The first Letter was long, Mr Richardson's answer 13 close Pages, Heck's reply 17; & Mr. R-s 39.' In later life she became the celebrated bluestocking Mrs Chapone, and when her works and correspondence were posthumously published there was not a single mention, affectionate or otherwise, of Busser White.[12]

*

Gilbert was no ascetic, and didn't stint any of his worldly enjoyments though mindful of his limited resources, he recorded their costs minutely, down to the smallest gambling loss and plate of radishes. He played chess, went to the races, and continued to enjoy gossiping in coffee-houses. Even when he was struck down by smallpox in the autumn of 1747, he managed to keep up a semblance of the good life. It was a severe attack, for which he needed the attention of two doctors at the immense cost of £31,[13] and – home comforts being the best – nursemaid Goody Marshall, specially sent up from Hampshire. (She was given a pair of shoes as a reward.) But his diet was still the sweet and sour mixture of a *bon viveur* determined not to let sickness ruin the style of life to which he had become accustomed. In a special list in his account books headed 'Expenses in the

Small-pox, 16 October', his purchases include three bottles of white wine, half a pound of Corinth raisins (probably dried blackcurrants), an ounce of green tea, a pint of wine, a pound of rushlights, and a dish of tripe.[14] But the regime seemed to work, and he was sufficiently recovered by the end of December to invest in a new pair of ice-skates.

Gilbert kept up his term-time residence until the summer of 1748, but in the vacations his life was almost nomadic. This was a common experience for young people in the eighteenth century, despite the myth of village confinement, and gentry and labourers alike frequently undertook a spell of travelling in search of work, fortune or just broadened horizons, before they settled down. Between 1745 and 1750 Gilbert roamed widely about lowland England, from the East Anglian marshlands to the wooded combes of Devon. No descriptive writing from this period survives, but the experience was crucial to him in later years. It gave him an insight into the variety of natural landscapes and their wild inhabitants that threw those in Selborne into sharp perspective.

Many of his trips were to relations and family friends. He became a regular visitor at his Aunt Rebecca Snooke's house at Ringmer, on the South Downs, and to his brothers Thomas and Benjamin, who had settled in London. Less frequently he went to Lyndon, in Rutland, where his future brother-in-law Thomas Barker lived, once going a roundabout way through Shrewsbury. Then there were expeditions to old Oxford friends. In the summers of 1746 and '47 he stayed with Tom Mander in Todenham, on the edge of the Cotswolds. Tom was now a budding physicist, but still apparently full of Oxford high spirits: 'You may give my Love to Him,' Mulso wrote, 'if his apparatus does not forbid your Approach' 'I presume You are popping & snapping so that a Farmer can't walk his own Fields in Security for You. Tom can walk farthest, but You shoot best; I fancy I have drawn your characters, tho' I may add, Tom drinks cyder longest but You take ye larger Glasses at first.'[15] In 1750 he journeyed down to see Nathan Wells in Devon, about 150 miles from Selborne, and entailing two or three days on the road.

His longest spells away from home were in East Anglia, where he was sent to help tidy up the affairs of his maternal grandfather's deceased half-brother, in the Isle of Ely. He was a distant relative, but the terms of his will had far-reaching implications for Gilbert. The only real money in the family was on Gilbert's mother's side. It had been passed down from her mother Miss Hyde, later Mrs Holt, to her widower, the Reverend Thomas Holt, and on his death to his half-brother, also Thomas Holt. When this Thomas died without obvious heirs early in 1746, he proved to have left his money not to Anne's eldest, but to her second son, Thomas, though the bequest was subject to so many annuities that Tom was not to see much benefit from it for another thirty years. The reasons for the tortuous path of this inheritance (passing through the lines of Thomases, as Anthony Rye has quipped) are buried deep in the arcane customs of eighteenth-century marriage settlements. The most important consequence was that Gilbert had missed his main chance of financial independence, though neither he nor any other member of the family appeared to see anything out of the ordinary in preference being given to a younger brother.

Gilbert was named as one of the executors of the will, and at the end of January 1745 he travelled east to begin the complicated task of cataloguing Holt's estates and effects, and settling matters with his tenants. He attacked the task with diligence and enthusiasm at first, reporting back to his father regularly with observations jotted down 'in my pocket book on the spot'. But it would have been a taxing job even for a trained surveyor. To begin with, the estates were divided between Thorney, in the Fens near Ely, and Rochford in Essex, and over the ensuing six months Gilbert was on an exhausting circuit between these two sites and London, Selborne and Oxford. The Rochford estates proved the hardest to cope with. They were occupied by forty separate tenants, and lay largely on low marshland near the River Roach. It was a landscape of perilous creeks, sodden pastures and limitless skies, as far removed from the wooded hills of Selborne as it was possible to imagine. Oysters were one of the accountable crops, and the inhabitants, then as now, doubtless saw themselves as having as much in common with fishermen as with inland farmers. Certainly they did not spare Gilbert the East Anglian's notorious reserve with strangers. At one point Gilbert wrote to his father in some disquiet, wondering how on earth he, as a 26-year-old clerical landsman, could persuade the tenants that he was empowered to collect rents.[16]

It is impossible to say how well Gilbert did the job, but he succeeded in 'getting wrong' with the family attorney, Mr Butcher, who seems to have been acting as agent for the estate. Years later Gilbert described Butcher as a 'very extraordinary man . . . He puts me in mind of Sarah Duchess of Marlborough, whose resentment Mr Pope says was the most formidable thing in the world – except her favour.'[17] In 1746 Mr Butcher's resentment was directed four-square at Gilbert, whom he regarded as a naïve and meddling outsider doing a job which should have been his. He complained of Gilbert selling the wrong animals, of his paying labourers too much, of his inexperience and ineptitude.[18] Gilbert wrote back in the most courteously apologetic of tones, but a more tight-lipped memo went into his pocket-book during one of his trips to Thorney:

> To sell the sheep as fast as possible. As many oxen as are saleable. Not to sell the Plate by auction at Thorney, but to reserve it to be disposed of at London by weight. The four men-servants not to be discharged 'till the will is proved, because they are witnesses. To take great care of the papers in the 'scrutore [sic] in the best Chamber, especially Bonds, Ledgers, &c. Use great secresy about money matters.[19]

Butcher finally wrote direct to Gilbert's father. Gilbert had sold off some of the wine at Thorney, he complained, and walked off with the keys. John White's draft reply, the only extant letter in his hand, is a timid and much amended apology. Like his son he clearly wished to be rid of the whole business, and especially of Butcher's interference. He ends by suggesting that the attorney should avail himself of the remaining wine at Thorney in compensation for his trouble.[20]

Gilbert's spell as an executor left him tired out, wiser about his native country and the ways of its inhabitants, and harbouring a deep-rooted suspicion of lawyers. It also brought to the surface a predisposition towards coach-sickness, which was to stay with him for the rest of his life. In August Gilbert wrote to Mulso with an account of how he had been overwhelmed during the middle of an earnest theological argument with a female friend. It sounds like a terrible attack, but he gets no sympathy at all:

> Lucretius's Suave mari magno &c.: was not ye Reason I laugh'd so heartily at your Stage Coach Sickness, which now you have recover'd I hope You will forgive me. I believe it was rather ye circumstances of the Sickness, than ye Sickness itself, that diverted me: I don't think there is a better Answer to ye Question of Original Sin than a groan; or a better satire on women's disputing it, than your cas-cading.[21]

Mulso relished Gilbert's tales of the road, especially of the kind of journeys he was too laggardly to undertake himself. The news usually arrived in the form of 'very exact and very entertaining' letters which were eagerly awaited by both Whites and Mulsos, and were sometimes read out loud after family dinners. The account which he sent of his long visit to Nathan Wells in August 1750 seems to have made an especially deep impression. Wells lived at East Allington, in the South Hams district of Devon, in the kind of broken, uneven country that Gilbert had learned to love in Selborne. ('I never see a Spot which lies much out of Levele but I think of you,' wrote Mulso, '& say "ay, now this would please White".') There were steep woods and sunken lanes, but also much that would have been strikingly new: the grey, looming mass of Dartmoor to the north-west, the

Devon cliffs, the warm south-east winds blowing in from the Atlantic. Gilbert's description of this foreign land made Mulso almost sigh for the dullness and lack of adventure of his own daily round.

> You live a scambling *[sic]* rantipole Life & have a great Variety of Objects to be painted upon Paper (at which Landscape Painting I think You a great & masterly Hand) & sent to your sedentary Friends; we receive them & think we are Travelling wth you for five Minutes, & then look up & find Ourselves in the same tedious Scene in which we have *rather* been acted *than* for a *Length of Days*.[22]

Reading Gilbert's despatches was the nearest Mulso was likely to get to such exotic scenes ('I, who have lately maintained that it is *up-hill from Hampton to Sunbury* should never bear the extreme Unevenness of that Country'), and he urged Gilbert to continue his 'Tours', and carry on writing about them. They would make an 'agreeable Pockett Volume', or better still, the basis for an epic poem. It should be called '*ye Progress* . . . It would make a fine Piece, & might tempt Gentlemen to examine their own Country before they went abroad & brought Home a genteel Disgust at ye Thoughts of England.'[23]

In fact Gilbert had already tried his hand at poetry of the pastoral kind, though the subject was not his rambles but the attractions of the place he had temporarily left behind. 'The Invitation to Selborne' had been written in 1745, while Gilbert was installed in the Fens, and the first version sent off to Mulso for his approval and comment. Since then it had become a kind of party piece, an all-purpose greetings card from what had come to be called 'the green retreat'. It was brought out on special occasions, amended and lengthened to keep it up to date, and sent out to a succession of friends and relatives. The earliest surviving version (already altered, apparently, from the original) dates from the early 1750s.

Later in his life Gilbert quite consciously used poetry as a way of sharpening his writing technique, or, more often, of releasing strong feelings that he felt unable to express in other ways, and this early exercise shows, embedded among some extravagant and unexceptional poesy, a sharp, almost sentimental longing for his 'native spot'. The body of the poem is little more than a tongue-in-cheek pastoral, with Selborne transformed into a part-Classical, part-Gothick Arcadia. The Hanger becomes 'the Pendant forest' and 'the mountain ground'. The shades of cowled monks and Crusaders float among the local ruins. But then a quieter more heartfelt note emerges, and Selborne becomes a real, personal landscape:

> Nor be the Parsonage by the Muse forgot;
> The partial bard admires his native spot;
> Smit with its beauties, lov'd, as yet a child,
> Unconscious why, its 'scapes grotesque, and wild:
> High on a mound th' exalted gardens stand;
> Beneath, deep valleys scoop'd by Nature's hand!
>
> Now climb the steep, drop now your eye below;
> Where round the verdurous village orchards blow;
> There, like a picture, lies my lowly seat
> A rural, shelter'd, unobserv'd retreat.[24]

Gilbert spent a good deal of his late twenties away from Selborne. His sojourn in East Anglia in 1745 was the longest period he had spent away from the village in his life. It is hardly surprising that, adrift in the vast inhospitable flatlands of Cambridgeshire, he experienced a pang of homesickness for the cosseted valleys of Hampshire.

Chapter Four
The Home Ground

Despite his wanderings and term-time attendance at Oxford, Gilbert had already taken up his first clerical position. He was ordained deacon in April 1746, and almost immediately became curate to his Uncle Charles at Swarraton, Hampshire. As Gilbert's stipend was only £20 a year he was presumably required only for Sunday services, and he continued to divide the rest of his time between Oxford and Selborne. Oxford was fifty miles away, but he kept a horse in stables there, and at first seemed quite undeterred by the weekly ride. But he was beginning to visit and stay in Oxford less frequently, and by the end of 1748 had given up his rooms there. In March 1749 he received his full ordination. A couple of weeks later his temporary curacy came to an end and, at the age of almost 30, he found himself out of work and back living in the family house.

Gilbert was never comfortable when he had nothing to do, and it was this partial vacuum that coincided with the beginning of a consuming passion for gardening that was to continue until his death. With his father still seemingly incapable of taking responsibility for the Wakes, Gilbert was effectively head of the household, and from late in 1749 he began serious work on the garden.

The land attached to the Wakes was perfect raw material for a combination of horticultural laboratory and pleasure-ground. Gilbert's father had done a little to improve its condition, but it was still a rather spartan patch, and lay on a sticky, chalky soil that was exceptionally difficult to cultivate. But it had the advantage of size, and of containing three quite distinct components.[1]

Nearest to the house was a smallish ornamental garden, with an area of lawn edged with flower borders. A wider border of bulbs lay against the house. Between this garden and the foot of the Hanger lay 'the Park', a few acres of meadow and pasture divided up into quite narrow fields by tall hedges. Just to the north of the ornamental garden, and projecting a little into these outer fields, was Baker's Hill, a curious mound that was probably a glacial relic. The soil on Baker's Hill was lighter and warmer than the surrounding clays, and this was the site chosen for the orchard, and most of the vegetable and melon beds. The whole estate could be viewed from the Wakes against a backdrop of the Hanger.

On 11 April 1750 Mulso wrote from Sunbury: 'You are now I suppose to be found, like Cyrus, ranging your Trees, & nursing your Plants,' and added a greeting that suggests that Gilbert had already admitted his special affection for the birds that visited the parish for the summer. 'I wish you Joy of ye arrival of ye Swallows & ye Swifts, & ye Nightingales, who have been with us about a week or ten Days ... I hope in Return for this important Account You will send me word how your Nurseries go, & the true State of Selbourne Hanger.'[2]

At times it sounds as if the educated cleric with a sophisticated taste for scenery was just a son of the soil after all. But Gilbert's fascination with the apparently mundane business of planting trees and raising seedlings wasn't simply an uncomplicated delight in the growth of things – though there is that, and a sharp botanical curiosity as well. The fact is that the garden had become one of the arenas in which the rapidly changing relationship between nature and humankind was being graphically expressed. On one hand was the idea of human dominance, and of putting nature – in this instance quite literally – in its place; on the other, the new notions of nature as worthy of admiration and celebration, perhaps even as a positive force or contributing partner.

By the beginning of the eighteenth century there had already begun to be moves towards more informal garden styles, and a greater interest in the plants that were used. Both Thomas Addison and Gilbert's acquaintance, Alexander Pope, were important influences on developing tastes, and scourges of the moribund forms of the old style. Pope had poked brilliant fun at their geometrical beds and trees clipped to the quick in a piece in the *Guardian*. His essay, entitled 'A Catalogue of Greens', purports to be a catalogue for a sale of topiary job lots:

ADAM and EVE in Yew; ADAM a little shatter'd by the fall

of the Tree of Knowledge in The Great Storm.
St George in Box; his Arm scarce long enough, but will be in
a condition to stick the Dragon by next April.[3]

In the emerging atmosphere where nature was beginning to
be regarded as intrinsically interesting and possibly more
benign than had ever been imagined, artificiality was giving
way to more subtly 'natural' discipline. Gardens – at least
those of the wealthy – became show cases for the whole
range of current aesthetic fads. Landscapes were construed
exactly as if they were paintings, with their wildness artfully
conjured into perspectives seen at their best from the house;
or, more prosaically, studded with clumps of exotic and
'curious' trees. Neo-classical scenes in which cattle grazed
among Arcadian groves were pitted against Gothick prospects of hovels and melancholy ruins. (In some places the
motif of decay was taken to bizarre extremes. In Vauxhall
Gardens there was a precursor of the twentieth-century
theme park, a Valley of the Shadow of Death, where coffins
replaced the crumbling columns and skulls were scattered
among the boulders.)
  Much of this excess came out of nothing more substantial
than the fashionable posturing of the nation's rich. Yet, amid
all the banter, there was a live issue facing anyone who was
concerned with finding ways of looking at, writing about,
and perhaps even reshaping nature. There was no question
yet of abandoning control, of allowing gardens to go wild. It
was more a matter of *how* humans regarded nature and how
this affected their involvement. Was the land a kind of
canvas where plants, rocks and even animals could be
ordered and disposed as if they were paints? Or did it have,
so to speak, a plan of its own which should be respected?
  Pope himself abhorred the more extravagant conceits of
the landscapers and professed to believe in an ideal state of
harmony between nature and humanity. But it would be
naïve to see him as a disinterested utopian or an early
ecologist. He believed in a rather uncritical way in the moral
good of Improvement, just so long as it was guided by

Reason and Taste, which in turn must be measured against Nature. Reshaping nature was natural to humans ('whatever is, is right'); its desirability was simply a question of scale and intention. In practice, Pope's views are so generalized and so blurred by his neat epigrams that he can be made to support any position. His famous lines in the 'Epistle to Burlington' (1731) are so sweetly reasonable that they can be read either as a moral prescription or an exoneration:

> In all, let Nature never be forgot . . .
> Consult the Genius of the Place in all
> That tells the water or to rise, or fall,
> Paints as you plant, and as you work, Designs.

Although Gilbert greatly admired Pope, he was never guilty of this kind of evasion or generalization, because his focus was always on the particulars of the natural world. Yet he can hardly have failed to be influenced by Pope's ideas, especially by his wit and his refusal to make a rigid distinction between the works of man and the works of nature. When it came to gardening, Gilbert found nothing incongruous about building picturesque arbours at the same time as observing minutely the germination of seeds.

In 1751 he began recording the results of his activity in what he christened *The Garden Kalendar*.[4] Books with similar titles had been published before this, notably Philip Miller's *The Gardener's Kalendar* (1732) and Richard Bradley's *The Gentleman and Gardener's Kalendar* (1731) but these were all prescriptive instructions as to what should be planted, pruned or picked on this or that day of the year. Gilbert's *Kalendar* differed in being an account of what he *had* done – the sowings and flowerings, the yields and failed crops, and, towering over them all, the effects of the weather. He began to make his entries on loose quarto sheets on 7 January, and as he outlined the sowing of 'two rows of early Spanish beans' in what was to remain a bold, straightforward and legible hand, he was beginning one of the very first horticultural documentaries.

The work in that first year was quite prodigious. Through-

out what turned out to be one of the most drenching springs
in living memory he was planting out the borders and the
beds on Baker's Hill. Vegetables were the first focus of his
enthusiasm. He grew more than forty different varieties,
including artichokes, endives, mustard and cress, white
broccoli, skirret and scorzonera, marrowfat peas, 'a remarkable long leek', squashes, cucumbers, all manner of let-
tuces, and 'a small crop of onions under Kelsey's Hedge for
picklers'. There were more experimental vegetables, too,
including maize, wild rice and potatoes. And in April 1751
he sowed a large bed of sea-kale, whose seed he had
gathered from the Devon beaches when he was visiting
Nathan Wells. Sea-kale was not brought into general
cultivation for another forty years, when it was popularized
by a near neighbour of White's, William Curtis of Alton.

Gilbert's efforts weren't directed solely towards vegetables. In the borders close to the house were planted crown
imperials, crocuses and pinks. Vines and roses scrambled
over the walls and the grass walks leading to the orchard and
vegetable beds were edged with tulips, wallflowers and
columbines. Even greater concentrations of flowers were
bedded out in one of the Park fields, in what Gilbert called
'basons'. These were large circular pits specially dug in the
sticky clay and filled with manure and the rich loam which
was brought up from the woods and wet meadows near
Dorton. Some basons were reserved for annual flowers –
love-in-a-mist, marigolds, marvels of Peru – but most were
used for clumps of more stately perennials, such as holly-
hocks or martagon lilies, and native wild flowers, like
foxgloves and St John's-worts, which had been transplanted
from the Hanger.

How much of the garden work did Gilbert do himself, in
the sense of actually wielding the spade? Not all, that is
certain. There are many specific references in the *Kalendar*
(and subsequent journals) to people from the village who
helped out in one way or another. Some were useful because
of particular skills. John Breckhurst planted trees. Will
Tanner, the shoemaker's son, was a crack shot, and was

brought in to dispose of birds which were supposedly damaging the fruit crops. Goody Hampton was employed as a 'weeding woman' in the summer months. She appears to have been a doughty worker, 'and indeed, excepting that she wears petticoats and now and then has a child, you would think her a man.' Less frequently, John Carpenter's wife also helped with the weeding. Other villagers such as Larby, Thomas Benham and John Carpenter himself were hired at day rates when there was extensive digging or hedge-cutting to do, and to help shift the immense quantities of manure that were used on the hot-beds. Presiding over them all was Gilbert's loyal retainer Thomas Hoar, who acted as his groom, gardener, scientific assistant and general handyman for forty years. He was a bachelor and slept at the Wakes, and would keep the journals up and write letters about events in Selborne when Gilbert was away. In the garden and in his treatment of plants and animals Thomas showed a delicacy and concern that is more than just a reflection of his employer's own sensitivity. Gilbert often mentions, with respect, the gentle way he would clear trees and shrubs of snow, or pick insects off the fruit bushes by hand, and his affection and care for Timothy the tortoise. But it's clear from a number of specific references, and the familiar tone of his descriptions, that Gilbert was personally and actively involved in most of what was being done in the garden – especially when it came to melons, which above all other products of the plant world held Gilbert's attention during the 1750s.

Melons seemed to hold a fascination for most gardeners in the eighteenth century. Philip Miller, whose exhaustive and influential *Gardener's Dictionary* was Gilbert's chief reference book (he bought copies in both 1747 and 1753) gave four of his considerable pages to them, and remarked: 'there is not any Plant cultivated in the Kitchen-Garden, which the Gardeners near London have a greater Ambition to produce early and in Plenty.'[5] It sounds a rather modish custom from this note, and there certainly is a sense in which melons were an embodiment of eighteenth-century enthusiasms.

They were exotic, knobbly enough at times to the point of being fashionably grotesque, and repaid hard work and technical ingenuity with enormous productivity.

Gilbert had been infatuated by melons for some years. After his attack of smallpox in 1748 his Oriel friend John Scrope wrote a bizarre satirical verse called 'Metamorphosis', which envisaged Gilbert bloated by fever into the very substance of his obsession:

Corycius long admired (a curious swain!)
The wealth and beauties of Pomona's reign;
The vegetable world engrossed his heart,
His garden lingering nature help'd by art;
Where in the smoking beds high heap'd appear
Salads and mushrooms thro' the various year.

But of each species sprung from seed or root,
The swelling melon was his favourite fruit;
Other productions kindled some delight
In his fond soul, but here he doted quite.
When others wisely to the grot retreat,
And seek a friendly shelter from the heat,
Anxious and stooping o'er his treasure, low
Poring he kneels, and thinks he sees it grow.

One day when Phoebus scorch'd the gaping plain,
Striving to rise at length he strove in vain,
Fix'd to the spot, exchang'd his shape and name,
A melon turned and what he view'd became.

Ovid would tell you how his roughen'd face*
Retains the network and the fretty grace;
His skin and bones compose the tougher rind;
His flesh compressed retains its name and kind;
Shrunk are his veins, and empty'd of their blood,
Which in the centre forms a plenteous flood.[6]

By the mid-1750s melon growing had become the major industry of the Wakes garden. The hot-bed (usually referred to grandly as the 'melon ground' and itself still something of

---

*Scrope's footnote: 'by the smallpox'.

a novelty in English gardens) was at its maximum 45 feet long and had some 30 cart-loads of dung dug into it annually. And each year, as he began the long ritual of preparing the beds and nursing these temperamental fruits through to maturity, Gilbert seems to have become locked in some personal struggle with the rigours and vagaries of the eighteenth-century climate. His melons hung in a precarious balance between succumbing to mildew or freezing to death and, later, between baking and flooding. The more they were threatened by frost or rain, the more he responded with elaborate concoctions of manure and oak tan-bark, deep digging, and scientific ingenuity.

The details were recorded in minute and enthralling detail in the *Kalendar*, and there are times during the 1750s (as there were to be increasingly through his life) when one has the feeling that the diaries are not just recording his daily life but in some sense *driving* it, that the work was being done – and done so deftly – because it had the momentum of a good narrative. There is not much to be gained by asking why he began writing a diary of this kind in the first place. He was inquisitive by temperament, and acutely sensitive to the influence of moment and place. For the present, it will suffice to say that the style of his writing begins to echo more and more the rhythms of his daily life.

A few of the entries from the melon saga for 1758 will give a feeling of the operation. There are more than sixty mentions of the melons and their hot-beds in this year, and it must count as the peak of his enthusiasm. It was also the year he noted in his account book 13s 8d spent in a single day on hired help for deepening the beds, and the year in which he built an extraordinary piped ventilation system for them.[7]

> Jan 17. Finished an earth-house in the melon-ground. It is worked in a circular shape with rods & coped over with the same, & then well thatched: is nine feet over & eight feet high: & has room to hold a good Quantity of mould & a man at work without any inconvenience.

Mar 4–6. Plunged nine melon-pots in the ten-frame, & three in the other frame. Contrived some wooden bottoms to the pots to make the earth turn-out more easily ... Sowed one melon seed from that curious Melon [a Cantaloup] brought from Waverley in 1756, in each of the twelve pots Bed heats well.

Mar 18: Melons up some in every pot; they look healthy, & grow apace.

Mar 21: Great snow all the day, & most part of the night; which went off the next day in a stinking, wet fog. Very trying weather for Hot-beds.

April 1: Unusual sunny, scorching weather for a week past. The heat drew the forward Cucumbers, notwithstanding they were constantly shaded; and would have spoiled the melons ... had not the pots been raised.

April 13: Worked-up a nine-light melon-bed with 18 good dung-carts of fresh, hot dung, & 80 bushels of fresh tan. I had made this bed just a week before, only two days after the materials were brought in; but finding it to heat violently I ordered it to be pulled to pieces, & cast back again, that it might spend it's violent Heat.

April 16: So fierce a frost with a South-wind as to freeze the steam which run out in water from between the panes of ye Melon-frames into long Icicles on the Edges of the lights.

April 21: Found the melon-bed so hot still that I did not trust the plants out of the pots. Earthed the bed all over an inch thick to keep down the steam, which in the night had spoiled three of the plants. Bored some holes very deep in the back of the bed to let out the violent Heat.

June 6: Earth'd the hand-glass melons the first time ... The plants are strong, & produce plenty of wood; but are strangely blistered in their second leaves by being exposed to the fierce sun while the night-dew was on them.

July 15: Found on my return from Dene about thirteen brace of Cantaleupes set; some very large. Plants in vast vigour with leaves near a foot in Diameter.

Aug 22: Cut the first Cantaleupe, the largest of the Crop: weighed 3pds: 5 oun: & half. It proved perfectly delicate,

dry, & firm [despite] the unfavourable weather ever since
the time of setting.

Sept 7: Eat a very delicate Cantaleupe: it had a bottle-nose,
& grew close to the stem. Sav'd the seed.

Sept 12: Held a Cantaleupe-feast at the Hermitage: cut-up a
brace & an half of fruit among 14 people. Weather very fine
ever since the ninth.

*

The melon feast was an indication of the way in which
gardening, for Gilbert, was not some isolated, academic
pursuit but a central part of the celebration of his native
ground, and an exceptionally sociable business too. Many of
his plants were presents from friends and neighbours. A
guelder rose came from John Berriman, artichokes and
Hypericums from the vicar. There are five different sources
for plants and seeds mentioned in the first dozen entries in
The Garden Kalendar. Gilbert was also in touch with a wide
network of professional gardeners and merchants. In 1756
he purchased a collection of conifers from Williamson and
Co. of Kensington, who had issued their first catalogue only
that year, and who went on to become one of the suppliers
to Kew Gardens.[8] Gilbert also had plants from the foremost
gardener of his day, Philip Miller, Fellow of the Royal
Society, author of *The Gardeners Dictionary* and curator of the
Chelsea Physic Garden for half the eighteenth century.
And, when he was visiting Oxford, he often took the
opportunity to bring back a few specimens or seeds from the
Botanic Garden.

But, gardening excepted, his life had begun to narrow a
little since he vacated his rooms at Oxford in 1748. Only two
temporary curacies had come his way in four years: his term
at Swarraton that ended in 1748 and a short period as curate-
in-charge of Selborne while the incumbent, Dr Bristow, was
ill. He took up this last position in October 1751 and, for the
duration, moved a hundred yards across Selborne street to
live in the vicarage. Mulso, who had recently taken the
living of Sunbury and become engaged to Miss Jenny

Young, congratulated him on his appointment, and encouraged him in the sermon-writing now to be one of his duties:

> I hear that You are snug at the Vicarage; where it is to be
> presumed that You are preparing Something for ye World.
> Sermons or Satyrs must come fm Him, who has left the
> — world. The latter will be ye Effect of his Contempt of It; the
> former (the better Part) his charity to & Pity of it. I had
> rather therefore that you was employed in ye latter.[9] [He
> means the charity and pity.]

It is worth noting, in the light of the frequent assumption that Gilbert's deepest regret was that he could never be vicar of Selborne, that it was at precisely the moment when he was occupying that position (albeit temporarily) and spending the winter in the spacious house where he was born, that he felt the pull of Oxford again. He had been informed that it was the turn of Oriel College to fill the office of Junior Proctor, and that he could have an option on the post. It was unusual for a non-resident to be offered such an opportunity, and Gilbert had no hesitation in taking it up. He resigned the Selborne curacy and took up his Proctorial office on 8 April 1752.

The Proctors' duties are neither very demanding nor very glamorous. They have responsibility for maintaining discipline among members of the University and officiating at certain formal occasions. There are a few apocryphal stories about Gilbert playing the diligent university policeman, including one which supposedly involved the chastising of a worse-for-wear Edward Gibbon, then at Magdalen College; but the attraction of the appointment for him was simply that he had an excuse for living in Oxford again, and being paid for it into the bargain. Mulso was not entirely sure he had done the right thing in accepting the constraints of this 'honourable Clog', but, as usual, he gave his support, and underlined it with yet another fanciful Scheme:

> I think You have paid the University a great Compliment in
> accepting of the Sleeves; for as I take your Genius, You are

rather Atticus than Tully ... and the green Retreats (for they begin now to be the *green* Retreats) of Selbourne afford more serious Pleasure to your contemplative Mind than ye frequentis Plausus Theatri can to your Ambition. I have a longing Desire to see You in your new Station; but then I want to bring in each Hand a Girl ... How prettily would they adjust ye Sleeve, & give a more rakish Air than suits the Academic Form, how would they admire ye Tuft, & how would they fancy *the Flap!*[10]

Gilbert was not quite such a committed contemplative as Mulso sometimes liked to imagine; enjoying the nonsense of cutting a dash in academic finery was just as much a part of his character. His purchases of clothes and food and entertainments in the early 1750s suggest a man who had a well-developed facility for adopting a style of life appropriate to wherever he was at the time.[11] In Selborne he lived frugally, with few inessential expenses beyond provisions for his pony Mouse and help for the garden. In Oxford he was the thoroughgoing man about town, buying 'a feather-top'd grizzle wig' and 'Norway-Doe gloves'. He had his crest engraved on a set of 'large polished tea spoons' and treated the Oriel Masters of Arts to a huge box of biscuits. He went to concerts, gambled at cards (and usually lost), played chess and usually won. His taste in food – at least when it came to luxuries – was sophisticated and rather modern. He had a penchant for lobsters, oysters and crabs, olives and almonds, Seville oranges and baskets of strawberries, and he purchased a great number of salads from the Botanic Garden. (On 16 August 1752 he catered for both present and future appetites, and added to an order of 'Spinage-seed, garlick, & half a Gallon of Mazagon Beans from Mason ye Garden'r' two ripe melons for a shilling.)

But this seemingly healthy diet didn't entirely make up for the outdoor life he had left behind in Selborne, when there was scarcely a day he didn't walk or work in the garden, and in the autumn of 1752 he had his 'mens room' fitted with a dumb-bell. This wasn't the weighted bar of modern gyms, but it had much the same function. It was, almost literally, a soundless bell – a flywheel with a weight and a rope attached, the user alternately pulling at the rope and being lifted into the air.

Gilbert's friends and relatives paid him frequent visits during his year as Proctor, and he enjoyed showing them the sights. His sister Becky dropped in on her way to Rutland, was whisked off to see the Radcliffe Camera and Great Tom (the famous bell in Christ Church) and entertained to a choral concert in the evening. Benjamin (then 27) travelled up with his future wife, Anne ('Nanny') Yalden, daughter of the Vicar of Newton Valence, accompanied by her brother Will as chaperon.* (Ben brought six bottles of olives up from London, for which Gilbert repaid him the considerable sum of fifteen shillings.) They stayed a whole week and took in visits to the University Museum and Magdalen College and trips out to landscape gardens at Blenheim and Stowe. The Mulsos came for a holiday in August and Gilbert broke his summer vacation in Selborne to play host. 'We all agree that the Proctor understands how to give ye most agreable Turn to every Thing,' wrote grateful Mulso a few days later, '& to improve every Scheme of Tast.' Thomas White called in occasionally, and young Henry White was permanently about, having himself been in residence at Oriel since the autumn of 1749.

The only one of the brothers conspicuously absent was John. He had followed Gilbert to Oxford and entered Corpus Christi College in 1746, but had later been sent down for some unspecified variety of disorderly conduct. He had been allowed to take orders, but was preoccupied at this time (or so his family believed) in digging the new Zig-zag track up the Hanger. Working on this sticky and perilous slope must have seemed an appropriate way of making

*

* The Whites' relations with the Yaldens are a good example of what a very close circle family and friends formed. Benjamin married Anne in 1753. When she died, he remarried, at the age of 61, her father's widow Mary. Meanwhile Thomas White had married, in 1758, the widow of William Yalden (Anne's brother).

amends for his Oxford indiscretions. But with hindsight there is a lingering suspicion that the subscriptions he was soliciting from Gilbert and other members of the family were being put to quite a different use.

*

Attempting to piece together a pattern of life from the evidence of account books is an exercise as deeply and hopelessly immersed in speculation as an archaeological dig. There are a few shards of certainty and mounds of possibility. A shilling 'lost at commerce'. Sixpence for 'mending a frock'. Hints and puzzles. Then frequent small payments to 'Mrs Croke's man' – and suddenly the girl that Gilbert had been so fond of ten years before, Mrs Croke's daughter Jenny, drifts back into view. Indeed Mulso's sisters (who must have met her during their August trip) were

> quite clear that the affair between You & *One Jenny* is quite serious ... but You was so grave wth me in the Post Chaise that I dare not add to their Opinion any thing but my Applause of the Lady. However that be, I dare say that She is very instrumental in soft'ning the Rigour of your Oxford Confinement, & often prevents your forgetting family Life.[12]

But as to the nature of their relationship there is nothing more than suggestive clues. The payments to Mrs Croke's manservant were probably simply tips, paid when Gilbert visited her house and haberdashery, but they may have been rewards for a messenger. The considerable bill he settled with Mrs Croke at the close of 1752 for his official velvet sleeves and silk trimmings, for suits and waistcoats and '20 yards of blue check'd linen' for curtains (it came to £36.15s, almost a third of his proctorial earnings) may have been an entirely necessary expenditure, yet, spent all at one shop, it may conceivably have been an attempt to curry favour with Jenny's mother. But what was happening between the tantalizing lines of the entries for 25 and 26 October?

> Spent in Journey from Selborn to Oxon in a post-chaise with Jenny Croke 01 03 11

Gave Jenny Croke a round China-turene, being prevented
paying for ye post-chaise ...... 01 16 04[13]

Had Jenny been to stay with Gilbert in Selborne or was she
more prosaically delivering Oxford rents to Grandmother
White? What transpired during the journey to prevent
Gilbert paying his fare, and earned Jenny a soup tureen as a
reward? Knowing Gilbert's usual reaction to coach travel and
his taste for black humour, it is tempting to think that this
was, in the most literal sense, a sick joke. There was
Gilbert, prostrate with nausea and giddiness, unable even to
settle with the coachman, and there was this competent 30-
year-old woman taking care of everything. She wouldn't
hear of being paid back with cash, of course, and so next
day, Gilbert buys her this unambiguous memento of the trip
and his 'cascading' ...

*

Gilbert's year as a Proctor came to an end in May 1753, and
almost immediately he set out on the road again, visiting
London and Sunbury during the remainder of May and
June. In July he had a bout of 'inward heat' – probably a
premonitory attack of the gout that was to trouble him in
later life – and set off for a seven-week sojourn at the Hot
Wells at Bristol. But he was not so ill that he couldn't pun
with Mulso, linking his condition with the name of his old
friend and sparky intellectual sparring partner, Hecky: 'My
Uncle laugh'd heartily at your *Hectic Heat*,' Mulso replied,
'& my Aunt said that half such a Joke was a serious Proposal,
& we laugh'd before hand at the Fright we suppose You in at
ye reading of this, by which You find that You have drawn
yourself into a Praemunire.'[14]

Gilbert was remarkably free of illness by the standards of
his day. Mulso, on the other hand, was scarcely ever well.
He was only in his early thirties but already had the
demeanour and failing constitution of an ageing invalid. He
suffered from disabling migraines, piles, gout, arthritis and
vague, idiosyncratic 'fits'. A walk in a cool September

evening laid him up in bed for a week with a swollen face.
When he was eventually married he found the pains of his
wife's labour too much to bear, and retired with 'a violent
Headach and Hysteric Complaint'. His general health
wasn't helped by the large daily doses of the potent (and
occasionally addictive) herb valerian that he took as a
sedative. 'From your Heights of Health You look down on
me, & pity me ... ' he wrote to Gilbert. 'I envy You your
bold Flights, your Eagle Ranges; but see You deserve them.
I am a poor sculking Quail, whose very Love-Song is
plaintive.'[15] In fact Gilbert did not really pity Mulso at all.
He suspected that his friend was caught in a vicious circle of
inactivity, malingering and malaise, and needed 'crisping'.
He recommended a more energetic outdoor life, preferably
on horseback. But when Mulso asked him to procure a
suitable horse, Gilbert couldn't resist a jape at his friend's
expense, and delivered a pony (nicknamed Grub) that was
'intolerably shabby ... He is so broken-winded & wheezes
so bad that my Heart Ache will do me more Harm than ye
Air Good.'

In the mid-1750s there is scarcely a letter from Mulso that
does not dwell at some length on the multifarious ailments
endured by himself or his family (his 'Set of Crocks' as he
called them) and at times Gilbert's patience with this
concentrated hypochondria appears to flag. Certainly his
letters to Mulso became less frequent, and this was another
cause for complaint from Sunbury. 'Am I to suppose that
your Life has in it a great deal of Sameness, or a great
Variety, that You are so bad a Correspondent? ... by your
Description of your own Way of Life [you] must have
Leizure Hours in plenty.'[16] Mulso's slight pique – it was
never real disgruntlement – was probably unwarranted, but
there were times when he was genuinely and seriously ill,
and on these occasions Gilbert's inattentiveness probably
had more complicated causes. He was under stress himself,
trying not very successfully to find a place and a position that
suited him, and the infrequency with which he visited his
friend may have been part of a growing tendency to cling,

for security, to familiar places. In fact his affection for Selborne was not so much a fixed, inherent quality, as something which seemed to grow in proportion to the lengthening list of jobbing curacies he occupied; and it would be oversimplifying matters to see it as the major obstruction to his settling down. He had three different positions in as many years. In September 1753 he took over the curacy of Durley, near Bishop's Waltham, Hampshire. He had lodgings at the vicarage for £20 a year, but with only Sunday services to attend to, was able to commute the twenty miles to and from Selborne on Mouse. He kept up this position for a year and a half, and in May 1755 took up another curacy in West Dean, near Salisbury, Wiltshire. This appointment was through personal contact: West Dean was one of the livings of Edmund Yalden, vicar of Newton Valence. This time Gilbert was more than thirty miles from Selborne and was forced to spend some time in the parish. He did a little desultory exploration. He went truffle hunting, and visited Stonehenge, where he watched the jackdaws nesting in the gaps between the great stones. But he was far from happy. In June 1751 he broke off his duties for another seven weeks in the Hot Wells at Bristol. In the autumn of 1755 he began helping Mr Yalden in Newton Valence as well as West Dean. By December he was finding his increased duties irksome, and some time early in 1756 he resigned from the West Dean position.

From the end of February the *Garden Kalendar*, which had been almost dormant for the past ten months, was taken up again with a new vigour and warmth, and began to be entered on an almost daily basis. And to Gilbert's continuing interest in melons and vegetables was added a growing passion for flowers and for landscaping. That spring he began to build a range of bizarre follies and conceits in the fields below the Hanger. The ideas were partly prompted by the theories and example of the pioneering landscaper, William Kent, but most seemed more like tongue-in-cheek parodies of his suggestions. In May Gilbert had two huge vases (once oil jars) set up on nine-foot-tall pedestals, in

conspicuous positions in the Park. He cut a vista through the
tall hedges in the outer field, ranging six gates so that they
would be seen as receding images, one within the other, and
terminating in a figure of Hercules, twelve feet high,
painted on a board. Goodness knows what Pope would have
made of it, but Mulso, attempting to conjure up the scene in
his mind's eye, managed to find the right note of perplexed
delight:

> You see me wth my hand over my Brows & retiring to the
> prescribed Distancs, I wave my head about, & take them in
> with a critical Survey ...
> I believe the gaining of six Gates one above another in
> Perspective is full as new, as it is agreable; Missy desires me
> to tell You that She is charmed with this happy Circumst-
> ance; a Six Bar Gate in the Country being One of her
> favourite Coups d'Oeils; but to have Six at once ye
> happiness of a Century.[17]

By this time the Zig-zag track had also been completed,
but not without leaving a sour aftertaste. The idea was John
White's, and he had begun soliciting contributions towards
the project in September 1752. Most of the work was done
during the winter of that year, and in a few more years the
track was well enough established to be decorated with
'obelisks' – fancifully rugged pieces of sandstone rock carted
from Woolmer Forest. The southern end of the Hanger was
much less wooded then, and the Zig-zag became a landmark
visible from many parts of the village.

Successful though John's scheme was, the rest of his life
was proving as turbulent and difficult as his spell at Oxford.
Somehow – by gambling or simply incautious management
of his affairs – he had managed to fall disastrously into debt.
With no money to speak of beyond the small change he had
collected for work on the Hanger and an income of £40 a
year (chiefly from occasional clerical duties in Barnet and
London) he borrowed money indiscriminately from friends
and relations. His rather lame excuse was that 'An expectation of relief from my Father flattered me with a view of

requiting these obligations soon, till he affectionately informed me how little it was in his power.' One of his debtors, Dr Bristow, the Vicar of Selborne, then threatened to sue him, and to prevent a scandal, John was rapidly packed off overseas. Some time during the early part of 1756 he became Chaplain to the Garrison at Gibraltar. He was virtually ostracized by his family, and, from the autumn of 1756, did not hear a word from any of them for nearly two years – in fact, not until the death of his father, the news of which he first learned in unfortunate circumstances while browsing through a paper in a coffee-house.[18]

Gibraltar seemed to settle John down a little. He had been married to Barbara Freeman not long before his departure, and they had a son, Jack, in 1757. Soon John began to emulate his elder brother and take a serious interest in the natural history of Gibraltar. But he never entirely lost the slightly unstable edge to his character. The guilt and resentment he felt about his relations with his family went very deep and were to flare up again much later in his life.[19]

*

In 1756 there was another important change in the circumstances of one of Gilbert's circle. After eleven years of engagement that at times had proved an obvious strain, John Mulso was married to Jenny Young. It was a sudden decision, brought about by a disturbing incident. Jenny had been travelling back to London after visiting Mulso in Sunbury. There had been exceptionally heavy rains, and just at the edge of the town her driver, trying to avoid floodwater, had overturned the coach into the Thames. Jenny and her companion escaped with no more than mild shock and a thorough drenching, but Mulso had been frightened out of his wits. So had Jenny's father, who was a widower and had apparently been one of the chief obstructions to their marrying earlier. Rather than put his daughter to any further risk from travelling between London and Sunbury, he gave his consent to the marriage, on the understanding that he could come and live with the couple till his death. John and Jenny were made man and wife on 18 May 1756, less than four weeks after the accident.

The abruptness with which his best friend abandoned his bachelorhood may have made Gilbert more aware of the insecurity and singularity of his own life. At any rate, after Mulso's wedding a chain of events only partly beyond his control was set in motion that took Gilbert to the nearest approximation to a crisis that he encountered in his life.

In the mid-fifties Gilbert began casting round aimlessly, and at times almost recklessly, for a place that suited him. There were further spells assisting at Selborne and West Dean, and he wondered if he might, after all, be able to put up with the Wiltshire living. There was talk of a position in the Isle of Wight, the mere thought of which made Mulso feel seasick. Then an opportunity came up through his Oriel connections. The perpetual curacy of one of the College's preferments, the parish of Moreton Pinkney in Northamptonshire, became vacant and was offered to Gilbert, as a Senior Fellow. He agreed to take it on, provided he did not have to be a resident there and could put in a deputy.

But he still regarded a situation in Oxford as being the ideal solution to his problem. He liked the city, the academic atmosphere, the civilized and cultured life that was available to a don. He liked the fact the he would be rewarded rather better than he would be for occupying a draughty and isolated rectory somewhere in middle England. The long vacations, too, meant that he could still spend much of the year in Selborne. So, when the Provost of Oriel, Dr Walter Hodges, died in January 1757, Gilbert, nervously hoping his seniority in the College would see him through, decided to become a candidate for the post. He was not successful, and, in the election of 27 January, Chardin Musgrave was chosen. Musgrave had been an acquaintance of Gilbert's since their undergraduate days together, but as the correspondence with Mulso hints, there was little love lost between them. Gilbert felt bitter about Musgrave's appointment, and thought him quite unsuitable for the post of Provost. Musgrave for his part regarded Gilbert as rather unscrupulous, in being both a non-resident Fellow and, it now seemed, a potentially non-resident curate. When Musgrave confirmed Gilbert's appointment to Moreton Pinkney in October 1757, he added a proviso in his memorandum book, unusual in that residence had never before been demanded for this preferment, but effectively making Gilbert appear a supporter of sinecures and an opponent of reform: 'Dec 15. Moreton Pinkney given to Mr White as Senior Fellow, tho' without his intentions of serving it, not choosing to waive his claim ... but [I] agreed for the future that in any of the Tenable preferments Preference shall be given to any Fellow who will undertake to serve the cure, before a Senior who would put in a Deputy.'[20]

Gilbert's health began to deteriorate soon after his disappointment in the election for Provost and for once it was Mulso's turn to act as confidant and medical adviser. But his housemasterly prescription – cold baths and self-discipline – was no more understanding or helpful than Gilbert's panacea of horse-riding:

> And now, my dear Friend, what can be the matter wth You? for Mrs. Mulso and Myself think your Case, as You state it, unaccountable: You are not ill but in your Limbs, no Affection of the Spirits, & yet Blisters, Valerian & Assa Foetida: If any thing of this Sort remains, be a Man of a more constant Courage than your poor Friend has been, &, after Leave obtained to get into the Cold Bath, persevere in it.[21]

Whenever Gilbert sank below his usual level of self-confidence and activity, Mulso became concerned about his lack of a secure berth. 'Curate or not Curate still I find You will travell; a restless Animal you will still be 'till I find You squatted down in a Fat Goose Living,' he wrote, with the slightest shake of the head, on 12 May 1757. By the middle of the next year, just after the vicar of Selborne, Dr Bristow, had died, he was moved to elegiac tones about the possibility of his friend and Selborne itself falling from grace:

I beg of you to contrive to get a great Estate, to be enabled to live on at Selbourne, to be the Friend of the Poor who have now lost one & may in a few Years lose another [Gilbert's father]; & prevent that Sweet Place, which is already sunk from a great Town to a Village, from decaying into the very Den of Poverty & Misery: Capable as it certainly is of the highest Improvements, & of being one of the most enchanting Spots in England.[22]

Unhappily Mulso's prediction about Gilbert's father proved accurate, and John White senior died on 29 September 1758. The news soon reached Oxford, and those who made up the anti-White faction at Oriel assumed that Gilbert had come into a wealthy inheritance and was duty bound to quit his Fellowship. Chardin Musgrave made a note in the Provost's memorandum book that he had 'hinted to Mr White's friends that I was ignorant what his circumstances really were, but suppose his Estate incompatible'. It is important to understand that there were real feelings of resentment, and quite possibly jealousy, among certain sections of the College. The legend of White as a self-interested pluralist survived at Oriel for more than a century, and was spelled out with undiluted venom in an essay on the college published in 1891:

Gilbert White, of Selborne, among the fellows of Oriel at this period has left the most lasting name, yet his college history is in curious contrast to the reputation which is popularly attached to him. Instead of being, as is often supposed, the model clergyman residing in his cure, and interested in all the concerns of the parish in which his duty lay, he was, from a College point of view, a rich, sinecure, pluralist non-resident. He held his Fellowship for fifty years, 1743–1793, during which period he was out of residence, except for the year 1752–3, when the Proctorship fell to the College turn, and he came up to take it. In 1757 he similarly asserted his right to take and hold with his fellowship the small college living of Moreton Pinkney, Northants, with the avowed intention of not residing. Even at that time the

73

conscience of the College was shocked at this proposal and the claim only reluctantly admitted. White continued to enjoy the emoluments of his Fellowship and of his College living while he resided on his patrimonial estate at Selborne, and, although it was much doubted whether his fortune did not exceed the amount allowed by the Statutes, he acted on the maxim that anything can be held by a man who can hold his tongue, and he continued to enjoy his Fellowship and his living till his death.[23]

This is an extraordinary level of acrimony to have persisted for over 130 years, and it is fair to assume that it had become magnified in the telling. But the College was being perfectly reasonable in taking precautions against its Fellowships being retained by those that had no real need of them. Gilbert saw their opposition in a very different light though. He felt he was being victimized, and insisted that Oriel must take his word about his still meagre circumstances, and permit him to hang on to his Fellowship.

It was a vain hope, given the level of rivalry in the college. Even Mulso could not understand why Gilbert seemed so reluctant to back up his assertions with a clear and open statement about his financial position. In November 1758 he wrote a friendly but cautionary note to Gilbert reminding him of the purpose of Fellowships and urging him to do nothing that might alienate the Oriel Fellows still further:

> Tho' I have talked with your Brother Ben: and wth Mr. Cane, I can form at present no Judgement upon what Plea You can keep your Fellowship wth your Estate, so that I cannot give advice of any Value to your present Purposes. I cannot but conclude from my Knowledge of You, that the Reasons must appear very strong to You; & that You could not be tempted by Interest to do anything contrary to the Statutes of the University, or of your particular Society; and not only so, but that You can never forget that Fellowships are a sort of temporary Establishments for men of good Learning and small Fortunes, 'till their Merits or some fortunate Turn pushes them into ye World, and enables

them to relinquish to Men under the same Predicament.[24]

Some time during that month Gilbert did make a private representation to the Provost in which he set down the precise nature of his circumstances. The letter, a draft of which came to light early this century, includes the following:

> As to the freehold Patrimony to which I am entitled by my Father's decease I am very certain that the clear yearly income, upon which I depend from it, will fall short of the sum above supposed compatible by ye Visitor's determination £66.13.4 ... And I am certain that the income arising from my freehold-land will fall considerably short of what I am entitled to receive in virtue of my Fellowship.[25]

The Provost (though obviously not all the Fellows) seemed satisfied by Gilbert's plea that he was indeed a man of 'good Learning and small Fortune' and was therefore entitled to retain his Fellowship. He said as much to Mulso when the two met while strolling in St James's Park the following February: 'he said it was in your own breast to keep or leave your Fellowship; for Nobody meant to turn You out if You did not choose it Yourself.'

From the evidence that is now available it looks as if Gilbert was being perfectly correct in insisting that he had not come into anything remotely resembling a fortune on his father's death. The pattern of inheritance in the family was, as we have already seen, murky, idiosyncratic and complex, but at the beginning of this century Rashleigh Holt-White examined the wills and deeds and published a thorough account in his *Life and Letters*.[26] In essence the situation seems to have been as follows.

Most of the money in the family was on Gilbert's mother's side, and what little came down through the Whites themselves had completely bypassed Gilbert's father, John. Gilbert senior had left his estate, including the Wakes, to his wife Rebekah. After that it was to pass not to their eldest son, John, but to their youngest daughter, Elizabeth. But this bequest must have come to maturity on Elizabeth's marriage in 1730 to her cousin Charles White, since she died in 1753, two years before her mother. They had no children, and the Wakes therefore passed into Charles's hands for the remainder of his life. John's sole inheritance was a fifth of Rebekah's property, which amounted to little more than a share in the rent from some cottages in Oxford.

So, far from bequeathing patrimony, John did not even have the family house to leave to Gilbert. What Gilbert did inherit, in a very qualified way, was what had been left by his mother (and notionally held by her husband until his death). This consisted of a number of small farms in the southern counties, which were subject to various mortgages and charges. Most of these were immediately sold to provide the younger White children's portions of the bequest. The one property Gilbert did retain was Woodhouse farm at Harting, which at this time produced a rent of £34 per annum. The Farringdon curacy brought in a little over £30 a year, and the income from the curacy at Moreton Pinkney about the same. His properties in Selborne amounted to a maximum annual value (at his death) of £28.[27] So Gilbert's total annual income from sources other than his Fellowship (which earned on average about £100 a year) was at this time almost certainly little more than £100.

The mystery, therefore, is why Gilbert took such pains to keep this information confidential, to the extent of ensuring that his private note to the Provost was not kept in the college archives. The only plausible explanation is the one suggested by Anthony Rye, that it was done to shield Gilbert's father from public scandal. John was in his thirties when Gilbert senior effectively disinherited him. Whether this was, as cause or effect, connected with the personality problems that became evident in his middle years can only be guessed at. But the story would probably have come to light if Gilbert had been less discreet with his disclosures. It's extremely doubtful if it would ever have been more than a minor piece of college gossip, but for Gilbert, who valued his position at Oriel so highly, that would have been a quite sufficient deterrent.

Chapter Five
Green Retreats

The year 1758 had been a very bad one for Gilbert. His father had died, he had failed in an attempt to return full-time to Oxford, and come close to losing his Fellowship and being publicly humiliated. This was the last occasion on which he was to make a serious and determined attempt to find a life away from Selborne. That autumn, as the Fellowship squabble was nearing its height, he had looked out towards the Hanger and seen something that moved him to make the first written indication of what was to become a lifelong fascination with the mysteries of territorial attachment:

> Nov 2. Saw a very unusual sight; a large flock of House-Martens playing about between our fields, & the Hanger. I never saw any of the swallow-kind later than the old 10: Octobr: The Hanger being quite naked of leaves made the sight the more extraordinary.[1]

From 1759 the garden again becomes the chief focus of his life. The first real day of spring was 13 April, and Gilbert was bursting with activity and hope for the coming season:

> Made an Annual-bed for the biggest one-light frame with 6 barrows of hot dung, & one of weeds: laid on the mould six inches deep. Finished-off, & raked very smooth the bastion, & sowed it very thick with rye-grass, & white clover. Sowed ye bare places in the fields, & orchard with the same. Planted two rows of slips of a very *fine sort* of double-bloody-wall-flower from my Dame Scot's of Harting. Made the ground very mellow with lime-rubbish. Sowed a plot of Holy-oak [Hollyhock] seed, & leek-seed. Planted some rose-campions, & Columbines in the new Garden.
>
> A perfect summer's day, that fetched ye beds finely to their heat after such gluts of rain.
>
> Saw seven swallows, the first this year, playing about James Knight's House.[2]

In the middle of November 1759 he left Selborne for six months, and vanished from view more completely than at any time during his adult life. Later he mentions that he had been in London and at his married sister Anne's house at

Lyndon, and it's fair to assume that he had taken a long break, in part to think about his own future. But there are no more solid clues as to how he filled his normally busy days. The garden was temporarily abandoned, the journals closed down, and Mulso, who had just become a father for the second time and was on the point of decamping to a new parish in Yorkshire, was left to ponder sadly how he would manage to see his nomadic friend again.

Gilbert returned to Selborne in mid-May 1760, to find the asparagus in season and his cucumbers and melons well cared for in his absence. The journal, which he always saw partly as a refuge, was able to continue its meandering progress. The day after his return, 18 May, it records 'a fierce storm of hail, which batter'd the vine shoots at the end of the Dining-room' – but was still preferable, no doubt, to last year's upheavals in the Senior Common Room.

Gilbert's sabbatical seemed to confirm his commitment to Selborne. Yet he was no nearer any practical solutions to his problems. He had no job and no prospect of any immediate increase in his small income. He was also still single, and Mulso would not let him forget it. In January 1761, his friend wrote with news of two weddings: Thomas Mulso, his brother, had married a Miss Prescott, and Hecky, Gilbert's old companion, had become Mrs Chapone. 'To these Brides & Bridegrooms,' Mulso wrote, 'I know You will give your good wishes that, that as they have long waited for *this happy State* (I don't know whether I speak to be understood by you who continue an old Batchelor) they may long continue happy in it.'[3] Later in the year Gilbert's sister Rebecca became engaged, and he was faced with the imminent prospect of being alone in the Wakes. He had almost certainly, in his heart, begun to abandon any serious thoughts of marriage. But the constant ebb and flow around him of weddings and births (and deaths: Hecky was widowed after just ten months) could hardly fail to highlight his own solitude.

But the garden, at least, was something for which he could make long-term plans. During 1761 he planted large numbers of fruit trees, and made a fruit wall for his espaliers.

This was the second piece of considerable stonework to be added to the garden that year:

> Jan 24: Long the mason finish'd the dry wall of the Haha in the new garden, which is built of blue rags, so massy, that it is supposed to contain double the Quantity of stone usual in such walls. Several stones reach into the bank 20 inches. The wall was intended to be 4 feet & an half high: but the labourers in sinking the ditch on inclining ground mistook the level, especially at the angls: so that at that part to bring it to a level it is 5 feet 8 inch: high, & 4 feet 6 inch: at the ends: an excellent fence against the mead, & so well fast'ned into the clay bank, that it looks likely to stand a long while.[4]

The Ha-ha was an ingenious and effective device consisting simply of a deep ditch between the garden and the park, pasture or farmland beyond. It was designed to provide a boundary and keep cattle out of the flower-beds without interrupting the view. Ideally it provided a way of visually merging the garden with the countryside beyond.

The Ha-ha at the Wakes was one of the earliest to be built in a small private garden here. In France they had been in vogue since the mid-seventeenth century, and began to form part of English landscapes in the 1720s. Horace Walpole, writing in 1770, thought them the cornerstone, as well as one of the most telling symbols, of the new gardening:

> But the capital stroke, the leading step to all that has followed, was ... the destruction of walls for boundaries, and the invention of fosses – an attempt then deemed so astonishing, that the common people called them Ha! Ha's! to express their surprise at finding a sudden and unperceived check to their walk ... I call a sunk fence the leading step for these reasons. No sooner was this simple enchantment made, than levelling, mowing, rolling followed. The contiguous ground of the park without the sunk fence was to be harmonised with the lawn within; and the garden in its turn was to be set free from its prim regularity, that it might assort with the wilder country without.[5]

Gilbert did not follow up his own entrenchment with such an elaborate manicure. But the extent to which, in more general terms, he saw no clear dividing line between the business of gardening and the life of the 'wilder country without' is shown by a remarkable entry in the *Garden Kalendar* for mid-May 1761. Quite out of the blue, after a run of short routine notes on disbudding vines and sowing broccoli, he launches into a long and vivid account of the lives of the local crickets. It was 20 May, a warm day in the middle of a wet spell, and Gilbert and his brother Thomas had wandered down to the pasture just north of the church known as the Short Lythe. It was at that time a steep, rock-strewn field, studded with furze and full of flowers and insects, and the two men planned to examine 'the nature of those animals that make a chearful shrill cry all the summer months in many parts of the south of England'. They had taken a spade to dig the creatures up, but it proved 'difficult not to squeeze them to death in breaking the Ground', and more gentle methods had to be worked out. In the rapt descriptions that follow, Gilbert's fondness for the crickets is as evident as his curiosity about them: 'they have long legs behind with large brawny thighs, like Grasshoppers, for leaping'. The female was 'dusky', with 'a long terebra'. The male was ' a black shining Colour, with a golden stripe across it's shoulder like that of the Humble bee'. He would, he felt, 'be glad to have them encrease on account of their pleasing summer sound.' The sketch carries on in this affectionate, discursive way. Yet behind it we can glimpse the emergence of what was to become the classic model for field studies: the patient, inquisitive watching, the changes of focus as questions multiply; then answers dawning, from flashes of intuition or plain hard reasoning, and these forming a framework to test against yet more watching. And all these processes not rigidly ordered but advancing together in a kind of continuous feedback:

> It is very likely that the males only make that shrilling noise; which they may do out of rivalry, & emulation during their

breeding time; as is the Case with many animals. They are solitary Insects living singly in Holes by themselves; & will fight fiercely when they meet as I found by some which I put into an hole in a dry wall ... For tho' they had express'd distress by being taken out of their knowledge; yet the first that had got possession of the chink seized an other with a vast pair of serrated fangs so as to make it cry-out. With these strong, toothed Malae (like the sheers of lobster's claws) they must terebrate their curious regular Holes; as they have no feet suited for digging like the mole-cricket. I could but wonder, that when taken in hand, They never offer'd to bite, tho' furnish'd with such formidable weapons. They are remarkably shy, & cautious, never stirring but a few inches from the mouth of their holes, & retiring backward nimbly into them, & stopping short in their song by that time you come within several yards of their caverns: from whence I conclude they may be a very desirable food to some animals, perhaps several kinds of birds.[6]

Nothing remotely approaching the vivid, sensuous, *attentiveness* of this piece exists in eighteenth-century prose on the natural world, and it is hard to explain its sudden appearance in the midst of the normally restrained pages of the *Kalendar*. Perhaps it was not as novel for Gilbert as it now seems, and represented a style he had evolved in, say, his early travel letters to Mulso, and which had momentarily strayed into the journals. Or perhaps it was a premonitory experiment, a try-out of an idea still only half-formed. If so, Gilbert was plainly not ready to follow it up (though he eventually used the note as a basis for the much longer account of crickets in the *Natural History*).[7] It is written up, with no covering explanation and the minimum of correction, as if it were a piece of outdoor work like any other. Later that same day he is back sowing French beans.

Yet all the characteristics that were to make White's writing stand so distinctively and originally apart are already there, simply waiting to be developed: the painstaking thoroughness; the eye for sharp and intimate detail; the mixture of animal sympathy and inquisitive science; the willingness to consider that animals had an 'inner' existence, independent of humans. Gilbert's vocabulary, which freely mixed scientific jargon and rural commonplace, followed naturally from these attitudes. The crickets might be able to 'terebrate', but they could also slip 'out of their knowledge'; be, as it were, both technologists and peasants. These sudden pitches into the vernacular were sometimes used by Gilbert for deliberate comic effect. Here they also make the crickets seem rather endearing, and heighten our sense of their distress without ever falling into sentimentality.

The most significant aspect of the essay is the way that Gilbert's affection for the crickets as fellow creatures is inseparable from his attitude towards them as objects of scientific study. On a later occasion, he worked out a way of encouraging the insects out of their holes without causing them harm: 'a pliant stalk of grass, gently insinuated into the caverns, will probe their windings to the bottom, and quickly bring out the inhabitant; and thus the humane enquirer may gratify his curiosity without injuring the object of it'.[8]

This is about as far as Gilbert went in the direction of experimenting on living creatures. He neither approved of, nor had much scientific faith in, the wilful distorting of animals' lives purely for the sake of gaining knowledge. He saw them as beings endowed with sensation and feelings, and as members of immensely complex and intricate living systems. Their secrets could not be forced from them without – philosophically just as much as physically – 'injuring the object' of the study.

Yet it's well known that Gilbert enjoyed hunting and shooting in his younger years, and until his late middle-age showed little compunction about killing all kinds of animals in order to identify or dissect them. His affection for them did not extend as far as an absolute respect for their existence as individuals. In this respect he was no different from most of his contemporaries, and it is perhaps only by modern standards that his outlook appears paradoxical. Yet it would be glib – and insulting to Gilbert's intelligence – to explain away his attitude as being purely customary. The eighteenth century saw an immense upswing of concern about the rights and welfare of animals among writers, philosophers and clerics. Some of these were known to White personally, and if he chose not to follow their arguments all the way, this must be seen as a conscious decision. Although he did not write directly about this issue until the last years of his life, his views on it underpin his attitudes towards scientific method and towards the nature of the relationships of humans with other creatures, and it is important to try and understand where he stood.

At one extreme in the eighteenth-century debate was Steven Hales, a noted physiologist, philanthropist, and one-time neighbour of the Whites, who is often assumed to have been partially responsible for Gilbert's scientific inclinations.[9]

Hales had been the non-resident vicar of Farringdon, a village three miles north-west of Selborne, between 1722 and 1741. He lived in Teddington, but during this period he spent a couple of months each summer at the Farringdon vicarage, and had been a good friend of both Gilbert's grandfather and father. Gilbert had met him when he was a boy, and seemed to have kept in touch in later years, perhaps when he was visiting his brothers, who then lived close by in south London. The autumn following the cricket-watch he became curate to Hales's successor at Farringdon.

Hales was probably best known as an inventor, and when Gilbert wrote a note about him to their mutual friend Robert Marsham years later, he appears as an ingenious, somewhat eccentric social benefactor.[10] His discoveries, Gilbert remembered, included ways of making wells safe, of preventing pies boiling over, destroying insects in fruit trees by the use of injected quicksilver, dissolving kidney stones with onion juice and, more seriously, ventilating the lower decks of ships. Most of these contrivances had come out of a life-long study of the circulation of fluids, especially in the bodies of plants and animals. Gilbert refers to his important book *Vegetable Staticks* (1727) on several occasions and made practical use of some of its findings in designing a ventilation system for his hot-beds. 'His whole mind seemed replete

brother Edward (Ned), Basil Cane (Gilbert's cousin), and Harry White, his brother, now very nearly 30, who had recently taken over the living of Fyfield, about thirty miles west of Selborne.

Gilbert was more or less master of ceremonies, and he put at his guests' disposal the tent-like pavilion which was regularly erected in the Wakes' grounds during summer (see Plate 1). Sadly, he makes almost no mention of the events of that summer. But one of the sisters, Catharine (usually known as Kitty), kept a diary during her holiday, which she entitled 'A little Journal of some of the Happiest days I have had in the happy Valley in the year 1763'. It is a breathless, naïve record, but so perfectly suggests the boundless energies and evanescent enthusiasms of these young girls – and the impact they had on the assembled bachelors – that it is worth quoting from at some length:[13]

22 of June in the afternoon Mr. White Mr. Harry White Mrs. Snooke & Mrs. Woods drank tea here; Mr H. White & Nancy sung & play'd at nine o'clock ... Went to bed between twelve & one o clock was very merry after supper the next day being Mr. and Mrs. Ettys' wedding day we kept it with mirth & jollity. The morn was spent at the Harpsicord a Ball at night began minuets at half an hour after seven then danced country dances till near eleven went to supper after supper sat some time sung laugh't talk'd & then went to dancing again danced till 3 in the morn; at half an hour after four the company all went away we danced 30, danced, never had I such a dance in my life before not ever shall I have such a one again I believe.

Gilbert was the only solitary male at this ball, and he always sounds something of an outsider among the young revellers. The vivacious Miss Kitty was paired with Harry, and to judge from the number of times his name appears, they made quite an impression on each other. The following day they all climbed the Zig-zag and had tea in the Hermitage. In the middle of the party Harry appeared, dressed up as a Hermit, and gave Kitty a delicious shock. They wandered round the High Wood till it was dusk, then went back once more to the Hermitage to admire its romantic prospects by lamplight. 'Never shall I forget the happiness of this day,' sighed Kitty, 'which exceeded any I ever had in all my life.' The next day, 25 June, was Harry's thirtieth birthday, and also a Saturday, when he needed to get back to Fyfield to prepare for the next morning's services. But Kitty and her sisters had other plans for this important anniversary: 'After breakfast ... Harry White came in to take his leave of us being in a great hurry to go but the 3 sorceresses ... so bewitched him that he did not go till four in the afternoon.' 'Poor Harry Tinderbox,' wrote Mulso, 'I pity his liver,' though it was his clerical decorum that seemed to be in greater danger. A few Saturdays later temptation got the better of him again: 'Sat 16 ... Mr. Cane & Mr. Henry White came on Horseback to the Door to take leave of us determined not to come in but he soon broke thro' his resolution & dismounted came in sang 3 songs & then took his leave.'

Gilbert observed these goings-on from the wings with a brave face and an avuncular smile. And he gallantly (or wishfully) made a bet with Miss Kitty that she couldn't persuade Harry to linger on. It was, needless to say, a hopeless gamble, but it may have been some comfort to Gilbert to know that Kitty preserved his settlement note, with its discreet hints and winks, inside her journal:

> MADAM – I make a point of paying my debts of Honour as soon as possible; but at the same time can't help remarking that it was not a fair wager. For it is plain, by some art magic best known to yourself, you have not only a power of detaining men that ought to be going; but also of keeping those away that ought to come. In the whole it is best that I have been the loser, as it would not be safe in all appearance to receive even so much as a pin from your Hands, – I am, with many a †††††††††††††††† and many a Pater noster and Ave Maria,[14]
>
> GIL. WHITE

And while the younger men danced and sang and acted out the roles of lovesick swains, Gilbert, too reserved for such antics, entertained the girls with more philosophical diversions – all thoroughly respectable, though they did seem to focus attention rather pointedly on the girls' physical attributes. They had their shadows taken, were measured, and as a special treat on 27 July were 'electrified', a newly popular parlour trick which involved standing on a stool whose legs were insulated by rubber, and having your hair brushed until it stood on end.

Tuesday 19 [July] after breakfast Mr. W [Gilbert] came in to ask us to go out a Riding we drest and went over to his house. but the weather grew so bad that it prevented our going We spent the morn together with much mirth & cheerfullness we were all weigh'd to see how much we were worth. I weigh 134lb oh monstrous afterwards we were all measured came home to dinner in the afternoon Mr. White the Mulsos etc. etc. came here with work singing & Playing we spent a very agreeable evening.

Wed 20 ... Mr. T Mulso gave us a discourse upon Natural Phylosophy & Astronomy we work'd he read some of Thomsons Seasons we walk'd in the Woods & then came home to dinner I hope I edify'd by his sensible discourse Mr. E.M. & Mr. White drank tea here afterwards we went out a Riding I rode double for the first time rode upon the sweet Commons & in the High Wood call'd at Newton, it was a most delightful evening I hope we are going to have fine weather.

Thursday 21. after Breakfast went into the Hay field toss'd the hay about a little then went to Mr. White's sat in the Alcove spent the morn most delightfully Mr. T. Mulso read Thomson & at Two came home to dinner at 6 we met again to walk went up to the sweet Hermitage sat viewing its various beauteous [views?] some time then walk round the wood back to the Hermitage, Mr. White read us an acrostick made upon Nanny. Miss Baker & I found a stone upon the Common which we carried to the Hermitage & placed it there as a memorial of our fondness for that place.

Reading Thomson, tossing the hay a little, viewing the prospect from a Hermitage ... what delightful, poetical treats! For these fashionable London girls, the Selborne interlude had become an opportunity to act out a rustic idyll in a setting as near to a classical Arcadia as they were ever likely to experience. As their holiday drew to a close, they were so taken with the fancy that they began calling each other after characters from pastoral drama and, occasionally, dressing up like them. Kitty was Daphne, and Harry, Ned and Basil were Strephon, Corydon and Collin, respectively. On the 28 July the whole company had a picnic on top of the Hanger. Gilbert, for once, was sufficiently moved to record the occasion in the *Garden Kalendar*.

> Drank tea 20 of us at the Hermitage: the Miss Batties, & the Mulso family contributed much to our pleasures by their singing, & being dress'd as shepherds, shepherdesses. It was a most elegant evening; and all parties appear'd highly satisfy'd. The Hermit appear'd to great advantage.[15]

Gilbert's dispassionate journal may have been more than usually evasive this time. He had apparently stage-managed the whole show, including the fancy dress, and a little while later wrote an ambivalent verse to Kitty, which she also kept carefully in her journal:

> Gilbert, a meddling, Luckless swain
>   Must alter lady's dresses
> To dapper Hats, & tuck'd up train
>   And flower-enwoven tresses.
>
> But now the Lout with loss of heart
>   Must for his rashness pay;
> He rues for tamp'ring with a dart
>   Too prompt before to slay![16]

On 3 August the Battie sisters departed for London, taking with them one of Gilbert's best canteloup melons as a gift for their father. 'Adieu happy Vale enchanting Hermitage much loved stump beauteous Hanger sweet Lythe,' wrote Kitty in the final entry in her journal, 'here the scene closes the play is done the pleasing dream is oer & tomorrow I must awake & find myself in London.' She also carried off a more personal tribute, a fulsome elegy from Harry (which he signed as 'Strephon') entitled 'Daphne's Departure'. One of its many stanzas ran:-

> Ah! wretched Selbourn! what avail thy Shades
>   Thy lofty Hills with waving Beeches crown'd;
> Their boasted Glory now for ever fades,
>   And endless Winter shall thy Vales surround.[17]

Gilbert too was moved to mournful – or at least mock mournful – verse by the girls' departure, but not into a direct admission of his own feelings: poetry for him played the role of a discreet escape valve rather than an open confessional. In this instance he recounts not his own sadness but 'Kitty's Farewell to the Stump beneath the Hermitage'. The poem generously includes Harry amongst the lamented views of Selborne – though more as 'The hoary Hermit' than as gilded Strephon – and it is that 'delightful stump', on which Kitty no doubt loitered in studied moonstruck poses, that Gilbert raises to the poetic centre of her affections.

Kitty may well have been momentarily infatuated with Harry, but she was sensible enough, even at 19, to understand about holiday romances, especially when so much of the summer idyll had been played out as a deliberate fantasy. The young men's ardour was slower to cool. Ned, his father reported in early October, felt '*cut to ye Brain*', but it would do no lasting harm, 'especially as it purges off in Poetry: when Passion is fancifull it is not dangerous. Ned requires these Brushings; being apt to have torpid & viscous Blood, if a Love Fit now & then did not quicken his Pulses.'[18] But Mulso sensed, either intuitively or from a confidence in one of Gilbert's letters, that it wasn't just the younger men who had been 'brushed'.

> It would not do you so much good, unless it was once to ye Purpose; for we, my Friend, begin to grow into a more serious Age, & to mean a little more what we profess. I beg you to get as much this Winter as possible into ye gay World;

for it will be of Prejudice to your Health & Spirits to employ
a Winter in putting on Wood in a Country Village.[19]

The 'Purpose', or 'certain Scheme', as it was variously
called, was Mulso's plan to marry Gilbert off, and he needed
only the slightest excuse to remind his friend that it was
making little headway. But this time the reference seems
more serious, and, as the autumn of 1763 gave way to a wet
and early winter, it became increasingly plain that all was
not well with Gilbert. His *Garden Kalendar* entries drop to
about half their usual frequency, and his letters to Mulso
become more urgent, to the extent that Mulso finds 'ye
tables are somewhat turned, & that you are like to be ye
Complainant, & I ye person complained of as a bad
Correspondent.' One note, which brought news of the death
of Mrs Thomas White and more evidence of Gilbert's
melancholy, made Mrs Mulso weep. In November Gilbert
took his friend's advice and went for a holiday in London,
staying at the Mulso family's town house in Rathbone Place.
Mulso thought it a wise move: 'a little of ye Bustle, and
Talk, & Variety of London is absolutely necessary for you,
and if you should have any *further Knowledge* of ye Miss B's:
it might have rather a salutary than a dangerous Effect; for it
is my Notion that they may be very safely taken either full or
fasting.'[20] Can Gilbert really have gone to town with the
intention of searching out the Batties? It was hardly the best
prescription for someone in his state of mind. The company
of these tireless heiresses, half his age and obviously marked
out for superior matches, was likely to drive him even
deeper into depression.

By the end of the year he was back in Selborne. He'd seen
little of the sisters and done nothing to improve his mood,
and in the unaccustomed quiet of the Wakes, with only the
company of his recently widowed aunt, Rebecca Snooke, he
began to sink into self-pity. He confessed as much to Mulso,
and made what was probably a morbid comparison between
his own circumstances and Mulso's proliferating (albeit
sickly) household. But his friend would have none of it, and

for once his gentle, teasing banter seems exactly the right response:

> I have but little Hope of your thinking much of any particular absent Female, because when you say – "while *I*, doing no good in my Generation, am still single!" – you did not insert the Lover-like word *Alass*! after *I*. There is a Sort of sentimental Sorrow in ye whole Sentence, but there is not Feeling enough for a Man in Earnest without the word *alass*.[21]

Behind the mockery Mulso's assessment was almost certainly right, and Gilbert's despondency probably had more to do with his age and a nostalgia for a last taste of youthful high spirits than any particular romantic longings. But the feelings were strong ones none the less, and when Gilbert came to express them in writing – to 'purge them off in Poetry' as his brother had done – he composed what is unquestionably the most effective of all his verses. 'SELBORNE HANGER   A Winter Piece. To the Miss Batties' is dated 'Nov 1, 1763',[22] just a couple of days after the *Kalendar* had noted the first autumn gales sweeping through the beechwoods. It starts off in anguished, heroic tones reminiscent both of Harry's elegy and Thomas Gray's ('How fall'n the glories of these fading scenes!/The dusky beech resigns his vernal greens;') and ends with a stanza that sounds like a declamation for the end of a masque:

> Return, blithe maidens; with you bring along
> Free, native humour, all the charms of song;
> The feeling heart, and unaffected ease,
> Each nameless grace, and ev'ry power to please.

But the heart of the poem is a powerful evocation of the storm-torn Hanger:

> The rushing woods with deaf'ning clamour roar,
> Like the sea tumbling on the pebbly shore.
> When spouting rains descend in torrent tides,
> See the torn zigzag weeps its channel'd sides:
> Winter exerts its rage; heavy, and slow,

From the keen east rolls on the treasur'd snow;
Sunk with its weight the bending boughs are seen,
And one bright deluge whelms the works of men.
Amidst this savage landscape, bleak and bare,
Hangs the chill hermitage in middle air;
Its haunts forsaken, and its feasts forgot,
A leaf-strown, lonely, desolated cot!

This is strong, physical writing, full of the rhythms of weather; but it hardly needs stressing that the loneliness and desolation are as much the author's as the landscape's. This projection of human feeling onto the external world of nature was to become a conventional and often greatly abused device of Romantic poetry. What is unusual – and, in a way, advanced – about this piece is that White does not turn the Hanger into an abstraction or an arena for fantastical Arcadian scenes. The beech groves, the hermitage, the feasts (and, stretching a point, the nymphs) are all *real*. So is their visible decline into winter. The Zig-zag breaking up in the rainwash, the whole hill and valley scene vanishing under 'clustering fogs' aren't just symbolic reminders of the transience of experience; they are actually part of the physical break-up of Selborne's summer playground. This glimpse that the links between the human and natural world were real as well as metaphorical was to become one of the key features of White's prose.

*

The winter of 1763/4 continued wet and stormy, but, by the middle of March, the cucumbers were in leaf, and the crocuses putting on a spectacular show, and Gilbert's spirits started to rise a little. He was soon back in energetic form in the garden, raking out the asparagus beds and planting rows of potatoes. There was not a great deal else to do during the week. He had still found no suitable living to replace his light duties as curate at Farringdon, and at times it is hard to believe he really wanted to. Oriel College livings at Tortworth in Gloucestershire and Cholderton in Wiltshire became vacant, were given a cursory glance, and passed over.

Nor could he be tempted out of the security of Hampshire by Mulso, despite a new openness and warmth in his old friend's letters from the north. Mulso was being mellowed by the joys of family life, and, perhaps, by his share of the tragedies. In the space of one month in 1764, he had lost his son George and gained a daughter. His wife Jenny was almost continuously ill, a prey to nervous debility and exhausted by three difficult confinements in the space of two years. But the pleasure of her company and of his surviving children more than made up for these disappointments for Mulso, and, throughout 1764 and '65, he sends Gilbert touching accounts of domestic life at Thornhill. He describes the rambling architecture, his eccentric fiddle-playing footman, the melons that had been planted in homage to Gilbert ('I had hope to have seen You, peeping at & pinching them, & laying your Head with my Gardener'), and himself and Jenny, valiantly trying to make the best of advancing middle age in the grip of a Yorkshire winter. They had been pinned down by the fireside together, these two near invalids, and had 'alternately taken up the Spectacles to read to one another'.

Mulso repeatedly pleads with Gilbert to come and share these homely pleasures with them. During the spring of 1764, and again in '65 and '66, he draws up elaborate plans for the journey north, discusses the sleeping arrangements ('We have one Room below Stairs where a Friend might lie, but he must be a Friend *indeed*' – or at a pinch, there was always the Melon frame) and dreams of the expeditions they will make together. His generosity and sense of excited anticipation are infectious, and as the years pass, Gilbert's failure to respond – and it was a failure, not a refusal – begins to seem a little miserly. Even the prospect of a carriage north with the now widowed Hecky Chapone failed to move him. Gilbert's evasiveness was hardly a momentous shortcoming, and it did not seem to strain the two men's friendship too seriously (though Mulso ends one of his invitations with the words 'I think you have used me ill, yet I am, as usual, Dear

Gil, Unalterably & afftely Your's'; and Gilbert begins one of his procrastinating replies 'Dear Sir').

But the reasons behind Gilbert's apparent inability to make a visit to the man who was his oldest and closest friend may reveal something about the way he was beginning to perceive his own future. He had, as it happens, plenty of excuses for not making the journey. He may have been discomfited by the prospect of 'the many Species of Satisfaction that attend Paternity' being pressed so closely upon him. He certainly felt some trepidation at the immensity of the journey – it involved at least four days on the road – and the inevitable bouts of coach-sickness that would accompany it. But he never suggested these as reasons for staying at home. The excuses he does offer seem, by contrast, rather thin. He has unavoidable clerical duties. He must supervise some 'musical Affair'. There are building projects unfinished at the Wakes. The image of Gilbert that is reflected in Mulso's letters at this time is that of a man who, from habit or choice, was beginning to see the life he already had as his one safe and reliable refuge and was digging in his heels.

And in June 1765, Mulso, now with a shrewd eye for the way Gilbert revealed his feelings in his prose style, concluded that even the possibility of marriage was receding fast, though he continued to urge Gilbert towards it for another couple of years. What persuaded him was Gilbert's reaction to a tragic accident in Selborne, in which a young boy had been killed:

> It seems however to have settled you in your Debates upon Matrimony, & confirmed you in your State of Celibacy: for you observe wth a Formality of Stile, which you drop in the next Sentence, that wedlock hath also numbers of Cares, &c: as if you had *excerped* the Observation fm a Treatise upon the Expediency of dying an old Batchelor.[23]

*

Later that year Gilbert began to take a serious interest in botany. He was in the mood for a new, absorbing, optimistic pastime, and it's clear from the *Kalendar* that he was

becoming increasingly intrigued by how plants coped with
the rigours of English weather: 1765 had been marked by
extreme conditions of all kinds. February had brought
severe frosts, and on the 28th a great snowstorm, the worst
in the village's memory: 'The wind was so strong, & the
snow so searching, that the Hotbeds were not uncovered
above two Hours all day.' Then there was a brief respite,
producing in the *Kalendar* one of those gems of terseness
and clarity that could capture the feel of a whole day in a
single sentence. 'March 4. A smart frost, & very strong
sunshine all day. The bees work very briskly on the Crocuss
amidst the banks of snow.' But the rest of March brought
gales, floods and heavy rain. So did April. The succade
melons were sickly, and the nectarines running to twigs.
During May and June an unrelenting drought set in. By
mid-July there had been no rain to speak of for ten weeks.
'The weeds are all kill'd,' noted Gilbert, looking out over
James Knight's baked plough-lands, and the soil was 'as
rough as the sea in an hard Gale'. On 6 July he was riding
back from his brother's house in Fyfield across the open hills
between Andover and Alresford, and was struck at how,
despite the privations of the drought, these downlands were
still green, often because of just one plant, the little salad
burnet. The poorer and chalkier the soil, the commoner it
became. And the more the sheep (which were very partial to
it) grazed it, the more thickly it sprouted back.

Gilbert was impressed by this plant, so 'tenacious of life',
and the long entry he makes on it in his journal that day, the
first on any wild plant, is a sign of his expanding interest.
Just over a month later he changed the title of the *Garden
Kalendar* to *A Calendar of Flora, & the Garden, from August 9th
1765*, and by the end of the month the garden was very
much in second place. With relieved sidelong glances at
what had turned into a bumper harvest in sublime late-
summer weather, and at the teeming broods of martins and
partridges, he was out scouring the woods and hedgerows for
new plants. He had nothing comparable to a modern
guidebook to help him, though John Hill's *Herbal*, which he

had purchased in 1765, was at least in English. Mostly he worked with austere Latin taxonomies like John Ray's *Synopsis methodica stirpium Britannicarum* and Hudson's standard *Flora Anglica*,[24] which he had bought that year. But he was eventually able to mark in his copy of Hudson 439 different species found within the parish of Selborne. His finds that first autumn are remarkable, given that he was a novice and prospecting in the tail-end of the flowering season. He discovered deadly nightshade, 'full of ripe fruit', on the steep chalk slopes of Wheatham Hill, near Petersfield; hellebores coming into early leaf on the Hanger; and sundew 'on the bogs of Beans-pond in Wullmere forest'. Plants, unlike more mobile creatures, could be given these exact addresses, and Gilbert's *Calendar* for the months that follow gives a vivid picture of the disposition of Selborne's flora in the eighteenth century – and, incidentally, of just how familiar he was with every corner and cranny of the parish. On 30 October he found sharp-leaved fluellen 'in my Ewelclose, a wheat-stubble', and the next day, wall lettuce, male and hart's-tongue ferns 'in a most shady part of the hollow lane under the cover of the rock as you first enter the lane in great plenty, on the right hand before you come to nineacre-lane'. (They can still be found in this exact spot today.)

The hollow lanes were Gilbert's favourite huntingground. Since they were the only thoroughfares through and out of the village he would have used one or more of them almost daily. But one senses a rather special fascination in the many references he makes to them over the years. Perhaps it was their combination of 'grotesque and wild appearances' with the feeling of a close, secluded intimacy; of secrecy with village conviviality. Lanes and flowers together formed a kind of enduring geography that was part of the identity of the parish. In the middle of a fierce November frost Gilbert found polypody and gladdon ('the stinking flag-flower') 'in the hollow lane between Nortonyard & French-meer just without the gate'. The gladdon, he remarks, 'was thrown, in all probability out of the garden which was formerly on the other side of the Hedge'. And as with many of his more interesting finds, he took its seeds back to grow on in the security of his own garden.

But Gilbert's botanizing wasn't done purely in the familiar surroundings of his home parish. He was every bit as inquisitive – and confident – when visiting the territories of friends and relatives. Late in September, down by the sea near his aunt's house at Ringmer, Sussex, he had found burnet rose, and was able to identify it from the leaves alone. On the way to Oxford in October he had walked the five miles between Streatley and Wallingford along the bank of the Thames, and noted comfrey and yellow and purple loosestrifes.

During 1766, Gilbert was sufficiently preoccupied with botanizing to devote a separate journal to it. On the notebook's flyleaf he inscribed its title and description: 'Flora Selborniensis: with some co-incidences of the coming and departure of birds of passage, and insects: and the appearing of Reptiles: for the Year 1766.'[25] The entries are little more than a bare record of dates and names, but they amount to a vast tally for just twelve months' browsing, and suggest some diligent work with his reference books. He had become adept at identifying plants when they were not in flower, and only occasionally made an out-and-out mistake like that confessed on 8 March: 'Discovered, as I suspect, the tuberous moschatel, *ranunculus nemorum Moschatella dictus*, in its radical leaves.' Later he adds: 'This was sanicle.' There are one or two notable records. On 16 April there was green hellebore flowering in the stony lane to Alton (still one of the only two clumps in the parish); and on 7 July Mulso's brother Thomas discovered the rare yellow bird's-nest in bloom near the Zig-zag: 'There were three or four plants together. It is allowed by all writers to be uncommon.' But the most engaging entries are those where Gilbert uses, with obvious pleasure, the evocative vernacular names for plants, so many of which have now become obsolete: wild williams (ragged robin); prim (privet); dwale (deadly nightshade); cammock (restharrow); arsmart (persicaria). Stinkhorns are spotted and listed, too, on 1 July, though here his smiles, slightly coy this time, are for the Latin name: 'Stinkhorns, or stinking morel, fungus phalloides, appear in the Lythe, and smell abominably. Lin: [i.e. Linnaeus] for a certain reason, calls it phallus impudicus.'

Gilbert had apparently already discussed this curiosity with Mulso in not wholly serious terms, for in April it had provoked one of Mulso's best wisecracks (quite possibly intended as a *double entendre*):

> Vegetation thrives apace now, & I suppose You are quite intent upon your new Study: You will not perhaps relish a Prospect the worse when we force you to look up, as I presume You will go wth your Eyes fixed on ye Ground most Part of the Summer. You will pass wth the Country Folks as a Man always making of Sermons, while you are only considering a weed. I thank you for your learned Dessertation on the *Canker* or *Stink pot*. I knew in general that all Flesh was Grass, but I did not know that Grass was Flesh before.[26]

In the summer of 1767 Mulso returned to the south, and took the living of Witney in Oxfordshire. He was now within riding distance of Selborne, and Gilbert went to stay with him in October. It is one of the very few occasions that John Mulso is mentioned by name in the journals, perhaps because he had the good fortune to share a habitat with one of the choicest local plants in the Midlands, the downy woundwort (now *Stachys germanica*).

> Octobr: 20. Being on a visit at the house of my good friend Mr: John Mulso Rector of Witney, I rode out on purpose to look after the base horehound, the Stachys Fuchsii of Ray, which, that Gent: says, grows near Witney park: I found but one plant under the wall: but farther on near the turnpike that leads to Burford, in an hedge opposite to Minster Lovel, it grows most plentifully. ... It was still blowing, & abounded with seed; a good parcel of which I brought away with me to sow in the dry banks round the village of Selborne.[27]

Chapter Six
A Man of Letters

In July 1767, Mulso wrote to Gilbert with the news that the Rector of Cromhall in Gloucestershire had died, and that this Oriel living was now vacant. He hoped, earnestly, that Gilbert would apply. For a start it might encourage him to visit Witney ('I lye in ye very Road'), and in any case it might be Gilbert's last chance:

> I am afraid that this is not the best Living of ye College: but nevertheless I think I collected by our last Confabulation, that You was inclined to secure to yourself the first Thing that fell, & get rid of your fellowship before your Fellowship got rid of you.[1]

And with memories of Gilbert's non-appearance in Yorkshire still fresh in his mind, he recommended that Gilbert should install a curate at the first possible opportunity. Being 'tied by the Leg as you are by your serving a Curacy yourself' was 'a Circumstance very hatefull to a Man whose Inquisitive Genius makes him love to change ye Scene often & search for Curiosities in various Regions'.[2] Mulso understood very well that Gilbert was bound to Selborne by complex ties of affection, circumstance and habit, not always voluntary and by no means always for his own good. 'I shall have you routed out of that Recess,' he wrote, 'where your Affections are too much engross'd for Yourself, & your friends at a Distance.'[3]

As might be expected, Gilbert made no real effort to secure the Cromhall position. When it became vacant again a few years later he described it as 'so dismally circumstanced that I think there can be no doubt which way I had best act ... no barn; I believe no stable; a wretched house; and all the parish offices for years past in the hands of an attorney'.[4] But on this occasion something had already happened to make the prospect of life in Selborne seem less lonely and aimless. On 18 April 1767 Gilbert had travelled to London for a long stay, no doubt visiting both his brothers, Benjamin and Thomas. Some time during the following two months he made the acquaintance of Thomas Pennant, the eminent traveller, writer and Fellow of the Royal Society, who was to become one of the correspondents of the *Natural History*.

It is not at all clear exactly how the friendship started. It isn't even certain if the two men met, and more than once in the correspondence that ensued between them Gilbert remarks how pleasant it would be 'to have a little conversation face to face after we have corresponded so freely for several years'. But Pennant had got word of Gilbert's skill and reliability as a natural historian and had passed on to him the suggestion that they share and discuss their findings. The intermediary was almost certainly Benjamin White. As well as owning a bookshop 'at Horace's Head' in Fleet Street that was a popular meeting-place for writers and scientists, Benjamin had just become Pennant's publisher. He had probably mentioned his brother's studies in Selborne, and even if he did not personally introduce them at his shop, he did enough groundwork for it to be easy for them to correspond.

And Gilbert, for one, was plainly delighted and excited by the opportunity. Within a couple of months of his return to Selborne he had composed a long and rambling letter to Pennant that would eventually become Letter X in the *Natural History*. It has, in its original, unamended state, all the energy of a long bottled-up enthusiasm. It chatters on about the possibility of hibernation by swallows, about the songs of warblers and how many species of water rat there were, and about the identity of the falcon found nailed to the end of a barn, which he was sending to Pennant forthwith. But it begins with an almost obsequious note of gratitude:

> Sir – Nothing but the obliging notice you were so kind as to take of my trifling observations in the natural way, when I was in town in the spring, and your repeated mention of me in some late letters to my brother, could have emboldened me to have entered into a correspondence with you: in which though my vanity cannot suggest to me that I shall send you any information worthy of your attention, yet the communi-

cation of my thoughts to a gentleman so distinguished for these kind of studies will unavoidably be attended with satisfaction and improvement on my side.[5]

Who was this man who could arouse such a show of awe in Gilbert, and galvanize a now rather lax correspondent into a fit of garrulousness? Gentleman he certainly was, born of a wealthy landowning family at Downing in Flintshire. And though Gilbert's compliments seem a trifle disproportionate now, there is no doubt that Pennant was beginning to acquire something of a name in the natural sciences. He had been elected to the Royal Society in February 1767, at the age of 41, and had completed the first edition of his encyclopaedia of mammals and birds, *British Zoology*, the previous year. It had not been particularly successful, and it was Benjamin's offer to republish the work that had brought them together in the first place. Pennant was also a doughty and open-minded traveller, and his various *Tours* were best-sellers in their time. Samuel Johnson thought him 'the best traveller I ever read'. But he had no great instinct or aptitude for field-work and nothing approaching White's critical intelligence. He was essentially an intellectual entre-preneur, a popularizer and compiler of other people's observations and ideas, and was able to produce a large number of very readable guides as a result. 'I am astonished at the multiplicity of my publications,' he exclaimed in his brief autobiography, *The Literary Life of Thomas Pennant*[6] ('by Himself'). Pennant's pushy and bombastic manner, and a reliance on second-hand information that at times came close to plagiarism, have left him with a rather tarnished reputation.[7] He was certainly not the most modest of men, and overestimated his prowess as a naturalist. But he was always an innovator as far as ideas for books were concerned, and he deserves credit for that. In the appendix to his *Tour of Scotland*, for instance (which gives an insight into his typical *modus operandi*), there is already a suggestion for the kind of book Gilbert was one day to write. It takes the form of a questionnaire about geology, rivers, birds, cattle, air, weather, echoes, and the like, addressed to Gentlemen and Clergy in North Britain, respecting the Antiquities and Natural History of their respective Parishes... with a view of exciting them to favour the World with a fuller and more satisfactory Account of their Country than it is in the power of a stranger and transient visitant to give ... It is to be hoped some parochial *Geniuses* will arise and favour the public with what is much wanted, LOCAL HISTORIES.[8]

This use of original reports from a wide network of field observers (including some famous ones, like Sir Joseph Banks and other Fellows of the Royal Society) blended with digests of already published works, was quite novel, though Robert Plot had tried a similar scheme on a much smaller scale.[9] Pennant was scrupulous with his references and acknowledgements, and his method would today be regarded as a thoroughly proper way of gathering material for a book. The results may have lacked the personal touch and insight of White's writing but they were highly accessible, and certainly in tune with the current fashion for natural history journalism, which by the 1760s was supporting at least half a dozen popular periodicals.[10]

With a new edition of *British Zoology* to prepare Pennant needed as many helpers and informants as he could muster, and he was no doubt pleased to discover an observer as original as White, especially one, as he confided later, who lived in 'the most southerly county'. It would be unfair to see all this as deceitful or cynical exploitation on Pennant's part; but equally so to imagine that it was simply friendship or the disinterested camaraderie of scientific enquiry that he was looking for.

Gilbert for his part can't have been under any illusion about what Pennant wanted from him. The deferential tone of his opening remarks was simply a polite acceptance of the terms of the relationship, and, once the correspondence was securely established, he was to become much more waspish. More to the point in that first letter was how he went on the explain the need he hoped Pennant's friendship would fill:

It has been my misfortune never to have had any neighbours whose studies have led them towards the pursuit of natural knowledge; so that, for want of a companion to quicken my industry and sharpen my attention, I have made but slender progress in a kind of information to which I have been attached from my childhood.[11]

Gilbert, in short, welcomed the arrangement whole-heartedly and thought it likely to provide a spur to his own observations and thinking. In this respect he was taking a fairly common view of the value of scholarly correspondence, for his comparatively isolated situation was not that unusual. All long-distance travel was slow and arduous. There were few learned societies, and correspondence provided something of the same framework for the intellectual community that con-ferences and journals do today. This may partly explain why, right from the outset, he regarded these letters as a special case, and began to make and keep copies of them.

The letters sent that year cover a vast range of topics. 'I forgot to mention ... ' one paragraph begins, and this exactly captures their gossipy, anecdotal tone. White talks about the fish to be found in the local stream, about the failure of the wild fruit crop, about a tame bat whose company he'd enjoyed the previous autumn, and which would take flies out of his hand. Almost by the way, he gives the first account in print of the harvest mouse – though this was achieved at the expense of whole families of young mice (the nests were 'perfectly round, and about the size of a cricket ball') being taken in the wheat-fields.

Much of the material in these early letters concerns events which happened some years before, and suggests that as well as an obviously retentive memory Gilbert may have kept rough notebooks for field notes and jottings. He would have needed no prompting to recall the feeding habits of his tame owl, or the summer the Wakes' garden was graced by a pair of hoopoes that 'used to march about in a stately manner, feeding in the walks'. But remembering precisely the date he once saw a late house-martin flying about the quadrangle of Christ Church in Oxford (it was 20 November) might have been less easy.

To cope with the kind of work he was now engaged in, Gilbert needed a more organized and permanent way of preserving his records. Fortunately, a solution became available at just the right moment. Towards the end of 1767 he was presented with a set of printed forms described as *The Naturalist's Journal*. They had been published by Benjamin White and were sent to Gilbert by their 'inventor', Daines Barrington, another prominent naturalist and one of Pennant's network of correspondents. Each page was meant to serve for a week. It was divided horizontally into days, and vertically into ten columns, for the recording of wind, weather, plants first in flower and other details. A final, broader column was included for miscellaneous observations.

Barrington provided suggestions about filling in the tables in the notes that accompanied each set of *Journal* pages. In the miscellaneous observations column, for instance,

> it may also be proper to take notice of the common prognostics of the weather from animals, plants, or hygroscopes, and compare them afterwards with the table of the weather, from which it may be perceived how far such prognostics can be relied upon ... Many other particulars will daily offer themselves to the observer, when his attention to such points hath once become habitual, and from many such journals kept in different parts of the kingdom, perhaps the very best and accurate materials for a General Natural History of Great Britain may in time be expected, as well as many profitable improvements and discoveries in agriculture.[12]

Barrington viewed the methodical logging – and, with luck, the deciphering – of nature as part and parcel of the great eighteenth-century drive to discipline the world, and this was echoed even in the sample entries he provided: 'Lost within the last week twenty sheep by the rot.' 'William was cured of the ague by the use of ... plants.' 'Swallows were found in a torpid state in ... cliff on the sea-coast.'

Specialized journals weren't uncommon in the eighteenth

century, though they were rarely laid out as meticulously as this. Gilbert's brother Harry kept one on the activities around his farm and household. His brother-in-law, Thomas Barker, had been making regular nature notes in Rutland since the 1730s. And Thomas Gray, the poet, began using Barrington's printed journal sheets in the same year as Gilbert. As Barrington freely admits in his preface, the idea for a naturalist's journal (though not the convenience of the printed forms) was not original. It had been inspired by the Calendar of Flora in Benjamin Stillingfleet's *Tracts*,[13] itself modelled on the *Calendar* (1755) of the Swedish naturalist, Alexander Berger. Initially, Gilbert did not seem to regard his new journal as in any way different from these records, or indeed as much more than a workaday notebook. He entered the weather diligently every day (a habit he was to continue to within a week of his death) and, with a great respect for the labelled columns, terse notes on the appearance of migrant birds and the opening of flowers. As for the garden notes that had once filled the *Kalendar*, these were now compressed into 'Miscellaneous Observations'. There is no surplus matter at all, certainly none of the explanatory filling-out that one would expect if the journal had been intended for outside reading. Sometimes it is left to the punctuation to provide the comment: '*Hirundo domestica*!!!' reads the entry for 13 April 1768, and the Latinism cannot hide Gilbert's sheer delight at the arrival of the first swallow. Sometimes there is one of those lucid, perfectly *selected* details that were to make the *Naturalist's Journal* the quintessence of White's view of the world:

> May 1: Great showers ... Wheat begins to look a little wan.
> Aug 10: White butter flies gather in flocks on the mud of the puddles.
> Sept 15: Rain all day. Black warty water-efts with fin tails & yellow bellies are drawn up in the well-bucket.

It's possible, from these early entries, to build up a picture of how Gilbert's field-work fitted into his daily round. Many of the observations were made in the garden of the Wakes, or in the parkland that lay on the other side of the Ha-ha. Some were doubtless the fruits of his regular ride to take services at Farringdon. This is only two miles as the crow flies, but at that time involved a tortuous meander through hollow lanes and overland tracks that could measure up to twice that distance. Yet from some of his records – of marsh harriers nesting in Woolmer Forest, for example – it looks as if he was also making trips specifically for the purpose of field study. He walked in the immediate vicinity of the village, but travelled by horse for preference. He may have carried a notebook, and perhaps a gun, though on most occasions where a bird is 'procured' away from the garden, it is for, not by, him. He was out in all weathers and quite frequently in the dark. On 3 June 1769 he 'Saw the planet Venus enter the disk of the sun. Just as the sun was setting the spot was very visible to the naked eye. Nightingale sings; wood-owl hoots; fern-owl chatters.' Each day the journal was written up in ink, probably in the study at the Wakes, with its view over the garden to the looming mass of the Hanger.

At first sight it seems a tidy, domestic regime. Yet one of the striking features of the journal is just how *un*methodical the records are collectively. By scientific criteria they are haphazard to the point of being whimsical. With the exception of the weather tables and the logging of the hirundines' movements, there is little rigorous, regular noting of places or species. A sudden fad or fit of curiosity will spring up – for parasitic insects or moulds or noxious fogs – dominate the entries for a week or so, and then peter out. Many questions are raised and reminders posted, but, in the pages of the journal at least, only rarely followed up. Whatever kind of record the *Naturalist's Journal* is, it is not the log of a systematic investigator. Nor is it a purely parochial record. During 1769, for example – not an exceptional year – Gilbert spent a total of fourteen weeks away from Selborne, and made entries for most of his usual retreats in Fyfield, Ringmer, London and Oxfordshire. The journal went with him on many of these trips, and is

sometimes written in a different nib when he is away
(though occasionally it remained in Selborne, and the
weather notes were completed by Gilbert's man, Thomas).
Then again, some of the most celebrated anecdotes in the
Natural History, even when they occurred within the period
spanned by the journal, aren't mentioned in it at all. His
account of a visit to Goodwood on Michaelmas Day 1768, for
example, to examine a long-dead and already putrefying
moose, went straight into a letter to Pennant written
eighteen months later; and the most blackly comic episode
in the whole book ('the length of the legs before and behind
consisted a great deal in the *tibia*, which was strangely long;
but in my haste to get out of the stench, I forgot to measure
that joint exactly'[14]) was either vivid enough to stick in the
memory, or was noted somewhere other than in the journal.

But at times Gilbert seemed unnerved by the responsibilities he had taken on. He wasn't yet confident that he
had the skill or the firmness of purpose to carry on this kind
of disciplined study, and as 1768 advanced he became
increasingly anxious for company and reassurance. On 30
March he invited Pennant to visit Selborne, and to bring
Joseph Banks if he could. The original letter ends: 'if he
[Banks] will do me the honour to come and see me he will
find how many curious plants I am acquainted with in my
own Country. I request also that you will be pleased to pay
my compliments and thanks to Mr Barrington for the
agreeable present of his Journal, which I am filling up day by
day.'[15] Pennant wasn't able to accept the invitation on this
occasion, and on 18 April Gilbert had another try at tempting
him down. 'I shall still live in hopes of seeing you, at this
beautiful season,' he wrote, 'when every hedge and field
abounds with matter of entertainment for the curious.' A
few days later he wrote directly to Banks, who was soon to
leave on his round-the-world journey with Captain Cook.
Gilbert took the trouble to make a copy of this letter in his
own hand, though there was little of substance in it beyond a
rather mournful anticipation of months of solitary work
ahead:

I was greatly in hopes that both you gentlemen would have honoured me with your company this spring; but now it seems that unless Mr. Skinner of C.C.C. [Corpus Christi College] should happen to come (as he has partly promised), I must plod on by myself, with few books and no soul to communicate my doubts or discoveries to.[16]

In May it was Mulso's turn to be invited, but he too had to refuse. He points out gently to Gilbert that it wasn't quite like the old days, when they were both relatively free agents:

No man beats you at playing the Master of a large family of friends, yet You do not yet know the Difficulties of managing a family of Servants & Children, & how hard it is to leave them prudently.[17]

Gilbert was depressed by this reply which seemed to portend 'a perpetual Embargo' on his friend's visits. Mulso reassured him that the obstacles were only temporary, but returned again to what he felt was the reason for Gilbert's unease:

How comes it to pass that You, who want to make Selborne your Residence, are afraid of a Living where your Residence would not be required? This is one of those Paradoxes in which you have always delighted.[18]

Mulso had raised this touchy issue again because the living at Cholderton – and another at Ufton Nervet, in Berkshire – had again become vacant and again been passed by. Gilbert seems, at this moment, already to have defined the limits of his own territory. He was reluctant to venture beyond its boundaries or to vary the kind of relationship he had already established with each place inside. He was quite happy staying in London, for instance, for weeks on end, and to have no more reminders of life in Selborne than the '12 brace of fair cucumbers' he had sent down from the village on May Day. But when Pennant invited him to Flintshire, 200 miles away, he might just as well have been suggesting an expedition to the South Seas, and Gilbert declined in terms which are very reminiscent of his evasiveness over visiting Mulso in Yorkshire. Pennant repeated the invitation at the beginning of 1769, and this time Gilbert realized that a more elaborate explanation was needed:

> You will not, I hope, suspect me of flattery when I assure you that there is no man in the kingdom whom I should visit with more satisfaction ... Besides your part of the world would not be without its charms from novelty; as I am not acquainted with the N.W. part of this island any farther than Shrewsbury. Your improvements, your mines, your fossils, your botany, your shores, your birds, would all be a matter of the highest entertainment to me. But then how am I to get all these pleasures and amusements? I have neither time nor bodily abilities adequate to so long a journey. And if I had time I am subject to such horrible coach-sickness, that I should be near dead long before I got to Chester. These difficulties, I know, will be matter of great mirth to you, who have travelled all over Europe; but they are formidable to me. As therefore the man cannot come to the mountain, I hope the mountain (since friendship will effect strange things) will come to the man: I hope you will have it in your power to meet me in London, and that you will gratify me with an opportunity of waiting on you in Selborne.[19]

Although Gilbert's coach-sickness was obviously no laughing matter (despite Mulso's occasional guffaws) it is hard to take this explanation at face value. Gilbert had gritted his teeth through journeys as extensive as this only fifteen years before, when the attractions at the other end had been far less. Was the worsening of his coach-sickness partly psychosomatic, a device for keeping him in the security of familiar territory? It certainly wouldn't be unfair to say that he was in a kind of thraldom to Selborne, and that the prospect of moving away – of being sited 'out of his knowledge' – filled him with as much unease as a displaced cricket. Yet perhaps he was beginning to accept and

Above: A view of the Hanger from the Lythes in the north-east. The Zig-zag path is visible amongst the then open scrub towards the left side of the Hill. In the foreground is the tent put up for summer entertainments.

Right: Gilbert's father, John.

Above: The Short Lythe and Dorton from Hucker's Lane, one of White's favourite views and walks. The gnarled tree roots, right, still survive. (Grimm, 1776)

Below: A more decorous view of Dorton and the Lythes, taken a hundred years later.

ROCKY LANE LEADING TO ALTON.

Above: Selborne's stream in Silkwood Vale, east of the church. (Grimm, 1776)

Right: The old hollow lane to Alton. (P.H. Delamotte, 1880). Both illustrations show the way the layered sandstone is worn down by water or traffic.

Above left: Gilbert's brother, Thomas, born 1724.

Above right: His daughter Mary, born 1759, and as 'Molly', one of Gilbert's favourite correspondents.

Right: Rebecca Snooke, Gilbert's aunt, who lived at Ringmer, Sussex, and was the original owner of Timothy the tortoise.

Above: A view of the Wakes from the foot of the Hanger in the 1770s, showing haymaking in the 'Park.' The lip of the ha-ha is just visible, and the alcove in the right-hand hedge. The tiny figure leaning on a stick just in front of the house is usually assumed to be White himself. (Grimm, 1776)

Below: A closer view of the Wakes, circa 1875.

Above: The old Hermitage on the Hanger, with Henry White (Harry), as the Hermit. (Grimm, 1776)

Harry (*below, left*) (born 1733) in later life, and (*below, right*) Catherine Battie, the girl with whom he – and quite possibly Gilbert, too – became infatuated during the 'festal summer' of 1763.

Above: View of Selborne
from inside the Hermitage.
(Grimm, 1776)

Right: A view from higher up the
Hanger. (P.H. Delamotte, 1880)

Above: Selborne church from the churchyard. The famous yew (foreground) was already twenty-three feet in girth when White measured it. (Grimm, 1776)

Below: The Plestor, or play-space, at the church end of the village street. The two boys on the right appear to be playing a form of cricket, which was very popular in the area. (Grimm, 1776)

understand a degree of confinement as a condition of his work. As Ronald Blythe has written of all great 'local' writers: 'Their feeling for nature and the landscape of man deepens when it remains hedged about by familiar considerations.'[20]

The extent to which Gilbert's relationships with places were becoming an important feature of his emotional and intellectual life, with an increasing timidity balanced by heightened sensitivity, is shown by two revealing passages to Pennant. The first, in the letter dated October 1768, was not included in the *Natural History*:

> I met with a paragraph in the newspapers some weeks ago that gave me some odd sensations, a kind of mixture of pleasure and pain at the same time. It was as follows: 'On the 6th day of August, Joseph Banks Esq., accompanyed by Dr. Solander, Mr. Green ... &c., set out for Deal, in order to embark aboard the 'Endeavour', Captain Cook, bound for the South Seas.'
>
> When I reflect on the youth and affluence of this enterprizing gentleman I am filled with wonder to see how conspicuously the contempt of dangers, and the love of excelling in his favourite studies stand forth in his character. And yet though I admire his resolution, which scorns to stoop to any difficulties; I cannot divest myself of some degree of solicitude for his person. The circumnavigation of the globe is an undertaking that must shock the constitution of a person inured to a sea-faring life from his childhood; and how much more that of a landman! ... If he survives, with what delight shall we peruse his Journals, his Fauna, his Flora! If he falls by the way, I shall revere his fortitude, and contempt of pleasures, and indulgences: but shall always regret him, though my knowledge of his worth was of late date, and my acquaintanceship with him but slender.[21]

Compare this, in both feeling and structure, with the following reflections on some other long-distance travellers, written to Pennant in February of 1769, but referring back to the autumn when Banks set sail:

When I used to rise in a morning last autumn, and see the swallows and martins clustering on the chimnies and thatch of the neighbouring cottages, I could not help being touched with a secret delight, mixed with some degree of mortification: with delight to observe with how much ardour and punctuality those poor little birds obeyed the strong impulse towards migration, or hiding, imprinted on their minds by their great Creator; and with some degree of mortification, when I reflected that, after all our pains and inquiries, we are yet not quite certain to what regions they do migrate; and are still farther embarrassed to find that some do not actually migrate at all.[22]

In 1768, the second edition of Pennant's *British Zoology* was published. It contained a certain amount of material supplied by Gilbert, particularly on house-martins and swifts, and he was properly thanked in the text. Gilbert obviously appreciated this, and it gave him the confidence to point out some of Pennant's errors. He had made 'several mistakes ... with respect to some birds of the *Grallae* order'. Gilbert's criticism is polite, exact and uncompromising:

But there is a passage in the article Goatsucker, page 247, which you will pardon me for objecting to, as I always thought it exceptionable: and that is 'This noise being made *only* in its flight, we suppose it to be caused by the resistance to the air against the hollow of its vastly extended mouth and throat for it flies with both open to take its prey.' Now as the first line appears to me to be a false fact; the supposition of course also falls to the ground, if it should prove so.[23]

This was White's very practical scientific touchstone: not the results of abstract argument or controlled experiment, but the evidence of patterns of repeated association in the real world. His attention to the circumstances under which birds sang had already produced some novel findings. He had noticed that snipes always 'hummed' as they descended in flight, and inclined towards the idea that the sound was not a song at all, but was made by the vibration of their feathers. He had tracked down the identity of the bird that made 'a clatter with its bill against a dead bough' by brusquely but decisively having one shot 'in the very act'. (It proved to be a nuthatch.) The times at which birds sang had even suggested an important and relatively new 'maxim in ornithology, that as long as there is any incubation going on there is music.'

As for the nightjar, he had dramatic first-hand evidence that it did not sing only in flight. One evening he and a group of friends were in the Hermitage up on the top of the Hanger, when a nightjar came and settled on the roof. It began to churr, and the company were 'all struck with wonder to find that the organs of that little animal, when put in motion, gave a sensible vibration to the whole building!'[24] He was sure that the note was produced in its windpipe, 'just as cats pur'.

Gilbert was only able to establish these facts by 'watching narrowly', which for him meant both close observation and the intimate study of small areas. Both approaches were novel at the time, and Gilbert believed that one reason Pennant made so many mistakes was that the style of his field-work was almost exactly the opposite. But he is always courteously indirect when it comes to such general criticisms. 'My little intelligence is confined to the narrow sphere of my own observations at home,' he wrote on 22 February 1770; and then, in September the same year:

> Monographers, come from whence they may, have, I think, fair pretence to challenge some regard and approbation from the lovers of natural history; for, as no man can alone investigate all the works of nature, these partial writers may, each in their department, be more accurate in their discoveries, and freer from errors, than more general writers.[25]

Gilbert was touched at how generously Pennant accepted his criticisms, and for his part was equally gracious when Pennant – rather quickly chancing on Gilbert's intellectual Achilles' heel – pointed out a slipshod argument about the migration of ring ouzels. 'You put a very shrewd question,' Gilbert admits, 'when you ask me how I know that their autumnal migration is southward? Was not candour and openness the very life of natural history, I should pass over this query just as the sly commentator does over a crabbed passage in a classic; but common ingenuousness obliges me to confess, not without some degree of shame, that I only reasoned in that case from analogy.'[26] Knowing with a fair degree of certainty that other autumn migrants came largely from the north, because of our milder winters, he had assumed that ring ouzels did the same. It was, he admitted, a fallacious way of thinking that he had only slipped into due to the virtual impossibility of ever truly *witnessing* migration.

The convivial tone of these letters reflected a general change for the better in Gilbert's life. In August, two Oxford friends, Richard Skinner of Corpus Christi and William Sheffield of Worcester College (shortly to become Keeper of the Ashmolean Museum) came to stay at Selborne for a fortnight. Gilbert was tremendously excited by their visit, as they were 'the only Naturalists that I have ever yet had the pleasure of seeing at my house'. When he wrote to Pennant about their visit, he recalled how exciting it was to walk out with these two scholars who seemed to know the identity of every living thing they encountered. (The living things themselves were not always so fortunate; Gilbert described how Sheffield 'went into Wolmer Forest & procured me a green sandpiper'.)[27]

The following month Pennant floated the possibility of launching a new periodical specifically devoted to natural history. Gilbert – rather surprisingly, given his close family connections with publishing – pleaded ignorance of such undertakings and expressed a worry that with the current public appetite for scandal and political controversy another new periodical specializing in natural science might have difficulty attracting a readership. But if Pennant did go ahead, he would be happy to help, though it could only be in a small way.

> I shall be ready to advance my mite: but then I shall expect you to be very charitable in your allowance, and to grant that my mite in one respect is equal to larger contributions, as it is all my stock of knowledge.[28]

The periodical never materialized, but a short while later another publishing idea was put to Gilbert. Some time during the spring of 1769, when Pennant had been off on one of his Scottish tours, Gilbert had met the Honourable Daines Barrington, the man who had presented him with the *Naturalist's Journal* the previous year. They began corresponding in June, and by the spring of 1770 Barrington, clearly impressed by what he was reading, suggested to Gilbert that he ought to make a book out of his observations.

It may seem curious that such a suggestion had not already been made to Gilbert by Pennant, given the latter's involvement with natural history publishing. But Pennant, of course, relied quite heavily on Gilbert's help and advice, and would not have relished having him as a rival. Barrington had no such inhibiting ambitions. He was an effusive man, an avid snapper-up of ideas and fashions, and in many ways a typical example of the wealthy dilettantes who straddled the worlds of art and science in the eighteenth century. Seven years White's junior, he was the fourth son of Viscount Barrington, a lawyer and a member of the Inner Temple, and like Pennant, a Fellow of the Royal Society, which, at this period, included many cultivated amateurs among its members. Beyond that there are not many similarities with Gilbert's first correspondent or, for that matter, with Gilbert himself. Barrington was neither field observer nor popularizer. His chief interest was in the theories of natural history and his way of thinking about these occupied an idiosyncratic niche somewhere between that of a medieval philosopher and a new rationalist. Like the earlier generation he was less interested in the routine, day-to-day workings of the natural world than in its great riddles and anomalies. Like his contemporaries he was eager to replace old superstitions with new truths. The paradox was that he seemed to think this could be achieved by the application of reason alone, much of it based on the assumption that the rest of creation ran their lives according to human notions of common sense. He acknowledged the need for carefully gathered factual evidence, but was curiously gullible when it came to assessing this. He read exceptionally widely, but seemed to have little interest in making his own critical observations – in 'watching narrowly' – in the world beyond his library. A glimpse of how his notional concern for rigour could collapse into a kind of offhanded woolliness when it came to considering evidence in practice is given in some of his remarks about migration. He thought, for instance, that the reason the Greeks and Romans handed down so little information about this subject was 'because their dress prevented them being so much in the field as we are'. Or if they did hear of an unusual arrival they had no guns to shoot it, 'the only method of attaining real knowledge in natural history depends almost entirely upon having frequent opportunities of thus killing animals, and examining them when dead.'[29] As for less tangible forms of evidence, their value rather depended on who was the supplier. Barrington accepted the testimony of most of his fellow naturalists without question, just so long as it coincided with his own beliefs. Where evidence was perverse or lacking he blamed the inattention or ignorance of the observer. He had no real understanding that evidence could be of different kinds and different degrees of accessibility. Migration certainly couldn't be happening 'beyond human sight'. He had met people

> who conceive they have lost sight of birds by their perpen-
> dicular flight; I must own, however, that I have always
> supposed them to be short-sighted, as I never lost the sight
> of a bird myself, but from its horizontal distance, and I doubt
> much whether any bird was ever seen to rise to a greater
> height than perhaps twice that of St Paul's cross.[30]

On vexed questions like this Barrington argues with the ingenuity and tortuousness typical of a bright man with a fixed idea. He was not really a dogmatist, more a rather blinkered intellectual sniper who would pot at any disruptive ideas, and his idiosyncratic stance led him from the best of questions to the most eccentric of answers. Finding the notion of a universal deluge hard to accept, he reasoned that fossils were accidental imitations of living things produced by burrowing insects. Appalled by the travesty of decent instincts that the cuckoo's behaviour represented, he tried to retrieve a shred of decency for its reputation by arguing that it probably did incubate and feed its own young, albeit in the foster-parent's nest.

But it would be unfair to judge Barrington's beliefs too harshly. At least he was alert to what the key issues in natural science were. If his disputations on these seem defensive and conservative, perhaps that is understandable at a time when science was constantly threatening to shake the most deeply-held religious and philosophical beliefs. Maybe the worst that can be said is that a whiff of self-righteousness seems to hang about him – as if he was constantly disappointed by nature's failure to live according to the tidy, moral scheme he thought appropriate for it – and that his care, his passion, was for the theory not the creatures. When Charles Lamb came to write a vignette on Barrington he caught this hint of imperiousness perfectly:

> – another oddity; he walked burly and square – in imitation, I think, of Coventry – howbeit he attained not to the dignity of his prototype. Nevertheless, he did pretty well, upon the strength of being a tolerable antiquarian, and having a brother a bishop. When the accounts of his year's treasurership [of the Inner Temple] came to be audited, the following singular charge was unanimously disallowed by the bench: 'Item, disbursed Mr Allen, the gardener, twenty shillings for stuff to poison the sparrows, by my orders.'[31]

But Barrington admired Gilbert, and mentions him with gratitude many times in his book, *Miscellanies*. And if his theories seem a little perverse today, they were important to Gilbert simply by giving him something to pit his wits against. As early as the fourth exhange of letters between them, Barrington surprised Gilbert with a new notion about the cuckoo. He had speculated that cuckoos did not lay their eggs indiscriminately in the first nest that came their way, but actually sought out foster-parents with habits 'in some degree congenerous' to their own. The observation, Gilbert replied, 'is perfectly new to me; and struck me so forcibly, that I naturally fell into a train of thought that led me to consider whether the fact was so, and what reason there was for it'.[32] And his way of considering the idea was not simply to meditate upon it, but to 'recollect and inquire' about local observations of cuckoo fostering. His neighbours were an observant bunch by now, and they reported seeing young cuckoos only in the nests of wagtails, hedge sparrows, pipits, whitethroats and robins – all of them, Gilbert realized, soft-billed birds like the cuckoo.

On this occasion Barrington and White's approaches proved to be complementary. But 'congenerous' was hardly a description which could be applied to their habits, and it is no wonder that when the idea of the book was raised, Gilbert's response was polite but circumspect. He was, as usual, coy and self-deprecating, and he repeats the slightly doleful complaint about his isolation. Yet given the significance of Barrington's proposal, Gilbert's reply has a composure that suggests the idea may have already occurred to him and been properly weighed up, and that for the moment he was keeping the verdict on it to himself:

> When we meet, I shall be glad to have some conversation with you concerning the proposal you make of my drawing up an account of the animals in this neighbourhood. Your partiality towards my small abilities persuades you, I fear, that I am able to do more than is in my power: for it is no small undertaking for a man unsupported and alone to begin a natural history from his own autopsia![33]

Whatever his private feelings about producing a book of his own, Gilbert's life after 1770 became increasingly involved with the labours of other writers. Pennant continued to be foremost among these, and during 1770–1, Gilbert began to comment on his illustrations and proofs as well as sending him new information. He had – in his letters at least – matured from a slavish novice to an accomplished (pedantic, some might say!) consultant. 'Your proof-sheet meets with my approbation,' he wrote at the beginning of 1771. 'I always was of the opinion that the stile should be in some measure adapted to the length of the composition, or the subject in all cases; and therefore long flowing sentences can't be suitable to short descriptions in a work that professes to be a synopsis.'[34]

Another sign of Gilbert's conscious movement towards a more literary way of life is the expansion in the range of correspondence he kept or copied. There are, for example, a sheaf of letters to his brother John, who since his ignominious departure in 1756 had been chaplain to the military garrison at Gibraltar. During the early 1760s communication between Gilbert and John had been sparse, but in November 1768, when Gilbert had begun to think seriously about migration, he told Pennant that he had 'written also to my South country correspondent at Gibraltar, & urged him to take up the study of Nature a little; & to habituate his mind to attend to the migrations of birds and fishes'.[35] This note comes, pointedly, after a paragraph extolling to Pennant the moral virtues of natural history:

> Happy the man! who knows, like you, how to keep himself innocently and usefully employed; especially where his studies tend to the advancement of knowledge, and the benefit of Society. And happy would it be for many more men of fortune if they knew what to do with their time; if they knew how to shun 'The pains and penalties of Idleness', how much dissipation, riot and excess would they escape; not without the complacency of finding themselves growing still better neighbours and better commonwealths-men.[36]

It looks very much as if Gilbert hoped his scheme for John would do them both some good.

John responded more enthusiastically than Gilbert had expected, and by the following year had conceived 'a design of drawing-up somewhat of a natural history of those Southern parts of Europe'.[37] Gilbert was glad to offer what help he could, and from the autumn of 1769 a voluminous technical correspondence about the peculiarities of Gibraltar's fauna and flora began. Only Gilbert's letters survive but they are full of bold and often quite uncompromising advice, and show not a hint of the naïvety he was apt to parade when discussing his own work.[38] John should 'Examine the Scarab-balls at different periods; perhaps at some seasons they contain maggots. Where are these balls found?' 'Where are your smelts caught? How are the montageo, or Spanish hams cured; in ye snow? are the hogs from whence they are taken fed with vipers?' He should remember that 'Wet insects keep incomparably better than dry' and that the Rock's plants needed to be included: 'A soldier sent out with an hand-basket in flowering time will collect many curious plants in a day.' Above all else he should watch out for reports on, and if at all possible collect 'yr winter Martin' (i.e. the crag-martin, which Gilbert initially thought might be overwintering house- or sand-martins).

There was editorial advice, too, terse, shrewd and confident, as if Gilbert was already an experienced hand in publishing. 'You are to remember,' he writes, 'that you will want an abundance of matter to fill up 200 or 300 pages: and no publication will make a reasonable appearance unless you can swell it to somewhat of such a bulk.' ... Beware of stating too dogmatically that a species is new ... Describe the vulture minutely ... 'get some account of the prickly heat, or fever, and the exact height of your mount'. Write to Scopoli; 'he is very clever: but ask him as gravely as you can how he is sure that the woodcock, when pursued, carries off her young in her bill'. Above all, deliver as many anecdotes and dissertations as possible 'to entertain the unsystematic reader'.

Of course this advice was far from disinterested. John's responses were invaluable for Gilbert's own work, and in November 1770, only six months after Barrington had raised the idea of a book, Gilbert suggested that they should, in some unspecified way, put together comparative diaries for a single year:

Pitch on some one year for yr Journal suppose 1769: & then

throw all the current observations you have made, & regular incidents into that year: by which means there will be some times 4 or 5 pages of observations to one of Journal. In that manner I shall manage my Journal for the same year: & thus we may compare the two climates.[39]

As well as letters, macabre bundles of dead specimens began to pour across from Gibraltar for identification or comment. Gilbert seemed to enjoy the discipline of examining these exotic objects, and when he had finished with them, they were labelled ('1, 2, 3, etc so you will be able to speak of them with precision') and sent off by waggon to Thomas White in London, to be collected by or forwarded to Pennant. The technical problems involved in the transport of these 'cargoes of curiosities' must have been formidable. Preservation techniques were still primitive, and though they may have been effective enough with insects, it is hard to imagine the state in which even salted-down fish must have arrived after a journey that could take as much as two months. Birds were scarcely better, and when only a wing or leg was sent over, it was usually because they were the only parts of the creatures that hadn't already decayed. But with one particular vulture it was all there ever was. 'The bird was found dead and floating in the sea; an accident it seems not very uncommon: some fishermen picked it up, and flayed it, eat the carcase, and threw away the skin, and gave him the head and feet.'[40] No wonder that one parcel became entangled with the quarantine restrictions at Stangate Creek, and that Gilbert, in the preface to his journal for 1770, writes out a recipe for 'A proper antiseptic substance for the preservation of birds &c'.

The objects that were subjected to this process of being stuffed, squashed, desiccated, crammed into boxes until they all resembled stoats, and then trundled over the stony roadways of rural England, were, needless to say, travesties of the original creatures, and Gilbert's interest in them seems a long way removed from his delight in the vitality of living things. But it proved to be a comparatively short-lived.

fad, a useful intellectual discipline, and perhaps the best way of taking advantage of John White's rather special resources. Very little of the content or style of these exchanges was to find an echo in either the *Natural History* or the *Journal*, and during 1770–1 the latter proceeds with its usual preoccupations.

Two themes were beginning to dominate the entries: the weather, and the arrivals and disappearances of birds, and all this suggested about the mysterious imperatives of instinct.

Early 1771 saw a long, severe freeze-up across much of Britain. In Skye, where snow covered the ground for eight weeks, it became known as the Black Spring. On 6 February it was cold enough in Selborne for a decanter of water to freeze solid inside Gilbert's bedroom. During the whole of March the thermometer barely crept above the low thirties (degrees Fahrenheit) and on 15 April dropped to fourteen degrees in the night. But the day before, the first, lone swallow had flitted over the snowbound village, barely delayed at all. The appalling weather continued, with harsh winds, fogs and dark freezing days. 'Cold & coughs universal' Gilbert recorded on 18 April, but he was still out and about, watching the spring fight back. On 20 April there was 'just enough rain to discolour the pavement' and he was able to watch multitudes of young frogs beginning their spring migration, miraculously unharmed by the severe frost. Swifts had returned by the 29th of the month and on 25 May the number dashing round the church had reached the usual eight pairs: 'they do not all come together, but in a straggling manner, a few at a time: perhaps a pair many days before the rest.' A fortnight later he noticed – and it had probably never been realized before – that the sitting hen swift leaves the nest to feed for a short while at dusk. By September ring ouzels were appearing on the chalk downs at Noar Hill, and families of martins and swallows were swarming in vast numbers below the Hanger. The 22nd proved a day to remember:

Tops of the beeches are tinged with yellow. Heavy clouds

126

on the horizon. This morning the swallows rendezvoused in a neighbour's wallnut tree. At the dawn of the day they arose altogether in infinite numbers, occasioning such a rushing with the strokes of their wings as might be heard to a considerable distance.[41]

That was the last occasion that month on which they were seen in large numbers. Only a few late broods and stragglers remained around the village. But then, out of the blue, many more appeared in the midst of stormy weather in the first week of October. They were gone by the middle of the month, migrated at last, or gone to ground in the village, he presumed. But while he was on a visit to Ringmer on a sunny day in early November, he 'saw three house swallows flying briskly at Newhaven at the mouth of the Lewes river!!' Their winter habits remained a tantalizing mystery.

Much of the material in the journals was soon reworked into his correspondence, even the rather cold-blooded dissection of two noctule bats which the journal records simply as 'procured'. The arrival of the swallow amidst the snow is announced to Pennant in the letter dated 12 May, and repeated almost word for word to Barrington nine days later. The idea of some kind of book based on his observations was beginning to take hold, though he was not letting on about this except to his closest confidants. His brother John was one of these. In January 1771, just after receiving a bizarre assortment of shirts, sweetmeats and dead birds from Gibraltar, Gilbert refined the suggestion he had made a couple of months before. 'As matter flows in upon me I begin to think of composing a nat: Hist: of Selborne in the form of a journal for 1769.'[42] But writing six months later to Pennant (who seemed to have echoed Barrington's suggestion) he was more cautious:

As to any publication in this way of my own, I look upon it with great diffidence, finding that I ought to have begun it twenty years ago. But if I was to attempt anything it should be somewhat of a Nat history of my native parish, an *annus historico-naturalis* comprizing a journal for one whole year, and illustrated with large notes and observations. Such a beginning might induce more able naturalists to write the history of various districts, and might in time occasion the production of a work so much to be wished for, a full and compleat nat history of these kingdoms.[43]

Mulso seems to have been given a hint of the new scheme much earlier, though for the moment he was too preoccupied with his own troubles to pay much attention. He was under siege by a florid array of new complaints – piles, 'rheumatism in the head', giddiness and a five-week confinement to bed after dislocating his ankle. 'A Winter is now become a serious Thing to me,' he wrote, 'who find that I cannot get thro' it, without Sufferings of one kind or Another.' Summers were not much easier, what with the heat and the exhausting social round. When the Mulsos visited Selborne in the middle of summer in 1770, transporting their cumbersome and ailing family had meant hiring a separate waggon for their 'great Boxes & Trunks', and a guide to take them through the hollow lanes from Alton. Some years later Mulso chided Gilbert for doing so little to improve access to the village, and urged him to lobby the local Member of Parliament, Sir Simeon Stuart. 'Think only of my knowing no Time of ye Year,' he wrote, 'for getting at You *without a Guide*; & seldom, with one ... If you lose this opportunity, I shall think that you love your Rosamond's Bower, *because* the Access is inscrutable.'[44]

That summer of 1770, tucked away in his bower, Gilbert felt secure enough to confide in his friend: Barrington's suggestion was looking more and more feasible, and he had begun thinking seriously about how to tackle it. By December Mulso was able to make a cryptic reference to some unspecified project on which Gilbert had been engaged since the summer:

Dear Gil:
There is not upon Earth a Man so hide bound in point of Letters as your honour. I wrote to you on ye Ninth of this Month, & I thought you would have been so glad to see my

Hand-writing again, that you would have mechanically caught up a Pen to thank me for it. But You preserve your old Sang froid. Have you been penning a new Sermon against Christmas Day? As to Charles ye 5th, I finish'd him in three Weeks, & You have had three Months, a solitary House, & a Fire to yourself: so that unless You purposely interrupt yourself in Order to prolong your Pleasure, It must be finish'd in all this Time. But you have an inexhaustible Fund in your Systema! true: but as That will never be over as long as you live, I will not admit it as an Excuse for not writing to me.[45]

*

Meanwhile, Gilbert continued to record life in Selborne with an increasingly sympathetic eye for exact, unexpected details. In July 1772 he watched a carder beetle working the garden campions. 'It is very pleasant to see with what address it strips off the pubes, running from the top to the bottom of a branch, and shaving it bare with all the dexterity of a hoop-shaver. When it has got a vast bundle, almost as large as itself, it flies away, holding it secure between it's chin, & it's fore legs.'[46] On 15 August, while he was riding back from a visit to Mulso's new house at Meonstoke, there was a slight earthquake at Noar Hill. White picked up the gossip about it later that day. A man in a field had heard a curious rumbling. A mother and her son had both noticed their house tremble at the same moment, while one was upstairs and the other down. And, White notes, 'each called to the other to know what was the matter.' It was a detail which captured exactly the sense of suddenness and surprise and yet was ordinary enough to put the authenticity of the report beyond question. This was the gift White was developing in his journal, of linking the strange and the unfamiliar with everyday experience. On 22 August, a day of heavy showers, he notes that vast swarms of black dolphin beetles were devouring the village's vegetables, even the tough outer leaves of cabbages. 'When disturbed on the cabbage leaves they leap in such multitudes as to make a pattering noise on the leaves like a shower of rain.'[47]

Sometimes more weighty matters find their way into the journal. Throughout the first fortnight of November 1771, Gilbert was observing his aunt's tortoise down at Ringmer, to see if its imminent hibernation could give any clues as to similar behaviour by birds:

> Nov 2. Mrs. Snooke's tortoise begins to dig in order to hide himself for the winter.
>
> Nov 15. Tortoise at Ringmer had not finish'd his hybernaculum, being interrupted by the sunny weather, which tempted him out.[48]

Even his family's travels were sometimes logged in the journal, as if they too were scarce migrants. For some time John White had been considering a return to England, and when a living in Lancashire became a possibility early in 1772, he set off home with his wife Barbara. As they made their laborious way across Spain, Gilbert tracked their movements alongside those of the mayflies. 'June 17. *Ephemerae* & *phryganaea* abound on the stream. Bror: John set-out on horse-back for Cadiz.' They arrived in England on 27 July with John in a sorry state, as he was to describe to Gilbert the following week:

> After being rolled in a tub across the Atlantic for 37 days, & suffering a severe fit of the gravel, together with an ugly fever, I landed at Gravesend last Monday evening extremely weak & emaciated. Providentially my wife was a stout sailor, and was able to nurse & assist me in my distress, else I had probably perished.[49]

His first task, once recovered, was to visit Lambeth Palace, where the Bishop presented him formally to the living of Blackburn, Lancashire. But as he could not take up residence until early the following year, he and his family spent the winter in Selborne, giving Mulso the line for one of his knowing quips. Writing in January 1773 he says 'I suppose your Brother John & his Lady are put up in Cotton with some of the Andalusian Rarities, for how they can stand agst this severe Weather after their broiling on the Rock so long, I cannot imagine.'[50] With them at the Wakes was their son John, born on the Rock in 1759 and universally known as Gibraltar Jack. He had been sent to England in August 1769, to attend a school at Holybourne, near Alton. Some of Benjamin White's sons were at this establishment, and both he and Gilbert kept an avuncular eye on Jack's progress. He was a bright 14-year-old, and soon began to help Gilbert with the transcription and copying of his letters. Gilbert got on well with young people, treating them with respect and intelligence, and never showing the slightest sign of condescension. (He had already begun a studious exchange of letters with his nephew Sam Barker, aged 15 that year.) During 1773, while John and his wife were in Lancashire preparing the new vicarage, Gilbert took full responsibility for their son's upbringing and education. He proved to be a fast learner. By the autumn he had consumed several volumes of the *Spectator* and learned to read tolerably well from Virgil. He had even, with great precocity, been 'much delighted' with that basic text of the Christian ecologists, Derham's *Physico-theology* (though it would be as well to make allowances for the fact that this was one of Gilbert's favourite books, too). He was well-behaved, obliging, and 'in his readiness to assist, and put an helping hand,' Gilbert confided to his brother, 'often puts me in mind of a gentlewoman that is very nearly related to him.' In August Gilbert treated him to a pair of lamb-skin breeches.

But his spell as a foster-parent was not without its share of anxieties. In June Jack had gone down with the measles, and Thomas Hoar had moved into a little bed alongside him to give him balm tea in the night. He 'behaved like a philosopher all through,' Gilbert reported, 'submitting to his confinement without reluctance or murmuring'. The attack seemed to leave him with an obstinate hoarseness which worried Gilbert at first, but he came to the conclusion that it was 'owing to a cause incident to young men about his time of life'. He was right to be concerned, none the less. Measles and whooping cough were rampant in the southern counties that year, and claimed the lives of five small children in Selborne alone.[51] (The Mulsos, even more fearful for their health than usual because of the epidemics, entered a pact with their neighbours to chance the novel – and still risky – practice of inoculation against smallpox.)

Accounts of all these domestic dramas were dutifully sent to Jack's father, and Gilbert seemed able to write in a more relaxed and intimate tone to John now the bulk of the groundwork for the Gibraltar natural history was complete. They exchanged descriptions of the progress of their respective house repairs, of brewing beer, of the celebrations accompanying the King's visit to Portsmouth (the cannon repeatedly shook houses at Selborne, thirty miles distant) and, of course, of the weather. But natural history was not forgotten. Gilbert was delighted that John had heard a sedge-warbler up in Lancashire. The bird was 'a wonderful fellow', and if only it could be 'persuaded not to sing in such a hurry would be an elegant songster'. There was plenty Gilbert could say about its power of mimicry, but he preferred his brother's one-word epithet: 'Your appellative of polyglott pleases me so much that I shall adopt it.' And adopt it he did, at least in the *Naturalist's Journal*. It also found its way into the entry on the sedge-warbler in Pennant's *Zoology*, in which virtually the whole description of the species is based on Gilbert's notes. 'I find you,' Gilbert wrote contentedly to John, 'as well as when you resided on the other side of the Pyrenean mountains, my most steady and communicative correspondent; and therefore it will be my own fault if our epistolary intercourse should languish.'[52]

But Gilbert's rather stilted phrasing is a sure sign that all was not as secure in the relationship as he was trying to make out; and that autumn a little of the underlying strain came to the surface. The cause – and it was not the first time it had been a source of difficulty – was Gilbert's reluctance to make long trips away from Selborne. On this occasion, though, he did seem to anticipate the likely outcome, and to make some attempt to forestall it. On 11 September he invited

John and his wife to come and spend another winter with him while their new house dried out. The previous winter he considered one of the pleasantest in his life, 'when I had my friends about me in a family way'. He had all the arrangements worked out. He would put a bed up in the drawing-room, and a grate 'where you shall have a constant fire, by which you may instruct your son, and fabricate your Fauna'. He would be more than happy for his sister-in-law to manage the house and see to the provisions. All in all, he believed, 'we shall . . . pass the dead season of the year in no uncomfortable way: and at the return of spring I will let you depart in peace; and will follow you in the summer into Lancashire.'[53] Gilbert assured John, perhaps a little too earnestly, that the proposal was 'a sincere intention', and that he and his wife should not be put off by the prospects of the long coach journey ('which is not so formidable to either of you as some others'). But this careful, diplomatic letter 'surprised and distressed' the touchy younger brother. He read it as an attempt by Gilbert to get out of a reciprocal visit to Lancashire. Gilbert immediately denied that he intended any such thing, and asked his brother to try to understand his position. 'You say I may easily throw up my church, and come down to you; which I ought to do, and fully intend: but then when I once relinquish my employ, I cannot reassume it when I please, even though I find myself ever so much becalmed for want of something to call me forth, and employ my body and mind.'[54] There was something in Gilbert's argument. Whether or not he seriously imagined he could make the journey north, having shied away from the prospect so many times before, he was certainly beginning to find the routines of the Farringdon curacy a mixed blessing. His first move was to try to resign the position altogether, but this was countered by Mr Roman, the rector, with a generous offer of a 25 per cent salary increase (to £50 per annum) to help Gilbert pay for an assistant when he wanted to be absent for any length of time. Gilbert promptly began canvassing Mulso, Skinner and other influential clerical friends to see if they could procure a locum for him. There was a good deal of manoeuvring and back-stage diplomacy, but to no avail. Gilbert failed to obtain a stand-in and, no doubt for many reasons, never travelled to see his brother in Blackburn. The slight misunderstanding between the brothers was soon healed, but Gilbert's lengthy explanations for his absence echoed on for some time, and his feeling of being 'becalmed' found little to relieve it that autumn.

In October he had to travel up to Oxford, where he was required to say his piece as a Fellow in a long-standing dispute over the holding of offices and residence. By chance Richard Skinner arrived in the city at the same time, and dragged Gilbert out – not unwelcomely, we can be sure – for a day away from the college wrangles. 'He made me dine and sup and spend the whole day with him; and is the same chatty, communicative, intelligent, gouty, indolent mortal that he used to be.'[55] Skinner, as it happened, with no reason to think he was going to meet Gilbert in Oxford, had just written to him with news of the adventures of their far-ranging friends, Joseph Banks, William Sheffield and John Lightfoot. The letter was waiting at Selborne. Given Gilbert's frame of mind, it was probably just as well that he first heard about their spirited travels over a few drinks.

But he still had his own, more limited territory to explore, and an increasingly agreeable companion in the shape of Gibraltar Jack. In December they visited Ringmer, where Gilbert's aunt, Rebecca Snooke, was recovering after a serious illness. Of all Gilbert's retreats away from Selborne, this was probably his favourite. Only half a mile from his aunt's house the South Downs began, and, going west towards Lewes, or south towards the Iron Age fort of Mount Caburn, it was possible to walk on the open hills, among wild thyme and ancient barrows, for miles on end.

Gilbert and Jack went for long tramps across the Downs, watching kites and buzzards, and keeping a sharp look-out for any late migrating birds flying out towards the Channel. Back in the house after their windswept walks they would listen to the rooks flying off to roost, and imagine Mrs

Snooke's ageing tortoise snoozing under the mud in the herbaceous border. Gilbert plainly enjoyed this fortnight in Sussex as much as any he had ever spent away from Selborne. He wrote to Barrington from Ringmer in the most cheerful and exuberant tones of their whole correspondence, and it is tempting to think that Jack's eager company was responsible. It is a very local letter, full of sharp and affectionate observations on sheep and shepherds, on the local gentry's taste for roast wheatears, and above all on the magic of the Sussex chalk-hills themselves, with their soaring and very un-Selbornian vistas. Gilbert was exhilarated by the South Downs. He had walked them for thirty years, yet still found 'that chain of majestic mountains' more beautiful each time he visited them. He reminded Barrington that John Ray himself, the father of physico-theology, used to visit a village at the foot of the Downs, and was 'so ravished with the prospect from Plumpton-plain near Lewes, that he mentions those scapes in his *Wisdom of God in the Works of the Creation* with the utmost satisfaction, and thinks them equal to anything he had seen in the finest parts of Europe.'[56] And as if that were not sufficient praise, Gilbert, apologizing rather nervously in advance, launches into a quite untypical flight of fancy about how the Downs might have been formed:

> Perhaps I may be singular in my opinion, and not so happy as to convey to you the same idea; but I never contemplate these mountains without thinking I perceive somewhat analogous to growth in their gentle swellings and smooth fungus-like protuberances, their fluted sides, and regular hollows and slopes, that carry at once the air of vegetative dilation and expansion ... Or was there ever a time when these immense masses of calcareous matter were thrown into fermentation by some adventitious moisture; were raised and leavened into such shapes by some plastic power; and so made to swell and heave their broad backs into the sky so much above the less animated clay of the wild below.[57]

A Man of Letters

It was to be another fifty years before James Hutton showed that scenery and rocks were formed in the past by geological processes identical to those that can be seen at work in the present, and Gilbert can be excused his rather extravagant fantasy, though seeing something 'analogous to growth' in chalk was not that far off target. What is surprising is that he was prepared to admit it to a colleague towards whom he had previously been so reserved. The trip to the majestic mountains had on this occasion quite gone to his head.

Chapter Seven
'Watching narrowly'

Gilbert had by now discarded his former reticence and modesty, even with Pennant. 'I have received a most violent complimenting letter from Mr. Pennant,' he gleefully announced to John that winter. 'He is going to publish a second edition of "British Zoology", and is to do wonders with the information extracted from my letters. I shall take the opportunity of laying before him the more glaring faults in the first edition.'[1]

But most of his energies were now largely devoted to long and lively exchanges with Barrington. 'My letters to Mr Barrington swell very fast,' he wrote, 'he has engaged me in a monography of the swallow genus.' Throughout 1773, the *Naturalist's Journal* had been carrying notes on these summer visitors to the village, and on 20 November 1773 he despatched a long essay on the house-martin to Barrington. Things then moved along with uncharacteristic despatch. In December Gilbert was able to tell John that, thanks to Barrington's influence, the essay was to be delivered as a paper before the Royal Society. 'An Account of the House-Martin, or Martlet' was read on 10 February 1774, and was well received. Gilbert was not a member of the Society, and didn't attend on this occasion, but he was able to see the paper in print in the *Philosophical Transactions* a month later.[2] Mulso was overjoyed that his faith in Gilbert was being vindicated at last: 'May your Hirundines, as I doubt not, bring in the Spring & Summer of your Fame! I am glad You have entrusted yourself to the Public that You reap your due Honour . . . You are Yourself the *richest* Man that I know; for You are the only Man of my Acquaintance that does not want Money.'[3]

On 16 March the following year the Royal Society heard a composite paper comprising Gilbert's letters on the swallow, sand-martin and swift (which was then still assumed to be a member of the same family).[4] Together these four essays are the high point of Gilbert's prose writing. By any standards they are models of lucidity and insight; by those of the eighteenth century they were revolutionary. Few such extended monographs of single species had ever been composed in the English language, and none which were drawn so closely and affectionately from life. Gilbert clearly regarded the subjects of his study as special and had already written a eulogy of them in a letter to Barrington in June 1773. In the edited version of the letters in the *Natural History* he converts this into a general introduction to the hirundine papers by inserting an explanatory note:

> (It will be proper to premise here that the sixteenth, eighteenth, twentieth and twenty first letters have already been published in the *Philosophical Transactions:* but as nicer observation has furnished several corrections and additions, it is hoped that the republication of them will not give offence ...) The *hirundines* are a most inoffensive, harmless, entertaining, social, and useful tribe of birds: they touch no fruit in our gardens; delight, all except one species, in attaching themselves to our houses; amuse us with their migrations, songs and marvellous agility.[5]

It would be hard to imagine a more glowing testimonial. There was nothing new in wild birds being given good references because of their practical usefulness; but Gilbert was breaking new ground in applauding them for sheer vivacity and entertainment value, and for their willingness to live on the most intimate territorial terms with human beings. Yet there was a fascinating air of mystery about them, too, especially about the instincts that governed their lives and put them beyond human sight for six months of the year.

The spectacle of these wild creatures, going about their perfectly yet inscrutably organized business inside the context of a human community, fascinated Gilbert, and must have seemed to him a perfect expression of Ray and Derham's vision of a harmonious Creation. Yet he never openly appropriated the birds' lives as evidence for any moral or theological theory, any more than he dismissed them as mere automata or human playthings. They are respected for themselves. In fact, if there is a weakness in Gilbert's account it is that the martins seem a little too bright – and with an intelligence very much in the human mould.

Martins teemed in Selborne during the eighteenth cen-

tury. Several pairs nested at the Wakes, and Gilbert was able
to watch them under the eaves of his brew-house and stable
without even leaving his garden. They arrived around 16
April, and once they had begun nest-building a month later
Gilbert must have found it difficult to drag himself back to
his desk and his parish duties. His journal entries on them
show a mixture of excitement and concern that is curiously
modern. Many of the intimate details of their lives that most
enchanted him (and which he was the first to set down on
paper) are the kind that can still touch anyone who has kept
the long summer watch over house-martins as they raise
their families. He noticed how they use their chins to plaster
new mud on the nests; their determination in rebuilding
nests when they are washed away by rain; the bewitchingly
inquisitive faces of the young birds, 'peeping out' of the
nest's hole all day when they are nearly fledged; and, finally,
how the young are fed on the wing by the parents, 'but the
feat is done by so quick and almost imperceptible a sleight,
that a person must have attended very exactly to their
motions before he would percieve it.' It would be foolish to
deny that Gilbert was thoroughly soft-hearted about his
'martlets', and sometimes he seems to ascribe human
emotions and purposes to them. The adult birds, he noticed
'are industrious artificers . . . at their labours in the long days
before four in the morning'; and when they carry off their
nestlings' droppings they do so with 'tender assiduity'. Yet
in the context of the whole paper, these reflections seem not
so much anthropomorphic as an affirmation that there is a
core of experience and challenge which is common to all
life. On the one occasion when he does explicitly compare
the behaviour of humans and martins it is the birds' skill
which is offered as the model. Gilbert is describing the
method used by the birds to construct their mud nests:

> The bird not only clings with its claws but partly supports
> itself by strongly inclining its tail against the wall, making
> that a fulcrum; and thus steadied it works and plasters the
> materials into the face of the brick or stone. But then, that

this work may not, while is is soft and green, pull itself down by its own weight, the provident architect has prudence and forbearance enough not to advance her work too fast; but by building only in the morning, and by dedicating the rest of the day to food and amusement, gives it sufficient time to dry and harden. About half an inch seems to be a sufficient layer for a day. Thus careful workmen when they build mud-walls (informed at first perhaps by this little bird) raise but a moderate layer at a time, and then desist; lest the work should become top-heavy, and so be ruined by its own weight.[6]

Such close-ups almost compel respect; they imply that even the smallest detail of the bird's life matters. When Gilbert turned his attention to the swallow itself a short while later, he moved further in this direction, and his essay includes examples of a viewpoint already strikingly realized in the journal. There are episodes which are not only acute insights into the bird's private lives and their part in the larger society of nature, but which are composed, almost as if they were parables or portraits. He had watched swallows and martins mobbing sparrowhawks as they glided down the Selborne valley:

As soon as an hawk ... appears he [a swallow] calls all the swallows and martins about him; who pursue in a body, and buffet and strike their enemy till they have driven him from the village, darting down from above on his back, and rising in a perpendicular line in perfect security.[7]

On the chalk downs he had seen horsemen followed by little flocks of swallows 'for miles together, which plays before and behind them, sweeping around, and collecting all the skulking insects that are roused by the trampling of the horses' feet'. There were the sounds, too. When a swallow hovered over one of the wide chimneys which were then their favourite nest-sites, 'the vibration of her wings acting on the confined air occasion a rumbling like thunder'; when one catches a fly, 'a smart snap from her bill is heard resembling the noise at the shutting of a watch-case.' And all this was noted in the face of bouts of increasing deafness, which at times, he confesses, made May 'as silent and mute with respect to the notes of birds, etc, as August', and for which he was soon to need an ear-trumpet.*

Only one of the anecdotes in the Royal Society papers seems slightly out of keeping and was perhaps inserted chiefly for effect, though it is an interesting enough story. It concerns an exhibit in Ashton Lever's famous museum in Alkrington, Lancashire (later transferred to London) – a swallow's nest, with eggs, built on the outstretched wings of a dead owl which had been hanging from a rafter. Lever was so struck with this curiosity that he gave the donor a large shell to put where the owl had previously been. This was done, and the following year swallows obligingly nested in the shell – which, needless to say, was whisked off to the museum just as soon as it had a full clutch of eggs. Gilbert certainly had not seen these exhibits himself when he completed the swallow paper early in January 1774. He had heard about them from John, who lived near the museum, and on 12 January 1774 he asked John to repeat the anecdote: 'Pray tell me over again the story of the swallow building on the dead owl's wings and on the conch &c. I think I could make good use of it'[8] A fortnight later it was installed at the end of the essay.

The paper on the swift, as well as containing magnificent descriptions of their evening races round the steeples and churches, records some wholly original observations. Gilbert had noticed that sitting birds and nestlings replied to the packs when they screamed past the nest entrances. He spotted, too, that they mated on the wing:

> If any person would watch these birds of a fine morning in May, as they are sailing round at a great height from the ground, he would see, every now and then, one drop on the back of another, and both of them sink down together for many fathoms with a loud piercing shriek. This I take to be the juncture when the business of generation is carrying on.[9]

---

* Dafydd Stephens, a consultant audiologist, has kindly pointed out to me a possible connection between Gilbert's fits of deafness and his predisposition to coach-sickness, perhaps in a disorder of the labyrinth (though he showed none of the disabling dizziness characteristic of Ménière's disease).

But their departure from the village in early August was 'mysterious and wonderful, since that time is often the sweetest season in the year.' And it posed problems about how the young could be made ready for long flights in such a short period. In the summer of 1775 he had the opportunity to observe a swift's nest at close quarters to see if this riddle could be solved. His brother Henry had been busy building a large new wing on his house at Fyfield, to accommodate his growing family and the small private school he was running. The extension ran between the kitchen and the brew-house, where a number of swifts nested, and Gilbert decided to take advantage of the general dismantling to take a look at one:

> I got Harry's bricklayer one evening to open the tiles of his brewhouse, under which were several nests containing only *two* squab young apiece; and moreover his workmen all told me that, when boys, they had invariably found only two eggs or two birds.[10]

He looked again ten days later, noted in his journal for 9 July that 'young swifts helpless squabs still', and the following year repeated the whole exercise, this time almost certainly in Selborne:

> On the fifth of July, 1775, I again untiled part of a roof over the nest of a swift. The dam sat in the nest; but so strongly was she affected by natural στοργη [affection] for her brood, which she supposed to be in danger, that, regardless of her own safety, she would not stir, but lay sullenly by them, permitting herself to be taken in hand. The squab young we brought down and placed on the grass-plot, where they tumbled about, and were as helpless as a new-born child. While we contemplated their naked bodies, their unwieldy disproportioned *abdomina*, and their heads, too heavy for their necks to support, we could not but wonder when we reflected that these shiftless beings in a little more than a fortnight would be able to dash through the air almost with the inconceivable swiftness of a meteor; and perhaps, in

their emigration must traverse vast continents and oceans as distant as the equator.[11]

Gilbert knew swifts to be resourceful feeders and flyers, and regarded them as being the most likely migrators among the 'swallow tribe'. But to the extent that he thought some of this tribe might stay behind to hibernate in the village (and to the extent that his views on migration were influenced by rational arguments), it was this image of small, inexperienced birds only a few weeks old crossing whole oceans that he found most distressing and incredible. And this was the argument he frequently put to Barrington, who believed, in a much less qualified way, in full-scale hibernation. To use the human analogies that were clearly always at the back of their minds, Gilbert, with his first-hand knowledge, saw the birds as good, industrious citizens, with complicated needs, considerable powers of adaptation, and an instinctive concern for their young. Barrington, who was largely ignorant of their domestic lives, regarded them much as he probably did the poor, as simple creatures lacking in flexibility and intelligence, and unlikely ever to make any effort that wasn't absolutely necessary. Migration over the sea was exceptionally unlikely, he believed, because birds would be unable to find food, and could not perform such complex navigation purely by instinct. In any case:

> Such a bird immediately upon its arrival on the Southern coast of Spain would find the climate and food which it desired to attain, and all proper conveniences for its nest: what then is to be its inducement for quitting all these accommodations which it meets in such profusion, and pushing on immediately over so many degrees of European continent?[12]

*

Gilbert frequently used information and anecdotes from friends and relatives to fill out his letters. In June 1774 he wrote to Samson Newbery, a Fellow of Exeter College who lived in south Devon, requesting any information he might have about the birds of the West Country. Newbery's reply is full of useful notes, many of which were quickly passed on to Pennant. But the correspondence with Pennant had by now almost run its natural course. The only two communications from Gilbert between November 1773 and September 1774 are a torrent of terse notes and anecdotes on birdsong, odd migrants, winter habits and the like, designed to give Pennant the maximum amount of factual information for the revised edition of *British Zoology* with the minimum of distraction from his now more absorbing correspondence with Barrington. 'I observe that my long letter carries with it a quaint and magisterial air,' he apologizes on 2 September 1774, 'but, when I recollect that you requested stricture and anecdote, I hope you will pardon the didactic manner for the sake of the information it may happen to contain.'[13]

His growing file of correspondence was beginning to strike Gilbert as a rather better (or at least more convenient) starting-point for his book than an 'annus historico-naturalis'. 'As to my letters,' he wrote to John at the end of March, 'they lie in my cupboard very snug. If you will correct them, and assist in the arrangement of my Journal, I will publish.'[14] One month later he is even more explicit about his plans:

> Out of all my journals I think I might collect matter enough, and such a series of incidents as might pretty well comprehend the Natural History of this district, especially as to the ornithological part; and I have moreover half a century of letters on the same subject, most of them very long; all which together (were they thought worthy to be seen) might make up a moderate volume. To these might be added some circumstances of the country, its most curious plants, its few antiquities; all which together might soon be moulded into a work, had I resolution and spirits enough to set about it.[15]

Gilbert's doubts about his resolution were to prove depressingly accurate. Although the description that he sent to John that May is virtually a prospectus of the *Natural History* as it was eventually published, the editing and arrangement were to take him another fourteen years. John did what he could to help, as requested, but it is doubtful if he was able to contribute anything substantial enough to speed up Gilbert's progress. Once he reprimands Gilbert for putting those traditionally most feminine of birds, swallows, into the neuter. 'I thank you for your strictures on my printed monography,' Gilbert replies, 'I *had* used the pronoun personal feminine to my swallows; but somebody objected, so I put *it* in its place; but I think you are right, and shall replace *she* and *her*.'[16] Dealing with editors was even then, plainly, a fractious and finicky business.

Indeed the problems involved in moulding a series of existing letters into a finished book raise the question of why Gilbert chose this particular way of preparing his text, rather than rewriting their contents as continuous prose. Was it nothing more than a realistic admission of his lack of determination and literary stamina? It is hard to see this prolific correspondent, who had kept a daily journal for nearly a quarter of a century and completed his elegant hirundine essays in a matter of weeks, as suffering from some kind of writer's block; yet the evidence of those fourteen years of prevarication is impossible to overlook. Perhaps – and the character of the journal entries might support this – he actually found immediate, first-time writing easier than revision. Max Nicholson has also pointed out that, since the idea for the book had arisen out of the correspondence with Barrington and Pennant, there was a kind of logic in 'following this line of least resistance' and simply editing the existing correspondence.[17] It would avoid the charge of pretentiousness, and enable Gilbert to use in its original state a good deal of material which had already been published by Pennant, and which could hardly have been reissued in any other form without a suspicion of plagiarism. Nicholson's suggestion that Gilbert also felt the need 'to shelter himself behind the then powerful names of Barrington and Pennant' is less convincing, given his growing confidence with both men.

Yet beyond these possible tactical considerations there is the plain fact that a collection of letters, datelined Selborne, was a well-nigh perfect medium for conveying the spirit of the seasonal ebb and flow of natural life in a parish, and Gilbert must have realized this sooner or later. The recording of one dramatic event earlier in 1774 shows the extent to which the letters were, in one sense, an extended form of village gossip. The saga of the Hawkley landslip is not a typical *Natural History* entry (especially as Gilbert was not even there to describe it first-hand) but it does demonstrate how the letters became a device for turning conversation into literature.

The year had begun portentously, with unprecedentedly heavy rains. On Sunday 9 January the flooding was so severe that Gilbert was for the first time in his curacy unable to get to Farringdon to take the services. 'Thomas and I were over the calves of our legs before we got to Peter Wells's' he wrote to John three days later, and 'were told that if we proceeded any further our horses would swim'. The exceptional weather brought a spate of unusual water-birds to the parish, including a number of bitterns. Three were shot in the parish (one in a coppice near the foot of the Hanger) and were brought to Gilbert's house, as was now becoming the custom with any natural curiosities which appeared locally. As the birds were already dead, he took a severely practical view of them. After weighing, dissecting and generally appraising them ('the serrated claw on the middle toe is very curious!') he cooked up the remains for his supper. 'I . . . . found the flavour to be like that of wild duck, or teal, but not so delicate.'[18]

The cold wet weather continued unabated during February and the underground springs ('lavants') began to break out of the chalk hills ominously early. Much of the early wheat on the low-lying clays was rotting in the ground. Lambing time was a disaster, with large numbers of animals, already weakened by a diet of sodden turnips, dying from exposure and drowning. Nor had Gilbert escaped with nothing more than a case of wet feet. He had been working hard on the swallow papers through the debilitating rounds of frost and flood, and had gone down with a complicated illness – probably influenza – of which he sent Mulso a 'terrible Description'. Mulso warned him to take the greatest care of himself, since the symptoms were liable to reappear; but not so much care as to become hypochondriacal. 'Do not fall into ye Extream of Fear on the other Side, like your Father; but consider, that by the Account of all the Faculty here, & indeed as seems a natural Consequence of the Peculiarity of our Seasons this winter, Extraordinary appearances of Illness, & new Modes of Suffering have happen'd.'[19] Fortunately Jack was still at the Wakes with his uncle, helping with his journal and correspondence and no doubt in keeping his spirits up, too. 'He is now of real service to me,' Gilbert wrote to John on 5 February, 'and a companion in my solitude.'

The deluge reached a climax on 8 March. Two days of unrelenting rain culminated in a snowstorm, and the resulting floods in the south of England were 'beyond any thing ever remembered before'. In the parish of Hawkley, a couple of miles south of Selborne, the mass of water accumulating below the chalk was reaching an unprecedented volume. Some time in the early hours of 9 March it finally found a weak spot and broke through. A huge section of Hawkley Hanger (ironically, land once owned by Gilbert's grandfather) fell away, toppling trees and cottages, and crashing with the force of a small earthquake on to the fields below. Gilbert's illness meant that he was in no state to visit the disaster, but Jack travelled down during the next few days and was able to report back to his uncle. His description was so vivid and perceptive for a boy of 15 – and not without a touch of his uncle's eye for detail – that Gilbert encouraged him to write it down in the form of a letter to his cousin, Sam Barker. This note remains the only first-hand account of the immediate after-effects of the landslip. Jack reckoned that eighty to a hundred acres had been affected:

> a large fragment of the Hanger . . . slipped away for near two hundred yards·in length, and fell down the steep to the depth of 40 ft,·carrying with it the coppice-wood, hedge, and

gate between the two fields, &c. The sinking of this gate is very strange, as it stands at present as upright as it used to do and is as easy to be opened and shut ... A lane which went down one side of this hill is sunk eight or ten feet, and very much pushed forward so as to be rendered impassable ... There is in one field that was wheat last year pretty well an acre so much sunk, that it is impossible to be ploughed. All the corn land which was affected by this event is full of large chasms and cracks, some two feet wide: the meadow land has very few of these cracks in it, but seems to be pushed forward; and is filled with large swellings of the turf very much resembling waves: in some places where the ground met with any thing that resisted it rose up many feet above its former surface.[20]

The landslip became a famous tourist attraction that spring, and one Sunday a couple of weeks after the incident, a crowd estimated at close on a thousand people gathered at the site. But Gilbert's continuing poor health kept him away from Hawkley till at least the middle of April. A trip to London later in March, while he was still suffering with the after-effects of his influenza, brought on first a rash and then a cough. By the end of the month he was 'feverish and faint', and not even up to making his usual April trip to Oxford.

But he was well enough recovered by the summer to visit the landslip and make his own investigations of the upheaval it had caused. He talked to cottagers who lived in the vicinity, and made meticulous measurements – to the nearest yard, in places – of the exact extent of the disturbance

Unusually, none of this evidence found its way into his correspondence. Perhaps it was too remote for Barrington and too much like old news for his relatives. But some time later he wrote up the story as one of the concluding 'false letters' in the *Natural History*. It takes the form of a letter to Barrington, but was never actually sent to him, and consequently bears no date.[21] With no need to hurry the telling, or to dwell on the sometimes rather dull necessities of real correspondence, Gilbert was free to fashion his account like a suspense story, and quite deliberately uses dramatic close-ups and cliff-hangers to bring an edge of Gothick horror to it.

Just as interesting, given how free Gilbert is in most of his writing with the niceties of sequence and order, is the extent to which the piece is structured. The details are accurate and telling, often touchingly so, and undeniably White; yet they are put together in a more controlled and recognizably eighteenth-century way than almost anything else he wrote. In places the essay's shape is as formal as a neoclassical landscape painting. There in the foreground are the hapless victims quaking in their cottages as seventy feet of wooded hillside collapses around them; in the middle ground, a world of familiar objects bent out of all order and sense; and beyond them, the shock-waves of the disturbance rippling away into the distance; and all seen, as it were, through the eyes of the main characters, the cottagers:

> When daylight came they were at leisure to contemplate the devastations of the night: they then found that a deep rift, or chasm, had opened under their houses, and torn them, as it were, in two; and that one end of the barn had suffered in a similar manner; that a pond near the cottage had undergone a strange reverse, becoming deep at the shallow end, and so *vice versa*; that many large oaks were removed out of their perpendicular, some thrown down, and some fallen into the heads of neighbouring trees; and that a gate was thrust forward, with its hedge, full six feet, so as to require a new track to be made to it. From the foot of the cliff the general course of the ground, which is pasture, inclines in a moderate descent for half a mile, and is interspersed with some hillocks, which were rifted, in every direction, as well towards the great woody hanger, as from it. In the first pasture the deep clefts began: and running across the lane, and under the buildings, made such vast shelves that the road was impassable for some time; and so over to an arable field on the other side, which was strangely torn and disordered. The second pasture field, being more soft and

springy, was protruded forward without many fissures in the turf, which was raised in long ridges resembling graves, lying at right angles to the motion. At the bottom of this enclosure the soil and turf rose many feet against the bodies of some oaks that obstructed their farther course and terminated this awful commotion.

*

For the remainder of 1774 life in Selborne proceeded on a more even keel. Despite the ravages of the winter, it proved to be a bountiful year. House-martins arrived, eventually, in even greater numbers than usual. A redstart took to singing from the top of the village maypole. In the Wakes garden, the peaches and nectarines set a bumper crop, and even the bees, still lethargic from the late spring, were persuaded into pollinating the melon and cucumber flowers by means of a little honey smeared on the petals. 'Sweet summer's day,' Gilbert wrote on 13 May, when he would plainly not have wished to be anywhere else in the world. 'Field cricket begins to shrill. Horses began to lie abroad.' And, inspired partly by Harry's ambitious projects at Fyfield, he began to think of extending and improving the Wakes by building a new parlour. Mulso approved of the plan, and understood the feelings that lay behind it:

> Pray, when you build, let it be a 'drawing Room up Stairs, that you may look on the Hanger; Let it be higher than the present, & let it be sashed – Monstrous! why this will be great Expence! True, therefore take two Years instead of One to do it in. As You want to decoy your family after You to make Selbourne a Place of Residence, as well as to enjoy it during your own Life, e'en do it in a tempting way.[22]

The Wakes had already become a holiday retreat for the White clan, and that April a new name joins the list of regular visitors. Molly, Thomas White's 15-year-old daughter, had come to spend the summer and be tutored by the vicar's wife, Mrs Etty. She adored Selborne, growing 'tall, fair and handsome', and no doubt enjoyed the company of her energetic cousin, Jack, who was still installed at the Wakes. Jack's stay had been extended, chiefly because it was proving difficult to find a suitable position for him now his schooling was over. Gilbert and Thomas had offered to help with the search while John was still in the north, but they were not finding much that lived up to their expectations for a favourite nephew. Chemistry was 'unwholesome'. Printers might earn a good deal of money, but their apprenticeships were 'low and servile'. Lawyers were overpaid and had never been popular with the family. Even where quite humdrum jobs were involved, employers were asking outrageous deposits for taking on young trainees. Gilbert reckoned, not entirely flippantly, that Jack would be most usefully employed assisting his father in the preparation of his *Fauna Calpensis*, which was beginning to falter for lack of help with the transcription: 'A writing master would take this trouble off your hands for a small sum, but with this disadvantage, that no man can transcribe his own works without seeing plans that he can alter for the better; a benefit which is entirely lost where a stranger is amanuensis. I wish Jack would earn your book; I mentioned the conditions, at which he smiled.'[23]

In fact John's book was beginning to run into an increasing number of technical problems. When he wrote to Gilbert about its progress in August 1774, there is an air of dejection in his letter, and the surprising admission – given the vast amount of work that seemed to have been devoted to it over the past four years – that he had advanced only a small way into the final text:

> I am drawing towards the conclusion of my insects; and shall then proceed to the quadrupeds, birds, and fishes. After all there must be a general correction and transcript of the whole, which will be no small undertaking.
>
> We have had a sad, gloomy, wet, chilly season. We are now sitting over a fire. I have brushed up my house as spruce as if it were for sale; but it is to give you as agreeable an idea of Lancashire as I can.[24]

There are close enough echoes here of some of Gilbert's complaints to suggest that John may have been slyly getting one back at his brother. Gilbert did not respond to this muted plea for encouragement and company. Perhaps he felt that too great a show of consideration would have obliged him to make the dread journey north. But he still seemed willing to advise John about the best way of presenting his work. The suggestions are as shrewd and effusive as ever. He should include as many plates as possible, since picture-books were now highly fashionable. So were accounts of tours, and John's volume would be the poorer without a 'pretty chapter' on his explorations. (Gilbert had just read Samuel Johnson's *A Journey to the Western Isles of Scotland*, and though he found it sentimental, it was 'full of good sense, and new and peculiar reflections'.) Gilbert, now the thoroughgoing literary professional, explained that Benjamin's hesitation in agreeing terms for the book might in part be due to a growing reluctance among publishers to take on new editions, in consequence of a confirmation that year of a drastic foreshortening of the legal term of copyright.[25] So, playing the role of the mediating elder brother, he suggests a way of appeasing Benjamin:

> Suppose you write to him, and ask him how much he will give you *downright* clear of the plates and printing for your copy; and then you will know your certain gain, and will run no risk. Anything in the naturalist way now sells well. Or if he chuses to go shares in profit or loss, enquire of him what proportion he should think would pay him for conducting the sale and publication.[26]

Hecky Chapone, he added, having sold her first two volumes for £50 the pair,[27] had now managed to squeeze her publisher for £250 for a third collection, *Miscellanies in Prose and Verse*, 'so that it is expected the man will lose considerably by the purchase.' ('We all abuse her this Time for cheating the Public,' commented Mulso, who had been the source of this particular snippet.) Gilbert revelled in the familiarity of this literary chit-chat, which must in several ways have shortened the distance between Selborne and the city. Hecky herself, having become a celebrated hostess, was rarely out of the gossip, and Gilbert had already risen spiritedly to her defence in a letter to his sister in the autumn of 1774. 'The insinuation that Mrs. Chapone is a papist is a foolish slander thrown out by somebody that envies her literary reputation: I have been assured since that she is an Italian stage-dancer.'[28]

*

The winter of 1774/5 began early, with snow falling in Selborne on 11 November. By the middle of the month repeated severe frosts had set in, and the papers were full of ominous reports of the weather conditions over the near Continent. Gilbert no longer relished the snow as he had done when he was younger, and confessed as much in letters to his sister Anne and to Mulso, who was sad to hear of this sign of the toll of advancing years:

> It was odd enough, that on the very Morning that I recd Your's, in which You complain of the Snow, that I had been revising a Lr from You, in which You tell me that You had rode out every Day to contemplate that beautifull Meteor, which shows itself to Advantage in your uneven Country. I am sorry You change your Note: No one bears Time better outwardly; and yet I know by Myself that Time has made some advances upon You, for Yesterday I was fifty three: I have one Pleasure however in this Increase of Years, It is the longer Date of our Friendship.[29]

In fact Gilbert was bearing the passage of time less well than Mulso knew. He had pains in his chest whenever he wrote for too long and, for a time, a 'heat and Stiffness' in his eyes from prolonged reading. His hands were beginning to show signs of gout. All these complaints made work on his letters and manuscript irksome and slow. And since Jack had finally left to join his father in November, Gilbert had no help at all with transcription. Technical aids to copying did exist, in the form of special inks and moistened, semi-transparent paper, but they were exceptionally expensive, and none of Gilbert's surviving correspondence appears to have been copied by any means other than laborious longhand.

Gilbert was no doubt relieved that he was able to spend the coldest part of December in London. But despite the fierce frosts of early winter, January and February of 1775 proved to be mild and exceptionally wet. It snowed on only two days, and on one of these the snow fell as sleet. From Hackwood Park near Selborne, Gilbert received a report that a large number of rooks had been brought to the ground during this fall, which had frozen their wings together. Rooks were one of a vast range of subjects – including wasps, frost-hollows, hops, the formation of dew-ponds and a great fall of gossamer cobwebs that he had witnessed in the village in 1741 – to which Gilbert gave special attention during 1775. He watched rooks eating grubs in the fields, squabbling over their nest-sites, courting, scrumping walnuts from his orchard, and finally how 'the twigs which [they] drop in building supply the poor with brush-wood to light their fires.'[30]

Many of his observations this year concern these kinds of interaction between animals, both with their own kind and with other species. He was fascinated by the sheer range and number of insects that were about during mild weather in the winter ('*lepismae* in cupboards, and among sugar *phalenae* in hedges') and how these were vital to the survival of our resident birds. He was also curious – perhaps for more practical reasons – about the lives of slugs and snails. He was puzzled as to why the seemingly better protected snail hibernated during the winter, whilst the 'shell-less snails, called slugs' were about all winter in mild weather, making havoc with garden plants and young wheat. Later in the year there was not much to choose between them in terms of the damage they caused, and Gilbert was pleased to find just how many were consumed by thrushes ('the walks are covered with their shells') – pleased for the thrushes, too, that there was such a provident food-source for them when the earthworms burrowed deep in hot, dry weather.

The exquisitely balanced economies of nature were one

of the subjects that Gilbert discussed at length with John Mulso when his old friend came to stay in late June. It was a visit that seemed to have been arranged at short notice and without any fuss, and Mulso thought it was probably the most agreeable time he had ever spent in Selborne. The two men had strolled about the village and the surrounding country (or at least the flatter parts of it; Mulso was no rambler) discussing physico-theology and the plans for the book, and Gilbert had shown Mulso his journals and some of the edited letters. Mulso seems to have been overawed by these. He does not quite know what to say, and his letter of thanks in July is untypically sober and formal:

> You have a double Felicity in your Manner of Entertainment; You can gratify your Visitors both wth beautiful Originals, & high Descriptions; Representations studiously copied from Nature & finished with a Masterly Hand. As You intend your Works for ye Public, I would not say so much in a Strain of Flattery; for tho' I would not tell an Author how much I disliked his Productions, yet I might slubber them over with a hasty careless Compliment, or lose them in Silence ... You have happily grounded Ethics on a stable & beautifull Basis, ye Works of God; & your Figures formed from naked & genuine Beauty, beat every finical Composition that would fascinate ye Judgement by adventitious Ornament. This is my real Opinion of your Work. But Mem: I do not mean by ye close of ye last Sentence a Slur on your Intention of employing the Art of Mr Grim, or any other more accomplished Designer: I wish he may add to ye Pleasure of ye World, as much as he will gratify my Partiality.[31]

This is the first mention of the possibility of using the up-and-coming Swiss artist Hieronymus Grimm, who had been working in England since 1768. Mulso sounds not wholly convinced about the need for such embellishments in a work already so finely drawn. But he would have been much more seriously perturbed if he had known what other additions Gilbert was planning, and which began to become apparent that autumn in a run of journal entries on the likely origins of Selborne place-names.

Gilbert had not yet settled the precise form and extent of the book, and in August, while he was staying at his aunt's house in Sussex, he took the opportunity to set down his thoughts about their respective projects in a long letter to his brother, John. Ringmer, that high summer, had the kind of youthful, familial atmosphere that invariably filled Gilbert with fresh energies. His sister Anne Barker was there, with her children Sally, 23 years of age, Mary, 15, and Sam, now 18 and already proving himself a valuable member of Gilbert's network of informants and advisers. 'The young people are clever and intelligent,' Gilbert wrote contentedly to his brother. 'Mrs Snooke is very well and a marvellous woman at 81.' Her tortoise Timothy had amused them all by consenting to be weighed for the first time, and multitudes of young swallows were gathering on the pine trees round the house. The only sadness in all this 'sweet harvest weather' was that Jack was not with them, but Gilbert was delighted to hear that he was now settled with a surgeon quite close to his father's house in Lancashire, though 'As to Jack's "venturing to draw blood from his majesties subjects," I do not so much wonder: I rather admire at the courage of the patients who permit him: however every young man must have a beginning.'[32]

But Gilbert points out that losing his amanuensis was having a decided effect on the progress of his work and he was resentful of John's insinuation that the *Natural History* was in a state of 'much more forwardness'. The truth, Gilbert insisted, was that while John's book was now completely finished, many of his own letters were still waiting to be transcribed, his journal 'is but just begun', and – here the new ingredient is spelt out for the first time – 'the antiquities of Selborne are not entered upon at all.' But he had made a start: 'Friends in Oxon., I hope, are searching for me amongst Dodsworth's collection of papers in the Bodleian library, 60 vol. folio; but the papers that I want to see most are immured in the Archives of Magd. Coll.'[33]

157

The scheme for using Grimm was also making progress. The artist himself was held up by work in the Midlands counties, but in the meantime he was being thoroughly checked out. The reports were promising. He had exhibited four pieces in the Royal Academy exhibition of 1769, only a year after his arrival in Britain, and had worked for some eminent patrons.[34] A deputation consisting of Thomas and Benjamin White, Thomas Mulso and Michael Lort (a friend of the influential critic Horace Walpole) who had 'been to his lodgings to see his performances', were all agreed that he was 'a man of genius'. He was especially good with prospects and buildings, though the two Toms felt that he took too many liberties with natural appearances, and that his trees were 'grotesque and strange'. Gilbert's chief worry was that he had a reputation for excessive delicacy in his manner of sketching and the use of light water-colour washes; whereas Gilbert wanted a style that would reflect the intensity of detail he was trying to capture in the writing: *strong lights and shades* and good trees and foliage'. White anticipates Gilpin here. The latter, in his *Northern Tour* (1786) writes:

> It is the aim of picturesque description to bring the images of nature forcibly and as closely to the eye as it can, by high colouring. High colouring is not a string of rapturous epithets, but an attempt to analyse the views of nature: to mark their tints and varied lights and to express all this detail in terms as appropriate and vivid as possible.

There is no doubt that Gilbert's continuing involvement with all aspects of publishing was a considerable influence on the character of the still embryonic *Natural History*. The shrewd editorial advice that he gave to other writers, for instance, always seems in part to be directed to himself. There are touches in it of both intellectual swagger and reflection. Yet he never openly stints or distorts the advice for his own ends. When his brother Thomas, who at long last had come into his inheritance from the Holts (see page 45), unexpectedly announced that he was thinking of writing on the natural history and antiquities of Hampshire, Gilbert responded with his usual mixture of encouragement and expert practical counsel. But privately the prospect must have made his heart sink. Thomas was unquestionably the most successful of his brothers and quite probably the brightest. He had already made a considerable amount of money as a partner in a wholesale merchant's business in London, and had shown some evidence, in his day-book and correspondence, of a confident and economical prose style.[35] Later in his life he was to contribute articles upon a huge variety of topics to the *Gentleman's Magazine*. He had a particular interest in Anglo-Saxon and medieval history, and it may have been partly at his suggestion that Gilbert decided to add a section on the antiquities of Selborne to his natural history. When Thomas made his somewhat cavalier announcement, Gilbert must have felt anxious over the possible competition and overlap between the two projects, but he is positive and hopeful about Thomas's idea. 'You are now at a time of life when judgement is mature,' he flatters him in January, 1776, 'and when you have not lost that activity of the body necessary for such pursuits.' He recommends employing an artist to visit 'the remarkable places' in the county, and outlines the subjects of which Thomas should make the most thorough study. But he has a warning about paying too much heed to the kind of approach typified by Robert Plot's work: 'he is too credulous, some times trifling, some times superstitious; and at all times ready to make a needless display, and ostentation of erudition.' Dr Plot had been the author of two of the earliest county-based natural histories – of Oxfordshire, published in 1677, and Staffordshire in 1686, the former interestingly subtitled 'being an Essay towards the Natural History of England'. In the absence of anything better they had become the model for local studies. But a new attitude towards the natural world – more alert, more self-critical – had been developing in the hundred years since, and Gilbert's strictures were certainly not an uncharacteristic show of sour grapes. Although Plot and his colleagues in the Royal Society had begun to stress the importance of direct observation, they had not yet begun to discriminate between different kinds of evidence. As a consequence, there is more than a trace of the medieval bestiary about his books. Observed fact, ancient fable and simple hearsay rub shoulders, and bizarre discoveries of the kind that crop up in many old natural history books – eggs within eggs and fossils shaped like human organs were two favourites – receive rather more attention than the common and typically local.

It had been a useful exercise for Gilbert to consider his opinion of Plot, but as far as Thomas was concerned it was so much wasted time. The Hampshire book proved to be a momentary whim, and Thomas, finding the management of his new estates a thoroughly fulfilling occupation, abandoned the idea as abruptly as he had raised it.

But John's book, the *Fauna Calpensis*, was becoming a cause for concern. By the autumn of 1775 Gilbert had managed to catch a glimpse of a fair proportion of the manuscript, and it was obvious that John had been paying little attention to the editorial advice he had been given. The text had a stuffy and bloated feel. It was still short of first-hand anecdotes and 'diversification', and was weighed down by Latinisms. It had grown to nearly a thousand pages but still had no index (which 'perhaps has never entered your head' chided Gilbert). The botanical sections looked shaky, and needed to be read over by an expert. Worst of all, the slight differences between John and Benjamin over the terms for the book had grown into a serious rift. Since John seemed disinclined to take Ben's advice on the title and general polish of the book, Benjamin had held back from buying it outright, and had apparently suggested that they share the costs. Whereupon John, always touchy and suspicious, announced his intention of publishing the thing himself, and accused his brothers of meddling with his work for their own purposes. Gilbert was alarmed by this souring of relations, and sent John a copy of one of his own best anecdotes (the fall of gossamer he described to Barrington in June that year) in the hope, maybe, of transfusing some new life into John's phlegmatic offspring. But he was exasperated by his brother's continued obstinacy and wild accusations, and when he tried to calm matters down in January 1776, he openly sided with Benjamin for the first time:

> Dear Brother,
> As you have enjoined me to speak my sentiments with respect to your work, you must not think me didactic and forward in the following pages ... Your Bookseller [Ben] must be consulted a little in the title page and advertisments; as he knows best how to throw in little savoury and alluring circumstances to quicken the appetite of your buyer. By no means should you print, brother Thomas and I both think, 'til you have sold your copy: booksellers know how to subscribe off an impression to the trade, and to throw cold water on a work lying on the author's hand ... We wish to see your papers, and to correct here and there, not out of vanity and a meddling temper; but because little errors unavoidably befall and escape every Author.[36]

John did what he could to patch the book up, but his heart was no longer in it. As well as being hurt by the criticisms, he had began to suffer from a debilitating and progressive rheumatic disorder. Gilbert did not learn of this until later in 1776, but he still did not go up to visit his brother. And his and Benjamin's constant flutterings over the progress of the book – however well meant – can't have done much to improve John's health or confidence. Gilbert did not seem to notice the condescension that occasionally crept into his letters, or the contradictory advice he was beginning to offer. In August he was urging the avoidance of arguments over the book:

> By your unusual silence I began to fear what has really been the case, ill health. You have perhaps by your attention to your book and other matters been too free with your constitution lately: you must therefore relax a little, and allow yourself more time for riding and walking. Particularly, I think, you should avoid contention though in ever so good a cause.[37]

Three months on, with John's condition not improved,

his advice was rather different. 'You seem a cup too low,' Gilbert wrote, 'and do not assume the importance of an author. If Mr Pennant had got such a work ready he would feel little diffidence.'[38] But John, of course, was nothing whatever like the self-confident and extrovert Thomas Pennant, and it is no wonder that by the summer of 1777 he had thrown aside the book in 'disgust and chagrin'.

Its final despatch came that autumn. In August Harry White had delivered a complete copy of John's manuscript to Selborne. At this stage it seems to have been read by all the brothers except Gilbert. Gilbert confessed that 'between an hurry of business, company and building' he had had little time to study it. But he had shown it to Dr Richard Chandler, a young writer and antiquarian, and a Fellow of Magdalen College, who had just been appointed to the livings of nearby Worldham and East Tisted and was helping Gilbert's research on Selborne's antiquities. His views and credentials, as relayed by Gilbert, were ambiguous, and John may not have thought much of the opinions of a 'traveller in Greece, who being no naturalist has no partiality for the Linn[aean] system; but avers that it will prevent your book from becoming popular'.[39] Chandler is sure, Gilbert continued 'that if you could perswade yourself to divest it of its quaint garb (those were his words) that he is certain it would be worth £200 of any body's money.' But what he was recommending in detail was nothing less than a complete restructuring of the book.

John must have felt crushed and humiliated by these comments, and a short while later Gilbert, glimpsing at last the damage that had been done, made a more generous attempt to restore his faith and determination:

'In the whole I *much approve* of your book. Your preface is neat; your history is what I call true Natural History, because it abounds with anecdote, and circumstance; and I verily think your dissertations on the *Hirundines* are the best tracts I ever saw of the kind, as they throw much light on the dark but curious business of migration ... I therefore pronounce as the Vice-chancellor of Oxon. does on similar occasions – *imprimatur*.'[40]

High praise indeed, from someone who had himself written so originally on the swallow family.

Yet Gilbert seemed unable to keep his professional doubts to himself and even this supposedly conciliatory letter has a sting in the tail. The book's sentences are too long, he complains. Sometimes the same verb is used five or six times in the same paragraph, and, in general, the style is 'rather diffuse'. Gilbert then makes the clearest declaration of his own interest: 'Being jealous of the honor of your work, I cannot admit of these inaccuracies, and have therefore presumed to amend some of them, but with what success I must leave you to judge. I must therefore desire you, who are so perfectly capable, to bestow a fresh and severe inspection on the language.'[41]

But it was too late. John was too ill and depressed even to reply. Little more is heard of the work, and when John died some two years later it succumbed with him, never to be published. All that survives today is a brief introductory section on the Rock of Gibraltar, rather cumbersomely written but too short to give much clue to the quality of the main text.[42] In its own way the *Fauna Calpensis* may well have been a valuable study, and in the hands of a more traditional publisher its fate might have been different. John's misfortune was not so much his writing style as his family background. He was the Whites' one-time black sheep, insecure, volatile and conservative, and his brothers were the most advanced and populist natural history communicators of the day. When they became locked together in the making of a book this was bound to lead to complex collisions of family loyalty and literary ambition. On more than one occasion Gilbert suggested trying another publisher, but never with the insistence with which he pointed out John's shortcomings. The most telling lesson of this sad episode is the commitment Gilbert and Benjamin had to their own literary aims and standards, to the extent that, in the end, they put them higher than their brother's peace of mind. There isn't any hint of a deliberate attempt to suppress John's book; but simmering fraternal rivalry can't be ruled out, and it does raise the question of what the effect might have been on Gilbert's own publishing plans had either Thomas's or John's book gone ahead to publication. Might his own motivation have been weakened or the focus of his book changed? Anthony Rye has gone so far as to suggest that if the *Fauna Calpensis* had appeared there would have been no *Natural History of Selborne*. 'Gilbert would have rejoiced at the *Fauna*'s success; it would have contented him; and since he never seems to have felt himself to be essential to the production of great nature books, and since John the naturalist was in a sense his child, perhaps he would no longer have cared to make the last supreme effort.'[43]

But Gilbert's dealings with various published works suggest that he relished the role of critic, and I think it equally likely that the publication of other family writings would have made him hone his own text that much more finely. Certainly the fact that John had at least *written* his book gave Gilbert an important, nettling, incentive to go on.

*

In what was becoming a long run of severe winters, the early months of 1776 were the most gruelling for years. 'Rugged, Siberian weather,' Gilbert noted on 14 January. 'The narrow lanes are full of snow in some places, which is driven into the most romantic, & grotesque shapes ... I was obliged to be much abroad on this day, & scarce ever saw it's fellow.'[44] Birds were suffering terribly and had begun to come into the house for shelter, only to be caught by the cats. 'The hares also lay sullenly in their seats, and would not move until compelled by hunger; being conscious, poor animals, that the drifts and heaps treacherously betray their footsteps, and prove fatal to numbers of them.'[45] They had been entering the Wakes garden and cropping the pinks. On 20 January, the fourteenth day of virtually continuous frost and snow, he wrote this short, sad epitaph in his journal: 'Lambs fall, and are frozen to the ground.'

Three days later Gilbert travelled to London, and found it

transformed into a frosted, silent citadel. The Thames was iced over, and the streets were 'strangely encumbered with snow, which crumbles and treads dusty, and looks like bay-salt. Carriages run without any noise or clatter.' On the last day of January, when snow had been lying on the roofs for twenty-five days, Thomas Hoar recorded a temperature of zero degrees Fahrenheit in Selborne. Gilbert subsequently wrote this record twice in the same paragraph in his journal, as if he could scarcely believe it. In London, the same day, the thermometer registered just six degrees F, despite the sun.

Gilbert was obliged to spend more time than usual in London this winter because of the continuing litigation over Thomas Holt's will. Thomas White had, after a thirty-year wait, come into full possession of his part of the bequest without any argument. But the precise position of the rest of the family was not at all clear from what proved to be a 'blotted' and contested bequest, and after two months of fruitless legal wrangling Gilbert returned to Selborne to pick up the threads of his book. The antiquities were now well under way, and he had taken advantage of his stay in London to commision the keeper of the Domesday Book to transcribe all the entries relating to Selborne, at the rate of four pence a line. Now the illustrations needed to be finalized. Grimm would cost him more, 2½ guineas a week, he reckoned. But he was determined to have him, despite Mulso's worries that 'that Ornament, which You seemed to set your Heart upon' might delay the completion of the book. 'I feel an impatience, & the more for your Sake,' he warned, 'as the Tast of ye Town in reading is capricious, & natural Observations have had a run, & at a high Price.'[45] But his reserve began to soften in the face of Gilbert's obvious excitement, especially when he was invited down to watch the great draughtsman in action. He ribbed Gilbert for behaving like 'an Italian Magnifico, with your Designer at your Elbow', and, declining the invitation, pointed out that he too was 'waiting for an Artist in his way, that may be as profitable, but is not half so agreeable to my Taste, I mean a Surveyor'. He had some lingering doubts about

Grimm's 'Stiffness of Expression' and 'religious Formality' but was, yet again, prepared to give Gilbert the benefit of the doubt: 'Your work, upon the whole, will immortalise your Place of Abode as well as Yourself; it will correct Men's Principles; give Health to those who chuse to visit the Scenes of Mr Grimm's pencil, in their Original.'[47]

Gilbert was taking his preparations for the artists' visit seriously, and among the several building works planned or in progress at the Wakes (which included 'fitting up a garret for any young person I may have with me') there was now a 'new hermitage' halfway up the Hanger, destined to figure in one of the views. Grimm arrived in Selborne on 8 July, and stayed twenty-eight days, '24 of which he worked very hard, and shewed good specimens of his genius, assiduity, and modest behaviour.'

It isn't clear whether Gilbert dictated the scenes which Grimm sketched, or whether he allowed the artist some leeway for his own preferences. Certainly the dozen scenes that Grimm eventually completed include most of Gilbert's favourite spots.[48] There is a panoramic view of the village and Hanger from the Short Lythe with the Zig-zag and Hermitage clearly picked out; another of the south-east end of the Hanger; 'a side view of the *old* hermitage with the Hermit [Harry White] standing at the door', and 'a sweet view of the short Lith and Dorton' from Huckers Lane, the prospect that he was later in life to describe as worthy of 'the first master in landscape'. The remainder are more orthodox vignettes which might have been drawn anywhere. There are two views of the church and Plestor; two of the meadows behind the Wakes; one of Temple Farm; a view of the village from inside the new Hermitage; Hawkley Hanger, still with its cracked ground and tumbled trees (though this 'does not prove very engaging'); and 'a grotesque and romantic' sketch of the waterfall in Silkwood Vale, which perhaps was meant to give an impression of the hollow lanes as well.

Gilbert was greatly tickled by the notion of being a patron of the arts, and, when Grimm had finished at Selborne, he joined forces with him for a while, as travelling companion and critic. They sauntered over to Lord Clanricarde's at Warnford (ten miles south-west of Selborne) to sketch a great antiquarian find, a hall supposedly built by King John; and to Richard Yalden's vicarage at Newton Valence to take 'a view of his house and outlet from the edge of this chalk-pit'. But here the two connoisseurs turned up their noses: 'The employer wanted and intended a view from the alcove; but the draughtsman as well as myself, objected much to the uniformity of that scene.' In August Gilbert wrote to John White with a detailed and enthralled account of Grimm's technique: 'He first of all sketches his scapes with a lead-pencil ... then he gives a charming shading ... and last he throws a light tinge of water-colours over the whole.'[49] It was a more conventional method than the excitable Gilbert realized, and the finished drawings, too, are somewhat mannered and formal. When Mulso saw a proof of the Hermitage scene the following year, he hardly recognized it. 'I declare that had the Picture come thro' any Hands but *a White's*, which might have directed me, I should not have guess'd at the Place. A Print in general does ill with Perspective; but in this, neither the Hill itself, or the neighbouring Country are in Character.'[50]

But judged as historical records, Grimm's vignettes probably provide a fair picture of the topography of eighteenth-century Selborne. The most striking feature of the landscape is the sheer quantity of woodland, much of it in precisely the same sites where it can be seen today. But there have been both losses and gains. The Lythes, now plantations, were then open grass and scrub; the south-eastern end of the Hanger was bushy rather than woody; and what is now pasture, just east of the church, was then a small copse. But there is one tree – the ancient beech whose roots grip like talons round a sandstone cliff in the Huckers Lane scene – whose remains are still recognizable today.

Chapter Eight
A Parish Record

Echoes of Grimm's visit, or of the beguiling notion of
Selborne as a model of the picturesque, returned to Gilbert
in the autumn of 1776. One mild day in mid-October he
notes that 'The hanging beech-woods begin to be beauti-
fully tinged, & to afford most lovely scapes, very engaging
to the eye, and imagination. They afford sweet lights and
shades. Maples are also finely tinged. These scenes are
worthy the pencil of a Reubens.'[1] It is, as *Naturalist's Journal*
entries go, a little arch, and a more typically personal image
of autumn crops up four days later: 'The redbreast's note is
very sweet, & pleasing; did it not carry with it ugly
associations of ideas, & put us in mind of the approach of
winter.'[2]

And perhaps of the advance of years. Gilbert had celebrated his fifty-sixth birthday in July, and Grimm's departure
marked the beginning of a mellower, more domestic phase
in his life. Much of the hectic literary activity of the previous
few years was now completed. John's *Fauna* was faltering.
The revised edition of Pennant's *British Zoology*, to which
he'd given so freely of advice and information, had been
published that summer. At last he was free to concentrate on
his own work, and though Mulso began to mount a barrage
of first disquiet and then dismay about the delay, he was
determined to see it though at his own leisurely pace.

There is no sign of middle-aged resignation or regret
about this change of gear; on the contrary there is a new
warmth in both his writing and his home life. He was
travelling less now (just five weeks away from Selborne in
1777) and finding that Selborne was repaying what, in so
many ways, he had invested in it. The fruit trees which he
had planted more than twenty years ago were now approaching their vintage years. There were new curiosities, too –
'ferrugineous foxgloves' and 'proliferous fiery lilies'. And
Selborne continued to be a gathering place for the Whites,
especially the younger members of the clan. In the autumn
of 1776, another 15-year-old nephew, Benjamin's son Dick,
endeared himself to Gilbert, though he was a very different
creature from the studious youngsters who had so far stayed

at the Wakes. 'It is well he is intended for trade,' Gilbert wrote to a maybe somewhat envious John White, 'since he loves anything better than [a] book: bodily labour he does not spare; for rolling, wheeling, water-drawing, grass-walk-sweeping are his delight. I have taught him to ride; and perhaps a good seat on an horse may be more useful to him than Virgil, or Horace.'[3]

The procession of energetic visitors was stretching the limited accommodation of the Wakes to bursting point, and the planned extension was long overdue. But on 6 June 1777 work began at last on the Great Parlour. It was to be a considerable piece of building, 23 feet long, 18 feet wide and 12 feet 3 inches tall, and Gilbert employed a team of local men under the foremanship of George Kemp. Kemp's wages were 2s a day, his assistant's 1s 6d, and the carpenters (who were using timber from woods near Winchester) received 1s 8d. The raising of the walls continued, with a few halts in deference to Selborne's capricious climate, until the end of July. Then the roof was put on. Gilbert slipped into his new role with gusto, and Mulso, who was recovering from the shock of one of his sons becoming a runaway, wondered wistfully if there might be a hidden 'Purpose' behind this unaccustomed zeal for improvement:

> and to say Truth I did not know but that this expatiating Scheme might depend upon Another, & that You was preparing to exhibit to Us Benedict the married Man. I knew such a Venture was too delicate to be explained even to an old Friend 'till it was quite resolved upon.[4]

Building was very much in the air in the district that summer. Three of Gilbert's near neighbours were planning extensions or wholesale rebuilding. Even the Wakes' house-martins seemed inspired to a burst of belated construction, and began a new nest above the garden door on 21 June. Gilbert was impressed by the domestic industry of the local swallows, too. He noted that at this midsummer season they were feeding their young from three in the morning till nine at night. (This suggests some long days on Gilbert's part,

too. Perhaps his gouty hand was causing him to sleep badly.)
He was still fascinated by the movements of these summer
birds. Between 15 and 21 August he wrote 'No swifts' in
every single day's journal entry. 'The latest swift I ever saw
was only once on the 21st Aug ... so punctual are they in
their migrations or retreat!' He was increasingly convinced
that a few, at least, might stay in the village. On 2
November, a mild, humid day, he saw more than a score of
martins

> playing about & catching their food over my fields, & along
> the side of the hanger. It is remarkable that tho' this species
> of *Hirundines* usually withdraws pretty early in Oct: yet a
> flight has for many years been seen again *for one day* on or
> about the 4th of Novr: ... These circumstances favour the
> notion of a torpid state in birds: and are against the migration
> of swallows in this kingdom.[5]

As usual when writing of house-martins there is not just
affection but familiarity in his voice: he takes it for granted
that these are Selborne's martins, the birds 'that belong to
this place', as he once described the village swifts (though
this did not prevent his having the occasional newly arrived
martin shot, to examine its condition). It's an indication of
the feelings he had for the 'parish birds' that he failed to see
the real explanation for these regular re-appearances. The
martins concerned were almost certainly not Selborne birds
at all, but part of one of the migratory streams of birds that
move slowly south across Britain throughout the autumn.

But the detached scientist and the romantic observer were
moving closer. On 27 December 1777, a 'dark & harsh' day,
Gilbert drew a delicious caricature of a wind-ruffled bird:
'No birds love to fly down the wind, which protrudes them
too fast, and hurries them out of their poise.' He was
intrigued by the idea of trying to capture what he called a
bird's 'air' (a precursor of our modern idea of 'jizz'), and, in a
letter to Barrington dated 7 August 1778, but probably not
sent, he gives thumbnail sketches of the characteristic
movements of almost fifty species or families of birds. The

result is White at his most dextrous, a rush of evocative images, with each bird caught, almost epigrammatically, by a few exact, unexpected strokes:

> Owls move in a buoyant manner, as if lighter than the air ... herons seem incumbered with too much sail for their light bodies ... the green-finch ... exhibits such languishing and faltering gestures as to appear like a wounded and dying bird ... fernowls, or goat-suckers, glance in the dusk over the tops of trees like a meteor; starlings as it were swim along.[6]

What is striking is the way Gilbert often arranges his sentence structure to echo the physical style of a bird's flight. So, 'The white-throat uses odd jerks and gesticulations over the tops of hedges and bushes'; and 'woodpeckers fly *volatu undosu*, opening and closing their wings at every stroke, and so are always rising or falling in curves.'

*

Back indoors, the Great Parlour also became a subject of scientific scrutiny. The plasterers had skimped their work by adding wood-ash to the mortar, and Gilbert worried that 'the *alcaline salts* of the wood will be very long before they will be dry at all, and will be apt to relax, and then turn moist again when foggy damp weather returns'. Luckily there were good drying winds during February, and the room was soon thoroughly aired. As the days grew longer, he could see how well it was aligned, and notes with satisfaction in February that 'The sun at setting just shines into the E: corner.' Its only real drawback was the echo, 'which, when many people are talking, makes confusion to my dull ears'.

The furnishing and fittings must have helped with this. They were lavish even for such a large and important room. The chimney-piece, '23 foot 7 in. of superfishal [*sic*] white and veined Italian marble', cost £5.17.11, and a large looking-glass, £9.19s. The wallpaper was 'flock sattin' in light brown with a coloured border, and was debited in Gilbert's accounts at £9.15. The room was finished with a 'fine stout large Turkey carpet' at 11 guineas.

That summer the newly-expanded Wakes was full of Gilbert's friends and relations. Molly White (now a regular visitor) was there, and thought the new parlour 'one of the pleasantest rooms I ever was in'. So were Anne Barker and Benjamin's two daughters, Jenny and Becky. Space had even been found for the studious Dr Chandler, although he lived only three miles away. He was a chronic wanderer, and years later Gilbert described him, with only the mildest hint of reproof, as 'an unsettled man [who] likes this method of procuring an habitation, because it looks so like *not* settling. Roaming about becomes a habit with Gentry, as well as mendicants; who, when they have once taken up a strolling life, can never be perswaded to stay at their own parishes.'[7]

But down in Ringmer, the following month, the atmosphere was less relaxed. The hostilities with France which had been smouldering throughout much of the eighteenth century had reached one of their periodic crises, and the south coast was buzzing with rumours of a possible invasion. 'I hope you can sleep without dreaming of ye French,' Mulso wrote on Gilbert's return. Neither man seemed to think much of the bellicose spirit in the air and the upset it produced in their communities. A Selborne man had just come into a £300 share in the bounty from a captured French merchant vessel. 'This will be some recompence to the poor fellow,' Gilbert commented to Molly, 'who was kid-napped in an ale-house at Botley by a press-gang, as he was refreshing himself in a journey to this place. The young man was bred a carter, and never had any connection with sea-affairs.'[8] Mulso declared that he would hate to see his hay-crop fed to French or Spanish horses, or to English troopers, for that matter, and quoted the conclusion of Voltaire's *Candide*, 'Il faut cultiver notre Jardin.'

Not that Gilbert needed any encouragement to look to his own plot. In mid-April the following year (1779) he was busy cutting cucumbers and sending a round-up of the village gossip to Molly.[9] He was lucky to have the cucumbers. There had been four months of drought, he told her, and the hot-beds were so cold and dry they were hardly working at all. Her father's present of a rain-measurer had been a kind thought, but a little ironic under the circumstances: 'There *was* a time when rain-measurers were very entertaining; and doubtless there *will* again.' But then one was always clearing up after the weather down here. The maypole had been blown down in a great storm on New Year's day, but was now mended and freshly painted. On an overcast night earlier in the month, burglars had broken into Burbey's shop, just over the street. They had made a mess of the window-frame but had been disturbed before they found the till.

These minor calamities were part of the everyday fabric of village life, and the constant stream of anecdotes that Gilbert was able to send to his relations shows how close he was to the parish grapevine. They are inconsequential stories for the most part, but Selborne's idiosyncratic landscapes and weather permeate them like a tangy local accent. All the local wells go dry in a bad autumn drought, then overflow during the deluges of the following spring. A great storm blows the tiles off Newton church roof, and hurls them through a farmhouse window, thirty yards away. A mad dog terrorizes the neighbourhood, and seventeen people and a horse – bitten or just nervous – are taken off in a waggon to be dipped in the sea. A bottle of brandy turns purple in Gilbert's cellar. A cow rolls down the Short Lythe, unscathed. Uncle Will slips on the Hanger and is knocked senseless by a tree stump.

The war with France and Spain created another kind of unsettled climate, as the rootless and sometimes glamorously alien life of the military clashed with village custom. On the common, a shepherd was attacked and robbed by a sailor. Two besotted local girls ran off with some of the soldiers billeted in Selborne in November 1781, and 'so that they might cut a figure in their new way of life' broke into Robert Berriman's farm and stripped his wife's wardrobe bare. The twenty-eight kilted Highlanders that were later quartered in the parish and gazed on as curiosities were altogether better behaved, and 'were never known to steal even a turnip, or a cabbage, though they lived much on vegetables'.

The humans in Gilbert's writings, their eating and migration habits minutely scrutinized, sometimes seem a little like biological specimens. Yet equally there are creatures who became known so intimately that they were looked on as humans, or at least as honorary parishioners. The most notable of these was Mrs Snooke's venerable tortoise. Timothy had lived in the walled garden as her much-loved companion for nearly forty years, and when she died on 8 March 1780, aged 86, it was unthinkable that he might pass out of the family's care.*

Gilbert was in London when he heard the news of his aunt's death, and travelled down for the funeral and the reading of the will on 12 March. He must have been sad to lose a relative who had been such a good and lively friend, and whose home was probably the favourite of all his retreats. But he was familiar with death and unperturbed by it, and on the journey down to Sussex it was the signs of spring and new life that he noted, crocuses in bloom, rooks building, and chaffinches beginning to sing ('but in a shorter way than in Hants'). In the will Gilbert had been left a small farm at Iping, near Midhurst, on condition that he paid legacies out of the rents to a number of other members of the family. The net income was little more than £50, and the seven-pound American tortoise must have seemed a much more welcome legacy, though it was not the kind of thing to be spelled out in the will. On 17 March, accordingly, Timothy was dug out of his 'hybernaculum' in the flower-border (he 'resented the Insult by hissing'), packed into a box full of earth and trundled back to Selborne in a post-chaise. He was shaken up enough by the journey to be thoroughly awakened by the time he arrived at the Wakes, and Gilbert described to Molly later that month how he 'walked twice the whole length of it [the garden] to take a survey of the new premises; but in the evening he retired Punder the mould, and is lost since in the most profound slumbers; and probably may not come forth for these ten days or fortnight.'[10]

---

*An eventual post-mortem examination of Timothy revealed that 'he' was a female. To avoid confusion I have kept the masculine pronouns in references to the tortoise.

It must have gratified Gilbert that, despite the trauma of enforced transportation, Timothy was still overwhelmed by the urge to hibernate. And as he slept away the succeeding weeks, drawn into his shell beneath the dark earth of the Wakes' flower-bed, he was observed with the same slightly distant but single-minded curiosity as he had been at Ringmer, a model of inscrutable instinct. 'The tortoise keeps under ground all day ... The tortoise puts-out his head in the morning.' He makes a breathing-hole; marches about the garden; shows a fortunate predilection for the garden's most prolific crop, cucumbers. When Gilbert gave an account of Timothy's habits to Barrington in April 1780 he expressed a rare note of doubt about the Creator's wisdom in bestowing 'such a profusion of days, such a seeming waste of longevity, on a reptile that appears to relish it so little as to squander more than two-thirds of its existence in joyless stupor, and be lost to all sensation for months together'.[11]

But as the summer advances and Timothy becomes more active, Gilbert's tone changes. He begins to refer to Timothy by his name, and to show a concern for him as an individual, not just as an unfathomable reptile.

> May 27: Sun. Cloudless ... Large blue iris blows ... Timothy the tortoise possesses a greater share of discernment than I was aware of; & is much too wise to walk into a well, for when he arrives at the haha, he distinguishes the fall of the ground, & retires with caution or marches carefully along the edge: he delights in crawling up the flower-bank, & walking along it's verge.[12]

He was still subjected to the indignities of some of Gilbert's knockabout experiments, but no harm was meant him. His pulse was searched for, he was taken to Burbey's shop to be weighed (much to the amusement of the village children) and was shouted at, to his complete indifference, through a speaking-trumpet. On one occasion he was dunked in a tub of water: 'he sank gradually, and walked on the bottom of the tub. He seemed quite out of his element and was much dismayed,' Gilbert says, with apparent surprise, 'This species seems not at all amphibious.' The revelation proved a life-saver years later, when Timothy 'was flooded in his hybernaculum amidst the laurel-hedge; & might have been drowned, had not his friend Thomas [Hoar] come to his assistance, & taken him away.'[13]

During the spring of 1784 Timothy went missing for more than a week, and his imagined adventures formed the substance of the well-known letter from 'Timothy the Tortoise to Miss Hecky Mulso'.[14] Timothy describes his early life and experiences at length, and how he resolved one May, 'to elope from my place of confinement; for my fancy had represented to me that probably many agreeable tortoises of both sexes might inhabit the heights of Baker's Hill or the extensive plains of the neighbouring meadow'. Miss Hecky Mulso wasn't Mrs Hecky Chapone née Mulso as has sometimes been supposed, but her niece, John Mulso's second daughter, then 21 years old; and it would be stretching a point to see it – as has also been done – as expressing some wistful, romantic yearnings on Gilbert's part. In fact it was written as a reply from Timothy to some verses addressed to him by Hecky, after she and her family had been on a visit to Selborne in July 1784. If Gilbert does identify with Timothy at all, it is where he describes 'what I have never divulged to anyone before – the want of a society of my own kind.' But the letter is best read as a charming and whimsical indication of just how far Gilbert was now prepared to credit the 'sorrowful reptile' with a personality, especially where he mocks his own somewhat insensitive experiments:

> These matters displease me; but there is another that much hurts my pride: I mean that contempt shown for my understanding which these *Lords* of the *Creation* are very apt to discover, thinking that nobody knows anything but themselves.

By the autumn of 1780 a note of real tenderness had entered Gilbert's voice, and he described how Timothy, homesick for the New World perhaps, had taken to the border under the fruit wall, and 'sleeps under a Marvel of Peru'. When he finally went to earth in November, Gilbert put a hen-coop over him to protect him from dogs.

*

Familarity with the parish also meant, for someone of Gilbert's standing, a degree of licence in the use of its natural resources. He tended, for instance, to regard the Hanger as an extension of the Wakes' grounds, and that autumn, as well as observing the solemn antics of Timothy, he became involved in the construction of a brand-new path up through the hanging woods. The Zig-zag wasn't being abandoned; indeed it was 'nicely cleaned-out' at the same time. But it was a steep climb, and beginning to prove something of a trial for the ageing White family. Gilbert, especially, was finding physical exertion increasingly difficult. His gout was now complicated by gravel, and he had complained in September of 'shootings in my back and bowel ... that pulled me down very much'.[15]

So what he christened the Privy Council decided to cut a more gently sloping path up the face of the Hanger, just to the north of the Zig-zag. It was to be known as the Bostal. The money for the project had been put up by Thomas White, and it is quite possible that the original idea came from him too, out of his interest in local history, for 'bostal' was an old West Sussex term for the paths that were cut up through the woods on the South Downs. Gilbert's occasional helper Larby had originally been put to work on the path, but he was proving too slow, and in September Gilbert hired 'a whole band of myrmidons' to finish the job. These were chiefly young men from the village, but it is likely that some of the visitors staying at the Wakes that summer also lent a hand, and the excavation was carried out in high spirits.

Those that didn't work gathered round to watch what the diggers would turn up next. They found moles, living in the middle of the Hanger, large lumps of pyrites – 'round as balls' – in the clay and fossil ammonites in the layers of chalk beneath. There was a good deal of friendly banter about the virtues of the new path. Gilbert reported that 'there is a junto against it called *Zigzaggians*, of which Mrs. Etty is the head; but Mr. E. and Mr. Yalden would be *Bostalians* – if they dared.'[16] The squabbling, such as it was, seemed to be largely over the dreadful muddiness of the newly cut track, and, when Gilbert bedded out the worst patches with ferns transplanted from the Hanger, the feuding was settled. (Although the following summer, the doughty Mrs. Yalden, who had no time for these mollycoddled men and their soft options, made a point of waymarking the path between Newton and the tops of the Bostal and Zig-zag with sticks. Afterwards she 'took a cartful of chalk and a carter, and ordered him to lay lumps of chalk all the way, for direction posts, the whole length of the down, so that Mr. Etty who used to say he would not go over the common by himself in the dark for £50, might now venture for half the money.')[17] In the end everyone agreed that it was a 'fine romantic walk, shady and beautiful', and that it would make the journey to Newton much more pleasant. Molly was particularly delighted by this more decorous way up the hill. There was still no direct coach route to Newton from Selborne, and the previous summer she had walked all the way to a ball in Richard Yalden's barn, most probably up the Zig-zag.[18]

The two paths were distinguished by more than just their slopes. They had strongly contrasting characters, too. While the Zig-zag was a bracing climb through open scrub and grassland, like an alpine track, the Bostal was a secluded tunnel into the heart of the woods. Cutting this considerable swathe – it was more than 400 yards long and probably two or three yards wide – had meant a great upheaval on the Hanger. It's very clear from the state and position of the Bostal today that it could not have been made simply by brashing a path through the undergrowth. The soil on the slopes had to be excavated to a depth of four feet in places to create a level surface. And even the most serpentine route could not have avoided the felling of some beech trees and the grubbing out of their roots.

None of this work was out of the ordinary – there was time

and labour enough, after all – except for the fact that it was all being carried out, without any apparent by-your-leave, on someone else's property. Although the Hanger was one of Selborne's commons, and Gilbert, along with many other villagers, had the right to graze cattle and take firewood, soil and timber (or at least tree *roots*) were the prerogatives of the Lords of the Manor. Gilbert, not even acting curate of Selborne at this time, had only the most tenuous connections with Magdalen College; yet nowhere in his correspondence or the college records is there any suggestion that he bothered to obtain permission to cut the Bostal, or for that matter build any of his other constructions on the hill. In effect, he gathered a gang of men and flattened an acre of the Lord's wood. It says a good deal about the remoteness of Magdalen as an absentee landlord, and the freewheeling community that developed in Selborne partly as a result, that he was able to get away with it.

Nor did the villagers seem the least bit put out, though strictly speaking their common rights had probably been infringed through the destruction of a small source of wood and mast. They no doubt welcomed the work which constructing the track had provided, and the general benefit the finished route gave to the whole parish. But with land rights being increasingly threatened by enclosure and agricultural modernization, it may be a measure of the affection felt locally for Gilbert that his actions were judged by the spirit behind them, not by their technical legality.

That spring (1780) the parish had given an indication of how it felt about its history and traditional identity. Throughout the previous decade, the third baronet Sir Simeon Stuart, who had succeeded his father as Member of Parliament for Hampshire in 1761, and who was Lord of the Manor of the neighbouring parish of Hartley, had been rationalizing his extensive landholdings in the district. He had stopped off rights of way, and grubbed out hedges, not just around his tenancies in Selborne, but along the ancient boundaries between the two parishes. More seriously, he had encroached on the common at Dorton. He was upbraided repeatedly at the annual Manorial Court, but to no avail.[19] He died in 1779, and there is no record as to whether the lost part of Dorton was ever regained by the village. But during the ceremony of beating the bounds held from 3 to 5 May the following year, the villagers made a point of reaffirming the old field and parish boundaries. It was the first perambulation for nine years and the largest turnout since 1703. Fifteen local farmers and tradesmen did the walk, including John Hales, John Burbey, Thomas Carpenter and Robert Berriman, as well as a dozen boys, and on the way they drove in stakes of yew – that classic Selbornian timber – along the lines of the vanished hedges.[20]

There was, throughout the last half of the eighteenth century, a discernible attitude in Selborne that the parish land, and most of what grew or lived on it, was a communal asset. Free of the brooding and often censorious influence of a Big House, and – except within the bounds of Woolmer Forest – from the increasingly vindictive action being taken against trespassers and poachers under the cloak of the Black Acts, and the 1770 Night Poaching Act,[21] Selborne villagers simply helped themselves. It was a sign of a comparatively free community, though the consequences frequently seem shocking to modern sensibilities. Village women dug up stinking hellebores in the Hanger to grow on as herbs (they 'give the leaves powdered to children troubled with worms'); Gilbert transplanted them too, as ornaments for his shrubberies, along with mulleins, foxgloves and spurge laurel; blackbirds were shot by the dozen when they raided the gooseberries; a boy robbed a nightingale's nest from one of Gilbert's own hedges; adders were slaughtered on sight.

Sometimes the quarry was altogether rarer. In the middle of June 1781, a boy climbed to the top of a tall beech tree on the Hanger, and took the one and only egg of a pair of honey-buzzards – more widespread then than now but still a scarce bird. A few days later the female bird was shot. Both trophies found their way into Gilbert's hands for examination. So did one of the flock of black-winged stilts, which, making the mistake of stopping off at Frensham Pond, eight miles away, received the kind of welcome customarily given to any conspicuous rarities. 'The pond-keeper says there were three brace in the flock; but that, after he had satisfied his curiosity, he suffered the sixth to remain unmolested,'[22] Gilbert wrote to Barrington, without any apparent trace of irony. It was only the third recorded visit to Britain by the species. Gilbert was even able to see the funny side of these unfortunate birds, and his account went on to say:

> I ... found the length of the legs to be so extraordinary, that, at first sight, one might have supposed the shanks had been fastened on to impose on the credulity of the beholder: they were legs *in caricatura*; and had we seen such proportions on a Chinese or Japan screen we should have made large allowances for the fancy of the draughtsman.[23]

But the swallow tribe at least were regarded with affection round the village, and their messy nesting colonies were tolerated in cottage, church and farmhouse alike. Perhaps they were still regarded as bringers of good luck to the households they chose as hosts. In 1780 there were forty martins' nests under the eaves of the Priory Farmhouse alone, and in June Gilbert marvelled at the numbers of young raised on this one building. The first brood, gathering to sun themselves on the tiles, covered one whole side of the roof. There were probably some of this colony among the large numbers that were feeding over the Hanger in mid-October. This has always been one of the great Selborne spectacles in late summer and early autumn, as families of martins, often joined by swallows skimming over the adjacent meadows, play in the thermals. Gilbert loved to watch these great acrobatic assemblies from his 'field alcove', a roughly built hideaway that he had put up in the fields between the Wakes and the Hanger. In the autumn of 1780 he resolved to watch them intently (probably with the help of his telescope) to try and settle once and for all the question of whether any went into hibernation. The notes he took during several consecutive days in the middle of October were worked up into an essay for the *Natural History* (though not sent to Barrington). Its conclusions would today be regarded as false, but it remains one of the finest insights into White's method of observation and feelings for house-martins, and is worth quoting from at length:

Having taken notice, in October 1780, that the last flight [of martins] was numerous, amounting perhaps to one hundred and fifty; and that the season was soft and still; I was resolved to pay uncommon attention to these late birds; to find, if possible, where they roosted, and to determine the precise time of their retreat. The mode of life of these latter *hirundines* is very favourable to such a design; for they spend the whole day in the sheltered district, between me and the Hanger, sailing about in a placed, easy manner, and feasting on those insects which love to haunt a spot so secure from ruffling winds. As my principal object was to discover the place of their roosting, I took care to wait on them before they retired to rest, and was much pleased to find that, for several evenings together, just at a quarter past five in the afternoon, they all scudded away in great haste towards the south-east, and darted down among the low shrubs above the cottages at the end of the hill. This spot in many respects seems to be well calculated for their winter residence: for in many parts it is as steep as the roof of any house, and therefore secure from the annoyances of water; and it is moreover clothed with beechen shrubs, which, being stunted and bitten by sheep, make the thickest covert imaginable; and are so entangled as to be impervious to the smallest spaniel... I watched them on to the thirteenth and fourteenth of October, and found their evening retreat was exact and uniform; but after this they made no regular appearance. Now and then a straggler was seen; and on the twenty-second of October, I observed two in the morning over the village, and with them my remarks for the season ended ...

I have only to add that were the bushes, which cover some acres, are not my own property, to be grubbed and carefully examined, probably those late broods, and perhaps the whole aggregate body of the house-martins of this district, might be found there, in different secret dormitories; and that so far from withdrawing into warmer climes, it would appear that they never depart three hundred yards from the village.[24]

The following spring, just about the time when the martins might be presumed to be coming out of hibernation, he put at least some of his proprietorial scruples aside, and hired a gang of young men to search the beech shrubs and root-cavities where the martins had apparently vanished six months before. But there was nothing – except that, a few days later (the search went on until at least 11 April), a lone house martin 'came down the street & flew into a nest under Benham's eaves'. This was an early date for the species, and Gilbert wondered if the bird might have been disturbed by the search-party on the Hanger.

The domestic affairs of the parish swifts were investigated with the same curiosity and determination. In the middle of August 1781 Gilbert noticed that there was still one swift, and perhaps a pair, flying regularly in and out of the church eaves. He debated whether 'a backward brood, delayed by some accident' had prevented them leaving with the rest. And on 24 August he was able to glimpse that they were indeed attending on two nearly fledged nestlings 'which show their white chins at the mouth of the crevice'. Gilbert was astonished. In forty years of close observation he had never encountered swifts with young this late in the year. It simply did not fit with their habit of punctuality that had so impressed him in 1777. He kept watch on the young for the next few days, and remarked how they began to look 'very brisk'. On 28 August, though, they had vanished, and on the last day of the month Gilbert and a helper climbed up to the eaves to see if they could unravel what had happened. It was soon explained. They found no live or hibernating birds, but 'in a nest two callow dead swifts, on which had been formed a second nest'.[25]

*

This story was quickly worked up into a short essay for the *Natural History*. It was included as a letter to Barrington, dated 9 September 1781, but was almost certainly never sent. Indeed the *Naturalist's Journal*, whose main entries had for some time been straying way beyond their allotted columns, was now acting as a work-book as well as a diary, a place where Gilbert could, in both senses, collect his thoughts. Occasionally he reports on matters of interest beyond Selborne, on, for instance, what sounds like a national epidemic of Russian 'flu in June 1782, and later that month on the large scallop shells his brother Thomas had nailed up under his eaves in South Lambeth to attract house-martins. (These prototype nest-boxes 'had not been fixed half an hour, before several pairs settled upon them; &, expressing great complacency, began to build immediately.'[26]) But chiefly the journal records, with an extraordinary clarity and concentration, the daily pulse of natural life in the parish. Many of these entries are like secular collects or miniature parables. A house-martin drowns in a water-tub. A lesser whitethroat – a 'pettichaps' – 'runs up the stem of the *crown-imperials*, & putting its head into the bells of those flowers, sips the liquor'. And at night, 'when the servants have been gone to bed some time, & the kitchen left dark' the hearth begins to swarm with young crickets, the size of ants. In just a few phrases, stripped of adjectival excess or elaboration, and often working by the simple contrast of two apparently incongruous images, he can catch the essence of a moment, or of a whole season. These are a few of the entries through which he mapped the progress of a heat wave in June 1782:

> June 14: *Ephemera*, mayflies, appear, playing over the streams: their motions are very peculiar, up & down for many yards, almost in a perpendicular line. June 15. Hung out my pendent meat safe ... A pair of partridges haunt Baker's hill, & dust themselves along the verge of the brick-walk. June 16. This hot weather makes the tortoise so alert that he traverses all the garden by six o'clock in the morning. When the sun grows very powerful he retires under a garden-mat, or the shelter of some cabbage ... June 20. The smoke from the lime kilns hangs along the forest in level tracks for miles.

It is the sense of selection in these entries that is so striking and which makes the *Naturalist's Journal* much more than a merely passive or casual record. They have a form and a rightness that makes them appear like answers to half-formed questions, or details coloured in an already partially outlined picture. Something is plainly on Gilbert's mind before he makes them. Earlier in the summer of 1782 he had been told of a strange congregation of swallows on a willow overhanging one of James Knight's ponds. It is almost certain that he never witnessed this himself, but he questioned his neighbour closely, and afterwards wrote a wonderfully evocative picture of the scene:

> His attention was first drawn by the twittering of these birds, which sate motionless in a row on the bough, with their heads all one way, & by their weight pressing down the twig so that it nearly touched the water.[27]

It is as simply and touchingly done as a Japanese print, and it isn't hard to understand the dense rush of associations that this scene must have aroused in Gilbert. Later he interprets it as suggestive evidence that swallows might hibernate near water. But the way he has composed his affecting description gives away much more tender feelings towards these favourite birds, huddled together for company and perched precariously over the water as they were. Gilbert openly admitted and described emotions of this kind in only about half a dozen entries over forty years. Yet in the later journals they are never far from the surface, and are arguably the stronger for being implicit. Gilbert may not always have been aware of just how much of his feelings he was revealing by his choice of details and of the language in which to capture them; but today they are all but impossible to read without an awareness of their symbolism and association and meaning.

The best journal entries are the sharpest and most evocative of all White's writing, and miniature prose-poems in their own right. Verse, as we have seen, he used either as a way of more honestly confronting and confessing his emotions, albeit in formal and sometimes devious ways, or as an intellectual diversion, a kind of literary circuit-training. In 1774 he had advised his nephew Sam that 'A little turn for

English poetry is no doubt a pretty accomplishment for a young Gent: and will not only enable him the better to read and relish our best poets; but will, like dancing to the body, have an happy influence even upon his prose compositions.'[28] For real writing, for honest accounts of the hard physical world around him in Selborne, he needed the spare immediacy of journal prose. In this he had the tacit support of both Jo Warton and the polymathic Dr John Aikin (a friend of Pennant's and a future editor of the *Natural History*). They had attacked both the stale images and the derivative phraseology of contemporary descriptive writing, as well as the poets who wrote naturalistic poetry 'without ever looking into the face of nature'. Ironically, as John Arthos has pointed out, it was above all else the influence of natural history and science that nurtured the 'stock diction' so characteristic of eighteenth-century writers:

> They knew something of the working of the universe, the harmonious balance of its elements ... the principles of vegetation, and their increasing knowledge pleased them for the proof it gave of a well ordered world. The sure constancy of things was the charm of nature; it was part of the pleasure of poetry to re-create that charm.[29]

In the journals of his mature years Gilbert White was one of the first writers to show that it was possible to write of the natural world with a fresh and intensely personal vision without in any way sacrificing precision. And, as his responses to a number of dramatic events in the parish were soon to demonstrate, he had begun to form a bridge between two different views of nature: the old superstitious view which none the less included humans as part of the natural scheme of things; and the more rational but also more alienated view of contemporary science.

*

At this time Gilbert was living rather comfortably at Selborne. After the death of his brother in November 1780, he had invited John's widow, Barbara, to come and live at the Wakes, and she was helping to keep house there. He was rarely short of company as he had sometimes been in his forties, and the house was often full of his friends and his growing clutch of nephews and nieces. In the summer of 1782 his guests included the Reverend Ralph Churton (a Fellow of Brasenose College, whom he had met through Dr Chandler), his brother Thomas White and his three children, his sister Anne Barker from Rutland and her two young daughters, and occasionally Gibraltar Jack who had settled at Salisbury as a surgeon, and who was now, in keeping with his age and position, always referred to as John. Gilbert especially enjoyed listening to Mary and Elizabeth Barker play the harpsichord.

But this was a pleasure for which he now had to pay a price. He had begun to suffer from a common annoyance of older people, known to psychologists as 'obsessional rumination' and after listening to his relations' recitals he found himself

> haunted with passages therefrom night and day, and especially at first waking, which by their importunity give me more pain than pleasure: airs and jigs rush upon my imagination, and recur irresistibly to my memory at seasons, and even when I am desirous of thinking of other matters.[30]

Though it was unconnected with the music in his head, he was also suffering from bouts of deafness and increasingly frequent attacks of gout. He had begun to show slight evidence of absent-mindedness, repeating himself in his correspondence, and on one occasion he signed off a note to Mulso with the words 'Your most humble servant G.W.'. These inconveniences were perhaps no more than a man of 62 should expect, but added to Gilbert's natural procrastination they must have slowed up his work on the *Natural History*, which at this stage included the writing up of a good deal of new material based on journal entries.

But Mulso, who in any case prided himself on his vastly more prostrating illnesses, would hear none of this. He was still convinced that it was the 'Rubbish of the Antiquities of your Native Place' that was holding matters up. Since he first heard about this extension of the book, he had become, first, anxious, and then quite furiously exasperated about it. 'A Farrago of Antiquities,' he railed, 'routed out of the Rusts and Crusts & Fusts of Time!' Later, 'Another Winter is pass'd without your *Essays*. I have no more to say than that You are a timorous, provoking Man: You defraud Yourself of a great Credit in the World . . . Your Porch will be bigger than your House; and You will clap a Gothic Front upon a Plan of Palladio, I mean this, if You *labour too much* at it.'[31]

I suspect that Mulso, with his intuitive understanding of Gilbert's ways, was warning him more generally of the dangers of losing touch with the vitality of his subject. Three years before he had advised Gilbert to make the book 'very clear, but very *short*. The Novelty, & Elegance, the Tenderness, & ye *Piety* of the Natural Part will be the Fort of ye Performance.'[32] And it was not only the tenacity with which Gilbert held on to his meagre curacy at Farringdon that Mulso had in mind when he wrote in June 1782: 'perhaps You are like an old Prisoner of ye Bastille, & would fear to catch Cold in your Leg if it had not a Chain on.'[33] Perhaps Gilbert had also sensed that he had to re-engage with his subject with the urgency that he had achieved when writing of the martins and swallows, ten years before. The stimulus he needed was not long in coming.

June 1783 had begun in a familiar style with spells of rain and cool winds. Then on the 23rd, Gilbert noted in the *Journal*, there was a vast fall of honeydew, and a 'Hot and hazy' mist. Over the following days (until 20 July, in fact) the air grew progressively more sultry and oppressive, and a blue fog hung about, persistently, day and night. 'Sun looks all day like the moon, & sheds a rusty red light' Gilbert wrote on the 26th. Soon there was an ominously premature leaf-fall from the trees, and as Gilbert's brother Henry recorded in his Fyfield diary, 'ye superstitious in town and country have abounded with ye most direful presages and prognostication.'[34] Gilbert eventually wrote up this phenomenon – 'a most extraordinary appearance unlike anything known within the memory of man' – as one of the set pieces that close the *Natural History*. His description, with its sense of insidious, creeping disaster, can still send shivers down the spine:

> The sun, at noon, looked as blank as a clouded moon, and shed a rust-coloured light on the ground, and floors of rooms; but was particularly lurid and blood-coloured at rising and setting. All the time the heat was so intense that butcher's meat could hardly be eaten on the day after it was killed; and the flies swarmed so in the lanes and hedges that they rendered the horses half frantic, and riding irksome. The country people began to look with a superstitious awe at the red, louring aspect of the sun; and indeed there was reason for the most enlightened person to be apprehensive; for, all the while, Calabria and part of the isle of Sicily were torn and convulsed with earthquakes; and about that juncture a volcano sprung out of the sea on the coast of Norway.[35]

It's now known that all these phenomena were due to the eruption of the volcano Skaptár-jökull in Iceland, noticed right across Europe. The sultriness broke up in a succession of violent thunderstorms over southern Britain. Mulso thought them the worst he had ever seen and had 'five fire-balls fall within sight'.

The 1783 summer – if such it can be called – was followed by a winter just as testing and protracted. The first snow fell on Christmas Day, and there was barely a day clear of snow until early April, 1784. When Gilbert was riding back from a visit to his brother in South Lambeth on 2 April, he had trouble getting through the drifts, and when he first glimpsed the village from the Alton path 'poor old Selborne afforded a very Siberian View ... I hardly knew my native spot.' A few days before, on the twenty-eighth day of continuous frost, he had confessed to Molly: 'I long for the weather described on the other side of the paper.'[36] On the reverse of the letter was a copy of a poem entitled 'On the Dark, Still, Dry Warm Weather occasionally happening in the Winter Months' that Gilbert had penned in one of

Selborne's brief respites from its pounding by the elements. The title (condensed and evocative enough to remind one of a journal entry) is the best thing about this poem, which for once reveals no more about his feelings than that he was distressed enough by the weather to write *something* in verse.[37]

The whole parish was still suffering from the combined effects of the summer tempests and the long freeze. Food was scarce, the price of mutton had risen to five pence a pound, and Gilbert's letters to London are full of pleas for salt-fish. Because the ground was so hard, there was little work to be had on the farms, and the poor-tax almost doubled. Illness was rife. Gilbert had a severe and protracted cold, and in the middle of it had to bury his friend Mr Etty, the vicar of Selborne, who died early in April of a serious infection.

Yet again, the summer migrants arrived in the midst of snow. A nightingale was reported singing at Bramshott, five miles from Selborne, on 2 April, and a farmer told Richard Yalden that he had seen two swallows at Hawkley on the unprecedentedly early date of the 7th of that month. This led to a bizarre exchange between Gilbert and Yalden. Gilbert asked the Newton Valence vicar whether he thought the farmer a likely man to know swallows, to which he replied – or so Gilbert reported – 'O, yes – for he was a married man.' It is as likely that Gilbert's hearing was playing him up as that Yalden saw natural wisdom as a reward for a conventionally moral life; but Gilbert had the last word nevertheless, and answered: 'Though a very unworthy batchelor, I presumed I knew swallows as well as most married men in England.'[38] Bats appeared on a 'sweet afternoon' on the 9th, and a pair of swifts were back in the village on May Day.

But not all the auguries were so promising. At eleven o'clock on the morning of 17 June, Gilbert met Mrs Etty on the Plestor. Rather surprisingly, the vicar's wife had a reputation locally as something of a sensitive, and she told Gilbert that 'by certain feelings she was sure storms were at hand.'[39] A couple of hours later 'a blue mist, smelling strongly of sulphur' began to gather around the Hanger. The storm broke over Hartley at a quarter to two, and soon reached Selborne. It began with large drops of rain, which were rapidly followed by huge hailstones, up to three inches in girth and 'somewhat in the shape of cockles, with a white nucleus in each'. Gilbert was sitting down to lunch at the time, and was alerted by 'the clattering of tiles and jingling of glass'.

The parish was devastated by the storm. Some men who could not get back from the field were injured, and John Burbey was badly cut in the hand while trying to cover up his hot-beds. Vast numbers of windows were broken, orchard crops destroyed, and over an area about two miles square the torrential rains flooded fields and washed the topsoil away. Gilbert was out surveying the damage and gathering evidence and anecdotes from his neighbours as soon as it had passed. Later he wrote in his journal the full story of the gathering and breaking of the storm, and its effects on the parish:

> The hollow lane by Norton was so torn & disordered as not to be passable 'till mended; rocks being removed that weighed 200 weight. The flood at Gracious street ran over the goose-hatch, & mounted above the fourth bar of Grange-yard gate. Those that saw the effect that the great hail had on ponds & pools say, that the dashing of the water made an extraordinary appearance, the froth & spray standing-up in the air three feet above the surface! ... The rushing & roaring of the hail as it approached was truely tremendous.[40]

*

What is remarkable about Gilbert's records of the prodigious weather conditions in 1783–4 is the way he infuses an acute, detailed, objective account with a sense of wonder – of awe, almost – at the natural dramas with which humans were still inextricably involved, a feeling which might have come straight out of the medieval period. He shows the same feeling, though with a different emphasis, when he comes to describe the flight of Blanchard's balloon across the village.

Balloons were a source of great public excitement in the 1780s. De Rozier had made the first manned ascent in October 1783, and when Lunardi made his celebrated flight from Chelsea on 15 September 1784 (accompanied by a cat, a dog and a pigeon) it was in front of an immense assembly, including the Prince of Wales. The enterprising Whites had, by this date, already made some ballooning experiments of their own. Gilbert's nephew Edmund White and a friend had constructed a small hot-air device out of thin paper. The 'bag' was two and a half feet long, and twenty inches across, and 'the buoyant air was supplyed at bottom by a cotton plug of wooll wetted with spirits of wine; & set on fire by a candle.'[41] The air was cool and moist on the open part of the Hanger chosen for the flight, and the device refused to perform properly. But when it was tried out in the stairway in Newton Valence Vicarage it rose up to the ceiling and remained there until the fuel ran out.

But in many areas of the countryside there was still some suspicion about these new-fangled devices. When Lunardi's trip had come to an abrupt halt in North Hertfordshire the local farmworkers refused to come to his assistance, and it took the example of a young woman, who grabbed one of the mooring cords, to bring them round.

Later that autumn Gilbert heard that there was to be another flight from Chelsea, this time by the Frenchman, Jean Blanchard. (In good weather London newspapers arrived in Selborne no more than a day after publication.) On 15 October, the day before the proposed ascent, the weather was fine and the wind steady from the north-east, and Gilbert became 'possessed with a notion' that Blanchard would pass over the village the next day:

> The next day proving also bright and the wind continuing as before, I became more sanguine than ever; and issuing forth, exhorted all those who had any curiosity to look sharp from about one to three o'clock, as they would stand a good chance of being entertained with a very extraordinary sight.[42]

Gilbert was determined to introduce this scientific marvel to his parishioners. He toured the fields like an evangelist, urging the workers to keep a watch towards the north-east, and sent off an urgent note to Farringdon, in case the balloon passed further north than he expected. By two o'clock, a large crowd had gathered on top of the Hanger, and expectations were rising as a long cloud of London smoke blew in from the north-eastern quarter. Gilbert tried hard to contain himself. He made a last patrol of the Pound-field below the Hanger, then went home for dinner, laying 'his hat and surtout ready in a chair, in case of an alarm'. The call came at twenty to three, and Gilbert ran into his orchard, where twenty or thirty of his neighbours had gathered. He watched the balloon's transit in a state of near rapture, and the descriptions he put down in letters, the *Journal* and later an article for a newspaper, come closer to catching the breadth of his complicated personality than anything else he wrote. He saw the balloon appear as a small dot and gradually materialize into a burnished yellow orb, flashing in the afternoon sun; and as this vision of the scientific future passes overhead its passage is mapped and measured by the ancient and familiar geography of the village:

> From the green bank at the S.W. end of my house saw a dark blue speck at a most prodigious height, dropping as it were from the sky, and hanging amidst the regions of the upper air, between the weather-cock of the tower and the top of the may-pole. At first, coming towards us, it did not seem to make any way; but we soon discovered that its velocity was very considerable. For in a few minutes it was over the may-pole; and then over the Fox on my great parlor chimney; and in ten minutes behind my great wallnut tree. The machine looked mostly of a dark blue colour; but some times reflected the rays of the sun, and appeared of a bright yellow. With a telescope I could discern the boat, and the ropes that supported it. To my eye this vast balloon appeared no bigger than a large tea-urn.[43]

If this is reminiscent of anything, it is of Brueghel's painting of Icarus, where the 'winged boy's' fall from the sky is figured against a farming landscape peopled with labourers who have not the slightest interest or concern about what is happening above them. Here the feeling is reversed, and the contrast becomes a celebration, inside a fond and familiar setting, of what can be achieved by human initiative. (As Richard Jefferies was to dream, a hundred years later: 'My sympathies and hopes are with the light of the future, only I should like it to come from nature. The clock should be read by the sunshine, not the sun timed by the clock.'[44]) For Gilbert, the mixed emotions this scene aroused recalled those he had experienced when Joseph Banks set off on his momentous voyage in 1768, and those he felt about departing migrants every autumn:

> I was wonderfully struck at first with the phaenomenon; and, like Milton's 'belated peasant', felt my heart rebound with fear and joy at the same time. After a while I surveyed the machine with more composure, without that awe and concern for two of my fellow-creatures, lost, in appearance, in the boundless depths of the atmosphere! for we supposed *then* that *two* were embarked on this astonishing voyage. At last, seeing with what steady composure they moved, I began to consider them as secure as a group of Storks or Cranes intent on the business of emigration.[45]

*

Gilbert spent the final years of work on the *Natural History* continuing to guide, and be guided by, the villagers of Selborne. The vicar who had replaced Mr Etty, the Reverend C. Taylor, proved to have little desire to reside in Selborne, and from October 1784 Gilbert became curate-in-charge, a position he held until his death. His duties were not very strenuous – twenty to twenty-five baptisms a year, four or five marriages and about twenty deaths.[46] But he had under his pastoral care a battleworn community, physically and economically depleted by the continuing assaults of the weather. Work and food were still in short supply. There had been a number of thefts of corn from local mills and barns, and firewood was being cut at a damaging rate on Selborne common. By the spring of 1786 even hay had become scarce. 'My rick is now almost as slender as the waste of a virgin,' Gilbert joked to Sam Barker, 'and it would have been much for the reputation of the two last brides that I have married, had their wastes been as slender.'[47]

One of the few things that was in the power of the village to attend to was the state of the local roads, many of which had been ravaged by the repeated alternations of frost and flood. Over the autumn of 1784 special attention was paid to the lane that ran south-west from the village up to Newton Valence. On 23 November Gilbert was able to record in his journal that his brother Thomas and family had come into the village by coach along this road and that this was 'the first carriage that ever came this way!' (Local people were paid by the job or day for work on the parish highways, and for repairing bridges, hedges and gates. Women helped by picking stones to fill ruts and holes. The work was paid for out of a rent levied on the copyholders of the parish, usually between two and five shillings a year.[48])

But no sooner had this work been completed than Selborne was hit by another brutal winter. On the night of 7 December 1784 there was a massive blizzard across southern England, the worst since 1776. Snow continued falling with scarcely a break for the next forty-eight hours. At eleven on the night of the 10th, one of Gilbert's thermometers registered one degree below zero Fahrenheit and the mercury in another had vanished into the bulb. All the bread, cheese, meat, potatoes and apples that weren't in underground cellars were frozen solid. In Gracious Street the ice was four inches thick, and over in Fyfield Henry White found that iron stuck fast to his hand when he picked it up.[49] Gangs of men were regularly called to shovel snow out of the hollow lanes (the parish spent seven shillings on beer for them on one day that winter) until a brief thaw in the middle of January.

Yet there were compensations. A deceptively bright day on 1 February brought about a curious appearance, and one of Gilbert's most perfect journal entries: 'On this cold day about noon a bat was flying round Gracious street pond, & dipping down & sipping the water, like swallows, as it flew: all the while the wind was very sharp, & the boys were standing on the ice!'[50]

The church bells, which had been recast amid great festivities in 1781, were rung as usual to commemorate what were known locally as 'Crownation' and 'Powder-plot' days. Cricket matches were held on the common on top of the Hanger, and sound as if they were lively affairs: in just a single match two men were carried off, wounded by the ball, one with a dislocated knee and the other a badly wounded face and leg. Elsewhere on the Hanger one of Gilbert's female helpers (perhaps Goody Hampton) scattered beech mast among the scrub, partly to compensate for the heavy toll that firewood cutting, and heavy timber-felling by Magdalen, were having on the more wooded stretches to the north-west.

Gilbert has sometimes been criticized for not paying more open attention to the villagers in the pages of the *Natural History*. Richard Jefferies, for instance, made this complaint, at the end of an otherwise very affectionate introduction to an 1887 edition:

> He knew the farmers and the squires; he had access everywhere, and he had the quickest of eyes. It must ever be regretted that he did not leave a natural history of the people of his day. We should then have had a picture of England just before the beginning of our present era, and a wonderful difference it would have shown.[51]

It is not really sufficient to answer that the *Natural History* was simply not this kind of book, for there is a good deal about human behaviour and social custom in it, particularly in the closing sections. The problem is that those humans who are included are portrayed less as real people than as other kinds of biological specimen. They are curiosities, like the moose and the tortoise: lepers, a toad-witch, gypsies, an idiot boy who had lived in Selborne during the 1750s and

1760s, and who from early childhood had shown an extra-ordinary obsession with bees:

> He was a very *merops apiaster*, or *bee-bird*; and very injurious to men that kept bees; for he would slide into their bee-gardens, and, sitting down before the stools, would rap with his finger on the hives, and so take the bees as they came out ... As he ran about he used to make a humming noise with his lips, resembling the buzzing of bees. ... [52]

The full account is extraordinarily exact and detailed, like a clinical case history, but there is little sign of sympathy or understanding. The boy is not even given a name, which at least the tortoise was. Gilbert's chief regret seems to be that had the boy had more intelligence ('but directed to the same object') he might have been able to contribute to a greater scientific understanding of the life of bees!

Nor is the precise account of the making of rushlights – that 'simple piece of domestic economy' – which forms Letter XXVI to Daines Barrington, entirely free of similar moralizing. 'The careful wife of an industrious Hampshire labourer', who used this cheap and long-lasting source of light, was commendably thrifty; but it's extremely doubtful if Gilbert had used this poor man's candle since his penny-pinching days at Oxford, and it seems unfair of him to rebuke the very poor for preferring tallow candles, as he did himself.

In Gilbert's defence it must be said that he was a strong believer in cottage independence and self-help, and had no time for measures that kept labourers in a state of subservience. There is a letter from Molly (now nicknamed 'the young Antiquary' by Gilbert for the help she was giving him on the book) which contains an abstract from an Act of Parliament relating to rushlights. It specified the conditions under which small rushlights for home use could be exempt from tax: 'and so as such as be only *once* dipped in, or *once* drawn through grease or kitchen-stuff, & not at all through any tallow melted or refined, shall not be chargeable ... *once through the grease*!!!' Molly comments acidly, 'Pray, Observe the tender mercies of the Excise toward the Poor!'[53]

Yet none of this implies that Gilbert was aloof or remote from the community. I am sure that one reason why he did not feel it necessary to spend more time explicitly discussing ordinary village life was that the villagers were already part of the fibre of the book, as collaborators and, in a sense, co-authors. Gilbert, as we have seen repeatedly, relied on his neighbours for evidence, information and anecdotes. Occasionally he would go out and quite specifically interview them, perhaps about the nests in which cuckoos had been found, or the effects of a storm; but mostly the information must have been gleaned in the course of ordinary conversation. In one of the very few personal recollections of Gilbert that are trustworthy, his brother Benjamin's granddaughter, Georgiana, quotes Gilbert's neighbour John Neal, who remembered his animated conversations with villagers, 'standing in the middle of the road, flourishing his stick', and talking with 'his peculiar way of shrugging his shoulders'.[54]

It was in his study of birds and their movements that he found the greatest benefit from having such a wide and sympathetic network of collaborators. The villagers became adept at spotting and reporting early migrants, bringing to Gilbert any curious specimens they had shot or found. The journals are full of more specific instances of help. Thomas Benham, the smallholder who lived down the street from the Wakes, helped in the search for hibernating house-martins. Tim Turner, Gilbert's next-door neighbour, also assisted in the house-martin study. He showed Gilbert two nests built like long tunnels to fit into the shape of his eaves, confirming the statement Gilbert had made that the birds' nests were not always hemispheric. Dan Wheeler's son reported finding a young cuckoo in a hedge-sparrow's nest, and underneath it, one of the hedge-sparrow's eggs that had been thrown out. Richard Butler, a thatcher, took Gilbert to see a flycatcher's nest built behind the head of an old rake lying on a shelf. John Burbey watched a hawfinch breaking open plumstones with its massive beak and consuming the kernels.

Not all these birds got away with their lives. Many – silent witnesses by then – were taken to the Wakes along with the reports on their behaviour. Indeed it is likely that Gilbert's well-known inquisitiveness actually provoked the 'procurement' of some of the rarer species. Some of the villagers acquired the habit of examining the crops of dead birds, and this may at least have put paid to a few damaging myths and superstitions. (John Burbey's hawfinch was subsequently shot on the suspicion – shared by Gilbert – that it was destroying the buds of fruit trees; but all its crop contained were the plum kernels he had watched it eating.) Gilbert's prize for initiative, though, would have gone to this farmer's wife: 'One of my neighbours shot a ring-dove on an evening, just as it was returning from feed, & going to roost. When his wife had picked & drawn it, she found its craw stuffed with the most nice & tender tops of turnips. These she washed & boiled, & so sate down to a choice & delicate plate of greens, culled & provided in this extraordinary manner.'[55]

George Sturt has pointed out how some of the more generalized descriptions of Selborne in the *Natural History*, particularly of the character of the soils, come out of not one individual's impressions, but the long collective experience of the villagers.[56] So does the language in which they are expressed. Gardens in the north-east of the village have 'a warm, forward, crumbling mould, called *black malm*'; over on the sandy soils of Woolmer Forest oaks grow '*shakey*, and so brittle as often to fall to pieces on sawing'. Farming and gardening jargon, vernacular names and dialect words abound throughout Gilbert's writings, sometimes in the same sentences as scientific Latin. But they are almost always words which have an evocative, often onomatopoeic, effect, regardless of whether their meaning is known. Skies can be 'muddled'; clouds 'flisky'; the ground 'chops' in dry weather; 'slidders' were the shallow trenches down which beech trees were dragged when they were felled on the Hanger.

*

In the autumn of 1787 this legacy of communal knowledge,

married to Gilbert's uniquely personal vision, began its journey into posterity. The first instalments of *The Natural History of Selborne* had at last been delivered to the printers. Mulso, who had given up harassing Gilbert about its protracted birth, was overjoyed, and promptly put in an order for a set of first editions. Two major decisions about the final shape of the book had already been taken. First, that 'the epistolary style' would be maintained throughout, and that even the notes and essays not sent to Pennant and Barrington would be presented as imagined letters to them. Second, some of these contrived letters should be shaped into an introduction and a conclusion to the book. The first nine 'letters' build up a picture of the setting of the book, the parish itself, its geology, scenery and history. The last six widen its scope and show the tiny village in the grip of the elements, whose influence had no geographical limits.

To some extent Gilbert's plan may have been influenced by Sir John Cullum's *The History and Antiquities of Hawsted*, which had been published in 1784 and adopted a similar structure. But the way Gilbert arranges his material makes a vastly greater impact than this rather mundane survey of an East Anglian parish. His opening and closing sections give form and scale and even a semblance of narrative structure to what would otherwise have been a shapeless anthology. The *Natural History* has, as a result, an epic feel, a sense of being an exploration of a whole world, not just a single parish. 'No novelist could have opened better,' wrote Virginia Woolf:

> Selborne is set solidly in the foreground. But something is lacking; and so before the scene fills with birds, mice, voles, crickets and the Duke of Richmond's moose ... we have Queen Anne lying on the bank to watch the deer driven past. It was an anecdote, he casually remarks, that he had from an old keeper, Adams, whose great-grandfather, father and self were all keepers in the forest. And thus the single straggling street is allied with history, and shaded by tradition.[57]

The working manuscript that Gilbert was slowly assembling for the printers is still extant, and by comparing its text with that of the surviving original letters to Pennant and Barrington it's possible to get an idea of the extent of his editing and additional writing. It's clear, for instance, that it is not just the opening and closing 'letters' that are literary devices; as many as forty of the sixty-six 'Letters to Daines Barrington', and fifteen of those to Pennant (amounting to almost half the total text) were probably never sent through the post. It is difficult to be more exact than this because of the extent of the editing. A few letters bear dates even though they were never sent. More have had their original dates changed, sometimes, bafflingly, by just a few days, though on one occasion by a whole year. Parts of other letters are deleted, chopped up, amalgamated, redistributed. A long communication to Pennant dated 8 February 1772 is split into three shorter ones dated, respectively, 8 February, 9 March and 12 April 1772. A note on soft-billed birds sent as part of a letter to Barrington on 15 January 1770, is presented in the *Natural History* as Letter XLI to Pennant. The letters written on 8 July 1773 went through an even more complicated transformation. From surviving transcripts it appears as if Gilbert wrote identical drafts to both Pennant and Barrington that day; but in the *Natural History* the first half of this communal text (discussing the whitethroat and other small birds) appears at the end of the otherwise 'false' letter XL to Pennant, dated 2 September 1774. The remainder forms Letter XV to Barrington, under its correct date.

Although some of these changes and reshufflings seem to be almost gratuitous and beyond any obvious explanation, most of them were sensible measures – for example, to remove personal messages and bring together material on related topics. There was also a good deal of new material to be written, much of it based on *Journal* entries. These amendments and additions, along with the copies of the original letters, had to be transcribed, and the final manuscript is in at least four hands: Gilbert's, Gibraltar Jack's, what looks like Sam Barker's script, and other, so far unidentified, autographs. Yet despite all this help, and the years he had spent on the book, these last stages of work still faced Gilbert – as they do most authors – with a hectic rush for the line. Molly White, who had been such a sterling source of help and advice for the past ten years, now began to have an even more active involvement in the book. In 1785, at the age of 26, she had married her cousin, Benjamin White's eldest son (also Ben), who had taken over the management of his father's publishing house in Fleet Street. Molly saw herself as part of the family business, and she soon took on the role of Gilbert's sub-editor. From the middle of 1787 Gilbert was sending his concluding essays (probably beginning with Letter LVI to Barrington) direct to her for checking and marking-up. Gilbert, understandably, fussed and fretted about his offspring – 'Pray let this letter stand *the last*, *before* the letters to Mr Barrington describing the weather of Selborne, in number, I think, *four*' – but he had no real cause to worry.[58] Back from Molly came clean sheets of proofs 'so well corrected, that I have not met with one error!'

The Wakes was a hive of cottage industry during the early months of 1788. While Molly was checking proofs in town, her new son Benjamin was being looked after in the Selborne crèche. 'In return for your care about my brat', Gilbert wrote on 13 March, 'I have pleasure to inform you that your boy is perfectly well, and brisk: and that his nurse is better.'[59] Gilbert himself was compiling his index, 'an occupation full as entertaining as that of darning stockings, though by no means so advantageous to society'. Ralph Churton was staying at the Wakes as well, and was also working on an index, to Dr Townson's *Discourse on the Gospels*, 'so that my old parlor is become quite an *Index manufactory*.'[60] Despite all this activity Gilbert still found time for his journal. He records shearing his mongrel Rover, and using the white hair in plaster for the ceiling; and notes the sad death of John Burbey's brown owl, 'a great washer', which was drowned in a water-butt. And on still nights at the beginning of March he had heard, in a respite from his deafness, the urgent flight-calls of migrating stone curlews returning to breed on the sheep-walks:

> On March 1st after it was dark some were passing over the village, as might be perceived by their quick, short note, which they use in their nocturnal excursions by way of watch-word, that they may not stray, & lose their companions.[61]

There were a few last-minute changes to the proofs ('procurers' in XXIV to Pennant is tactfully changed to 'neighbours'); and some final queries and requests to Benjamin junior. Should the *Antiquities*, also composed as a series of letters, be addressed to somebody? Shouldn't quotations be printed in italics? And would he, please, not be 'offended at the vague spellings of the names of *men*, and *places*, but to take them as you find them in their places, because centuries ago men had no criteria to go by, but spelt just as it happened.'[62] Then, some time during the spring, it was all done, and after nearly twenty years of daily work Gilbert had no more to do than wait for the finished copies. It is no wonder that, on the point of being launched into the public eye at the age of 68, he found himself in an unaccustomed state of jitters. He felt, he wrote to Churton in August, 'like a school boy who has done some mischief, and does not know whether he is to be flogged for it or not'.[63] He passed the time as best he could, sowing winter vegetables and recording the progress of the hop harvest. In November he watched, without any obvious enthusiasm, the King's stag-hounds' unsuccessful search for a stag in Hartley Wood, and seemed more moved by the 'Swarms of sporting gnats come streaming out from the tops of the hedges, just as at Midsumr'.[64] In the end, he decided, as he had often done before, to 'purge off' his anxiety in verse. The result, a little self-mocking piece entitled 'To Myself Commencing Author,' was posted off to friends and relatives in London:

> Go, view that House, amid the garden's bound,
> Where tattered volumes strew the learned ground,

Where Novels, – Sermons in confusion lie,
Law, ethics, physics, school-divinity;
Yet did each author, with a parent's joy,
Survey the growing beauties of his boy,
Upon his new-born babe did fondly look,
And deem Eternity should claim his book.
Taste ever shifts; in half a score of years
A changeful public may alarm thy fears;
Who now reads Cowley? – The sad doom await,
Since such *as these are now* may be thy fate.[65]

Copies of the *Natural History* began to be delivered well in time for Christmas. Mulso was honoured with an advance copy, and though he had read most of the text before, he was generous with his praise, even of the section on antiquities which he had reviled for so long. But the most touching tribute in Mulso's letter of thanks was the inclusion, for the first time in more than thirty years of correspondence, of an astute and nicely crafted natural history vignette. It is so well done one wishes Mulso had tried his hand before:

A Circumstance struck me the other day in *your way*, it seem'd a novelty to me, but it may be usual & constant, for ought I know. We have great Numbers of Jackdaws, which get under our Tilings. Out of my Study window I have the long Roof of the Deanery before me, and it was new to me that during this whole Month of Decr, as far as it is pass'd, the Jackdaws keep in Pairs. I observed on the Ridge Tiles that tho' a Number were there at a time, yet for the most part they left little spaces, & the Pairs were discernable & separated from the rest; they were likewise in different Pairs on the Declivity of the Roof. It wants much of Valentine's day, but the world is in a Hurry *to secure it's rights*.[66]

Henry White had received his copies on 3 December, and his journal for the day reads:

Hamper from London containing stock of Books, etc etc, & Natural History of Selborne, pres. by ye Author; a very elegant 4to with splendid engravings. Red-breast comes into the Parsonage.[67]

Sadly Harry did not live long enough to see how the world at large received his brother's book. On 27 December he filled in his diary for the day, noted 'the wind rather rough and fierce' and the poor yields from his coppice woods, and then quite suddenly died, aged only 55. Gilbert wrote to Sam Barker that the 'unexpected event ... has plunged a numerous family in the deepest sorrow and trouble'; and it cast a shadow over what would otherwise have been a happy time for Gilbert. His book was being complimented everywhere. His old friend Jo Warton was delighted with it. Thomas White gave it a long, appreciative but – coming as it did from a brother – properly restrained review in the *Gentleman's Magazine*. More important was a perceptive unsigned notice in the *Topographer* for the Year 1789:

> a more delightful, or more original work that Mr. White's History of Selborne has seldom been published ... Natural History has evidently been the author's principal study, and, of that, ornithology is evidently the favourite. The book is not a compilation from former publications, but the result of many years' attentive observations to nature itself, which are told not only with the precision of a philosopher, but with that happy selection of circumstances, which mark the *poet*. Throughout therefore not only the understanding is informed, but the imagination is touched.[68]

But the evidence of his own advancing years and the toll of another desperate winter were hard to avoid during the dark days at the start of 1789. The frost had been joined by northeast winds so piercing that labourers were finding it hard to stand up in the fields. The local ponds were either frozen solid or bone-dry from the previous summer's drought, and farmers were having to drive their cattle long distances to the local springs for water. When the thaw came Gilbert looked down into a freshly dug grave and saw that 'the frost ... appeared to have ent'red the ground about 12 inches'.

*

The few short years that Gilbert had left were inevitably clouded by the deaths of friends and relatives. Mulso's wife passed away in December 1790, and the following September Mulso himself succumbed to a long illness. At no other time does one become more acutely aware of the importance and value of Mulso's letters than when, quite abruptly, he is no longer there to record Gilbert's reactions to the death of his oldest friend.

But there is no sense of anticlimax about Gilbert's life after *Selborne*. He kept up his journal without any perceptible decline in energy or imagination, and continued to be an active gardener and genial host at the Wakes. A journal entry for 16 May 1790 shows a benign satisfaction at the fecundity of both charges: 'Mrs Edmund White brought to bed of a boy, who has encreased the number of my nephews & nieces to 56. One polyanth-stalk produced 47 pips or blossoms.'

This great army of nephews and nieces, whose regular increase is proudly logged in the journal, were frequent visitors to the Wakes, and Gilbert's natural history interests plainly rubbed off on at least some of them. In September he wrote to Molly about her second son's (3 years old and number 52 on Gilbert's list) fastidious attention to the hirundines. 'Tom talks much of mum's martin's nest; but complains that the young *poop* on the pavement.'[69]

One of the consequences of publication was the emergence of new correspondents. One of these was George Montagu, the Gloucestershire sportsman-naturalist who went on to compile the first dictionary of birds. Montagu was an energetic and efficient worker, and differentiated many British birds for the first time (including the harrier that bears his name). But his interests did not spread much beyond identification and classification, and his letters to Gilbert are little more than a shopping-list for specimens to add to his collection:

You are surprised at my requesting of you the Goat-sucker [nightjar]: 'tis true many parts of this county produce them, but they are not to be commanded, and one bird in the spring or before August is worth twenty after that time, as most birds are then out of feather, and the young ones are seldom in full, or proper plumage till the winter, and many till the ensuing spring.[70]

Gilbert no longer had the stomach to treat birds as so many bundles of collectable plumage, and though he replied politely to Montagu's first letter in the summer of 1789, the correspondence soon petered out.

Much more to his taste was a letter of congratulation that arrived the following July from Norfolk. It came from Robert Marsham, of Stratton near Norwich, a traveller and lover of trees who proved to have kept a natural history journal for more than forty years. He was 82, twelve years older than Gilbert, yet it was obvious from their very first exchange that the two men had much in common. Marsham's first letter is a lively, inquisitive, serpentine ramble around a vast array of topics, from the mating of frogs to winter-leafing hawthorns, that is reminiscent of Gilbert's early communications with Pennant, and Gilbert replied in kind. They kept up an affectionate and scholarly correspondence that was cut short only by Gilbert's death. Trees, their planting, care, size and uses, were always the chief topic of discussion, but the two men also found common ground in their growing distaste for the needless exploitation and killing of wild creatures, and in a shared fascination with the mysteries of migration. Marsham admitted early on that he was especially perplexed by what happened to young swallows during the winter:

> I have had 4 pair attending my house as many years as i can remember. If these produce two broods of 5 young, you see, Sir, one pair only, will in 7 years produce above half a million, 559870 birds: yet the number every Spring appears the same.[71]

Gilbert had a perfectly reasonable solution to this puzzle, but was curiously diffident with it, as if he found it hard to accept that his beloved summer migrants were subject to exactly the same perils as resident birds (like, say, the tits), whose stable populations he never questioned:

> With regard to the annual encrease of swallows, & that those that return bear no manner of proportion to those that depart; it is a subject so strange, that it will be best for me to say little. I suppose that nature, ever provident, intends the vast encrease as a balance to some great devastations to which they may be liable either in their emigrations or winter retreats.[72]

The mass death of such attractive and loyal birds was sad to contemplate. Even the loss of one was a cause for sorrow. When Marsham, discussing the possibility of torpidity in his reply, mentions that he had found a dead swallow under his window on 10 November the previous year, Gilbert admonishes him almost by return of post: 'It does not appear from yr letter that you endeavoured to revive the Swallow which fell down before yr parlor-window.'[73] (Marsham was innocent: 'the Swallow was dead, & a wing torn off.')

Gilbert's fondness for the swallow family was obvious in everything he wrote about them, and as he continued to debate their winter movements with Marsham, it begins to look as if there might be a very simple reason for his stubborn refusal – against an increasing volume of evidence – to come down off the fence on this issue: in an unscientific corner of his heart he did not *want* them to go. The possibility that a few of the birds whose presence so enlivened the parish during the summer might be sleeping away the cold months on the Hanger must, I am sure, have made the bleak Selborne winters a little more tolerable.

> Sep 7. [1791] Cut 125 cucumbers. Young martins, several hundreds, congregate on the church, & yew-tree. Hence I conclude that most of the second broods are flown. Such an assemblage is very beautiful, & amusing, did it not bring with it an association of ideas tending to make us reflect that

winter is approaching; & that these little birds are consulting how they may avoid it.[74]

A journal note on the state of the martin flocks a week later (subsequently worked into a letter to Marsham) shows an even more intense mixture of exultation and poignancy:

> during this lovely weather the congregating flocks of house martins on the Church & tower were very beautiful & amusing! When they flew off all together from the roof, on any alarm, they quite swarmed in the air. But they soon settled again in heaps on the shingles; where preening their feathers to admit the rays of the sun, they seemed highly to enjoy the warm situation. Thus did they spend the heat of the day, preparing for their Migration, & as it were consulting when & where they are to go![75]

Marsham shared his sentiments. 'I love the Swallows and H. Martins so well,' he replied, 'that i lament the want of their company in Autumn as heartily & as much as i do the warm weather.'[76] Although the two men were never to meet they were becoming firm friends. Gilbert confided that he was beginning to 'look upon You as a Selborne man'; Marsham returned the compliment by naming a favourite beech 'Mr White's Beech'. It was 'about 50 years old, & runs clear about 25 feet, then, about as much in handsome head'. 'O, that I had known you forty years ago' remarked Gilbert in that winter of 1791. It is tempting to speculate how Gilbert's writing activities might have been affected if he had met Marsham at the same time as Pennant and Barrington. The correspondence would certainly have been more intimate and affectionate, but perhaps a little too much so to make for compelling reading. My own suspicion is that the various kinds of frustration Gilbert felt with Pennant and Barrington were important incentives in sharpening his style.

*

It was a sign of just how little Gilbert's energy and enthusiasm had declined that he was actively preparing another monograph for the Royal Society, this time on the nightjar, or fern-owl. He had always been fascinated by this mysterious bird, even before the occasion when one shook the Hermitage with its churring song (page 117). He called it a 'nocturnal swallow', and thought it every bit as evocative of hot summer nights as swifts and swallows were of summer days. In 1789 he began looking at it more closely, in the hope that he might be able to defend it against the superstitious charges that it sucked the teats of goats, and infected calves with the parasitic disease known as 'puckeridge'. He complained to Marsham:

> The least attention & observation would convince men that these poor birds neither injure the goat-herd nor the grazier; but that they are perfectly harmless, & subsist alone on night-moths & beetles; . . . nor does it any wise appear, how they can, weak & unarmed as they are, inflict any malady on kine, unless they possess the powers of animal magnetism, & can affect them by fluttering over them.[77]

To try to build up a fairer picture of the nightjar's life, he began offering sixpence to his 'intelligent young neighbours' for every story they could bring him about the bird.

But more ominous stories were in the air. On 14 July 1789, the day that a woman who lived at the foot of the Hanger brought Gilbert two nightjar's eggs and a clutch of first-hand anecdotes about the bird's breeding habits, the Parisian workers stormed the Bastille. News of the French Revolution took some while to reach Selborne, but from the autumn of that year Gilbert's letters begin to contain anxious and bewildered notes about 'these strange commotions'. Gilbert did his best to understand what was happening, and read Arthur Young's *Travels through France*.[78] He couldn't feel comfortable with Young's reformist politics, but he was impressed by his sharp eye, and by his strictures on the French clergy's weakness for hunting and carousing. Knowing that Young lived in East Anglia, he enquired of Marsham whether they were acquainted. Marsham replied with a rare outburst of blimpishness. He decried the corrupting influence of the Revolution on English workers (thirteen of his own ungrateful villagers had joined a 'Jacobin' club!), passed on a string of libellous gossip about Young, and concluded that the man was 'an abominable coxcomb'. Gilbert, in his replies, seemed anxious to make it clear that, despite his respect for Young's warnings, he was very far from being a radical:

> You cannot abhor the dangerous doctrines of levellers & republicans more than I do! I was born & bred a Gentleman, & hope I shall be allowed to die such. The reason you having so many bad neighbours is your nearness to a great factious manufacturing town. Our common people are more simple-minded & know nothing of Jacobin clubs.[79]

It would be wrong to read too much into this statement. Gilbert, by his own admission, had no first-hand experience of English sympathy for the French cause, and was probably exaggerating his feelings in order to avoid a disagreement with a valued acquaintance. If he was no radical, he was also no uncritical defender of property interests. In Selborne politics he remained a resolute supporter of the rights of the 'common people'. He had personally helped to bring about an informal agreement between Selborne's commoners to make the cutting of firewood on the Hanger less intense and more equitable.[80] In 1789 he made a public stand on behalf of a local right of way, and wrote in the Parish Register an affirmation that one of the ancient trackways to the north of the village 'had been from time immemorial an undisputed bridle road', until Sir Simeon Stuart and his tenant had stopped it up some twenty years previously, 'and so deprived the neighbourhood of the advantage of that way'.[81] And even in the last year of his life he was prepared, if the need should arise, to help scupper a far more serious threat to local common rights. News of the danger came from his nephew James (one of Benjamin's sons). Early in 1793 James had met an attorney known to Gilbert, a Mr Fisher, 'a Man of a meddling disposition'. Fisher was a canny, speculative racketeer, and had been working through central southern England, drawing up enclosure schemes for different manors, and endeavouring to sell them to the landowners. He had his eye on Selborne, but had apparently been put off by Gilbert's assertion that the woods and commons in Selborne belonged to the tenants, not the Lord of the Manor, and that this had been confirmed by the 1719 Decree in Chancery. But James thought there was a chance that Fisher might come to Selborne to check the wording of the Decree; and recommended that if Gilbert thought there was any ambiguity in it (and there certainly was: see page 29) he might keep it judiciously hidden:

> I trust you will excuse my giving you a hint. If you will take the trouble to look into the Decree, and if it is what Mr. Fisher from conversation with you, supposes it to be, there can be no objection to shew it him when he asks to see it, but if there should be any thing in it which is different from his present ideas, or would induce him to revive this business, I think that you would wish to evade shewing him any thing which may, in the event, occasion much trouble and expence both to yourself and all the other copyholders of Selborne.[82]

Fisher never came, but the threat he briefly posed was a portent of changes that were soon to affect the independence and diversity of rural communities throughout southern England.

*

Gilbert's last few years passed comparatively peacefully. He was troubled by coughs in the winter, and by occasional attacks of gravel and gout, but not so much as to interfere with what was still an active outdoor life, and what seemed to be an increasingly rapturous view of the natural world. On 20 March 1792, he was in the middle of a letter to Marsham, describing how the first passage migrant, the chiffchaff, usually arrived on 20th March, 'when behold! as I was writing this very page, my servant looked in at the parlour door, and said that a neighbour had heard the *Chif-chaf* this morning!! These are incidents that must make the most indifferent look on the works of the Creation with wonder!'[83] That summer the village seemed especially blessed with birds. Two pairs of flycatchers nested at the Wakes, one in the Virginia creeper over the garden door and the other in the vine over the parlour window. There were eleven house-martins' nests under John Burbey's eaves, and three singing nightjars close to the track from Selborne through the High Wood, which Gilbert took when he was visiting his nephew Edmund at Newton vicarage. On the evening of 27 August 1792, one of these birds came down to the Wakes garden, and put on a spectacular show by 'hawking round, & round the circumference of my great spreading oak for twenty times following, keeping mostly close to the grass; but occasionally glancing up amidst the boughs of the tree', showing 'a command of wing superior, I think, to the swallow itself'.[84]

The winter of 1792–3 was mild by Selborne standards, and the house was full of visitors. Ralph Churton and Benjamin junior and Molly White came for Christmas, and various other nieces and nephews (now sixty-two in number) throughout January. Snowdrops bloomed before the end of the month. In March Gilbert went for what was to prove his last trip away from Selborne, to visit his brother Benjamin's new house at Mareland, between Alton and Farnham. The two brothers walked up to Bentley church, a long, steep climb, and from the top were able to see the crest of the South Downs. Gilbert watched Ben's lambs gambolling, listened to the Farnham bells ringing 'up the vale of a still evening', and filled his journal with nostalgic quotations. Back in Selborne in April, Gilbert and Chandler made one last unsuccessful search for hibernating swallows in the ragged thatch of a deserted cottage. But the mild winter had been followed by a harsh, backward spring. There were repeated snow-storms throughout April, and Gilbert's illnesses had begun to return, all together. On 2 May he wrote an almost desperately poignant note in his journal: 'Sad, blowing, wintry weather. I think I saw a house martin.'

On 28 May he noted that the hirundines had still not begun to build. But he was able to find some pleasure in the great showers of apple-blossom: 'My weeding-woman swept-up on the grass-plot a bushel-basket of blossoms from the white apple-tree: & yet that tree seems still covered with bloom.'[85] On 10 June he cut five cucumbers and read the funeral service over 'Mary Burbey, aged 16'. The next day 'A man brought me a large plate of strawberries, which were crude, & not near ripe. The ground all as hard as iron: we can sow nothing nor plant out.'

On the 15th he made his last short journal entry and wrote what was to be his last letter, to Marsham. It was a lively, inquisitive communication which pondered yet again the question of hirundine migration, and Gilbert's intellect seemed not to have been dulled one bit by the illness ominously outlined in the letter: 'I have been annoyed this spring with a bad nervous cough, & a wandering gout, that have pulled me down very much, & rendered me very languid & indolent ... The season with us is unhealthy.'[86] But his condition deteriorated suddenly. On 17 June Dr Webb of Alton was sent for, and from this date visited his patient every day. Gilbert was apparently in some pain, for Webb administered a number of 'anodyne draughts', presumably of laudanum.[87] Meanwhile Gilbert's bed had been moved into the old parlour at the back of the house, where he could look out over the garden to the Hanger, now in full, belated leaf. And it was here, perhaps watching the swallows skimming over the Park Meadows, that he died on 26 June 1793.

Epilogue

Gilbert disapproved of the 'improper custom of burying within the body of the church' and in his will specified in wonderful, alliterative prose that he should be interred 'in the church yard belonging to the parish Church of Selborne aforesaid in as plain and private a way as possible without any pall bearers or parade and that six honest day labouring men respect being had to such as have bred up large families may bear me to my grave.'[1] The covers had already begun to be drawn over his life.

Most of his close relatives soon joined him. Benjamin died the following year, Thomas in 1797. Gibraltar Jack, after losing his first wife, married Henry White's daughter Elizabeth, but died without children in 1821. Molly survived the longest, not dying until 1833 at the age of 74.

As for the *Natural History*, it did not at first fulfil its early promise. A curious, bowdlerized German edition appeared in 1792, and a selection of entries from Gilbert's journals was published as *A Naturalist's Calendar* by Dr John Aikin in 1795. But a full English second edition (also edited by Aikin) did not appear until 1802. The third (edited by Mitford) had to wait until 1813. In fact it was not until the 1830s, after the publication of the celebrated article on Selborne in the *New Monthly Magazine* (see page 7) that the book became first fashionable, then an established classic, with new editions coming out virtually every year.[2]

Its rise in popularity occurred as part of the growing public taste for escapist, and nostalgic 'country writing'. This in turn coincided with a period of great unrest and distress in the countryside, typified by the uprisings and machine-breaking of 'Captain Swing' in 1830. Swing reached Selborne itself in the middle of November that year, the first serious social disturbance the village had seen for four centuries.[3] A large gathering of farmworkers sacked the workhouse and besieged the vicarage, demanding a reduction of tithes from their unpopular, cantankerous vicar, Mr

Cobbold. Many of the rioters were subsequently arrested and transported. A few were hanged. The man who sounded the trumpet for them, John Newland, escaped and hid for some months on the Hanger. When he eventually gave himself up he was pardoned, but died in poverty years later, and was buried under the yew tree in front of the church.

In 1847 a new road was built from the village to Alton, and the hollow lanes gradually fell out of use. Selborne had now joined, in every way, the fast-moving world of nineteenth-century England. The narrow window of time and place through which Gilbert White had been able to see his unique vision of the natural world – supported by an independent community, in an atmosphere that was inquisitive about nature without as yet being touched by a sense of loss – was finally closed.

NOTES AND REFERENCES

Major sources and abbreviations used in references to them:

AS – Gilbert White, *The Antiquities of Selborne*, ed. W. Sidney Scott, 1950. (The most helpfully annotated edition.)

DB – Manuscript letters from Gilbert White to Daines Barrington, British Library Add. MS 31852.

GK – Gilbert White, *The Garden Kalendar*, British Library Add. MS 35139. (A facsimile of this was published by Scolar Press in 1975. A full transcription is forthcoming from Century-Hutchinson.)

GWM – Gilbert White Museum collection, The Wakes, Selborne.

HL – The Henshaw papers, bMS Eng 731 Houghton Library, Harvard University. (A large collection of White family papers.)

HRO – Hampshire Record Office, Winchester, Hampshire. (Selborne parish records.)

JM – John Mulso, *The Letters to Gilbert White of Selborne*, ed. Rashleigh Holt-White, 1906.

LL – *The Life and Letters of Gilbert White*, ed. Rashleigh Holt-White, 2 volumes, 1901.

MCA – Magdalen College Archives, Oxford. (Papers concerning the manor and parish of Selborne.)

NHS – The standard published text of: Gilbert White *The Natural History and Antiquities of Selborne*, 1789. (A facsimile was published by Scolar Press in 1970.)

NJ – Gilbert White, *The Naturalist's Journals*, British Library Add. MS NJ BL 31846–51. (A full transcription of the journals is forthcoming from Century-Hutchinson.)

Selborne – various editions of The Natural History, indicated by the name of the editor.

TB – Gilbert White, *The Natural History and Antiquities of Selborne*, ed. Thomas Bell, 2 volumes, 1877. (An important edition which also contains numerous letters, poems, account books, etc.)

TP – Manuscript letters from Gilbert White to Thomas Pennant, British Library Add. MS 35138.

Notes and References

1 INTRODUCTION – LEGACIES AND LEGENDS

1. James Russell Lowell, 'My Garden Acquaintance', in *My Study Windows*, 1871.
2. 4 June 1785, NJ.
3. Samuel Johnson, *A Journey to the Western Isles of Scotland* (1775), ed. R.W. Chapman, 1924.
4. Virginia Woolf, 'White's Selborne', in *The Captain's Death Bed*, 1950.
5. Mark Daniels, introduction to *Selborne*, 1983.
6. Edward Thomas, 'Gilbert White' in *A Literary Pilgrim in England*, 1917.
7. See Michael Rosenthal, *Constable: the Painter and his Landscape*, 1983.
8. *New Monthly Magazine*, Dec. 1830, vol. 29, p. 566.
9. James Fisher, introduction to *Selborne*, 1941.
10. James Russell Lowell, *Latest Literary Essays and Addresses*, 1891.
11. John Burroughs, 'Gilbert White's Book', in *Indoor Studies*, 1895, and 'Gilbert White Again', in *Literary Values*, 1903.
12. Edward A. Martin, *A Bibliography of Gilbert White*, 1934.
13. J. Wright, *'Saint' Gilbert*, 1909.
14. See Edmund Blunden, *Nature in English Literature*, 1929; Cecil Emden, *Gilbert White in his Village*, Oxford, 1956; H.J. Massingham, *Selborne*, 1938; E.M. Nicholson, *Selborne*, 1929; Anthony Rye, *Gilbert White and his Selborne*, 1970; W.S. Scott, *White of Selborne*, 1946.
15. John Ray, *The Wisdom of God Manifested in the Works of Creation*, 1691; William Derham, *Physico-theology*, 1711–12. See also, Charles Raven, *John Ray, Naturalist*, 1950, for an excellent analysis of physico-theology.
16. Rye, see note 14 above.
17. See Charles Dixon, *The Migration of Birds*, 1892.

2 'A PLACE OF RESPONSES OR ECHOES'

1. Letter 6, AS.
2. William Cobbett, *Rural Rides*, ed. George Woodcock, 1967.
3. James Mudie, in *Selborne*, ed. Edward Blyth, 1836.
4. Letter X to Thomas Pennant, NHS.
5. Parish Register 1703, 32 M 66 PR, HRO.
6. *The Sixth Report of the Commissioners appointed to enquire into the state and condition of the Woods, Forest, etc. of the Crown*, 1790.
7. Letter V to Thomas Pennant, NHS.

8. See J.E. Gover, *Hampshire Place Names*, 1961, manuscript in HRO, and Eilert Ekwall, *The Concise Oxford Dictionary of English Place Names*, 4th edition, 1960.

9. Letters 7 to 25, AS.

10. GW to Sam Barker, 2 Sept. 1778. LL vol. II p. 29.

11. E.M. Yates, 'Selborne and Wolmer Forest', in *Selborne Association Newsletter*, 2 Oct. 1978.

12. 132/27 MCA.

13. Selborne 397, MCA and also C 33/332 fo 143, Public Record Office.

14. Miscellaneous correspondence with tenants, MCA, and also 135/107, MCA.

15. Survey and Terrier of Selborne Lands, 1793, CP 3/18, MCA.

16. Ibid.

17. Court Books, 1726–91, V 56–60, MCA.

18. Ibid. and R. Haywood, 'Wood Rights in Selborne', in *Selborne Association Newsletter*, 3 Feb. 1979.

19. Arthur Young, *A Six Weeks Tour through the Southern Counties*, 1768.

20. A. and W. Driver, *General View of the Agriculture of the County of Hants*, 1794.

21. Charles Vancouver, *General View of the Agriculture of Hampshire*, 1810.

22. Gilbert White, 'Answers to the several questions respecting the parish of Selborne', 193, HL.

23. Letter V to Thomas Pennant, NHS.

24. Vestry Accounts, 32 M 66 PUI, HRO.

25. Cobbett, see note 2 above.

3 WIDENING HORIZONS

1. LL vol. I p. 31.

2. See, for instance, V.H.H. Green, *A History of Oxford University*, 1974, and Christopher Wordsworth, *Social Life in the English Universities*, 1873.

3. Joseph Warton, *Companion to the Guide*, 1760.

4. C.L. Shadwell, *Registrum Orielense*, 1893.

5. Joseph Warton (ed.), *Works of Vergilius Maro*, 1763. See also Edmund Gosse, 'Two Pioneers of Romanticism', in *Proceedings of the British Academy*, 1915, for a critical assessment of the Warton brothers' influence.

6. Warton, see note 3 above.

7. 18 July 1744, JM.

8. 8 Oct. 1744, JM.
9. 6 June 1751, JM.
10. 17 July 1749, JM.
11. 30 Aug. 1750, JM.
12. H. Chapone, *Posthumous Works* (with a 'Life drawn up by her own Family'), 1807.
13. Account Book, 1747, Oriel College Library.
14. LL vol. I p. 49.
15. 27 Oct. 1746, and 21 Aug. 1747, JM.
16. GW to John White, 9 and 16 April 1746, 102, 103, HL.
17. GW to Thomas White, 24 June 1776, LL vol. I p.321.
18. R. Butcher to (GW?), 17 HL.
19. LL vol. I p. 45.
20. John White to Butcher, 18 Aug. 1746, 211 HL.
21. 1 Aug. 1746, JM.
22. 30 Aug. 1750, JM.
23. Ibid.
24. Version in *Selborne*, ed. Frank Buckland, 1880.

4 THE HOME GROUND

1. David Standing, *The Wakes Garden: a Short Guide*, Selborne, 1985.
2. 11 April 1750, JM.
3. *The Guardian*, No. 173, 29 Sept. 1713.
4. A facsimile exists, edited by John Clegg and published by the Scolar Press in 1975. A full transcription is to be published by Century-Hutchinson in 1986.
5. Philip Miller, *The Gardeners Dictionary*, 3rd edition, 1737.
6. *Gentleman's Magazine*, June 1783, also in LL vol.I p. 50.
7. Account Book 1758, GWM.
8. John Harvey, *Early Gardening Catalogues*, 1972.
9. 29 Jan. 1752, JM.
10. 28 March 1752, JM.
11. Account Books, 1752–53, TB vol II.
12. 27 Jan. 1753, JM.
13. Account Book, 1752, TB vol. II p. 323.
14. 4 Aug. 1753, JM.
15. 4 Nov. 1751, JM.
16. 26 Mar. 1754, *et al.* JM.
17. 23 April 1756 and 4 Oct. 1754, JM.
18. John White to GW, 10 Jan. 1759, LL vol.I p. 110.
19. 222, HL. There is extant a curious poem – 'On the difference

between an ancient and a modern hermitage' – which is presumed to have been written by John in Gibraltar in 1758. This was the year the Whites erected on the Hanger the rustic summerhouse they called the Hermitage, and the poem's theme is a rather cynical discussion of how the original function of such retreats had declined. It is not easy to square such an up-to-the-minute knowledge of what was happening in Selborne with John's ostracism by his family. But if the poem has been correctly attributed, some of its sections do suggest that John was harbouring rather bitter feelings about his exile and enforced hardship:

> Some Ages ago when a Man was inclin'd
> To retreat from the Trifles which busy Mankind
> Bid adieu to all Business, Folly, Care,
> And devote himself wholly to Fasting and Pray'r,
> He retir'd to a Mountain, found, or made him a Cave,
> And shap'd out his Table, his Bed, and his Grave.
> Drank nothing but Water, eat nothing but Roots . . .

> But in these modern time 'tis a different matter,
> Our hermits can't live upon Roots and plain Water.
> When they have a mind to erect them a hut,
> They pick out the pleasantest place can be got,
> They stack it with Burgundy, Claret, Rhenish
> And with Tongue, Ham and Chicken, their bodies replenish
> But the D--l a bit do they e'er think of pray'r.
> They are wholly ta'en up with the Gay and the Fair.
> Each Hermit the praise of some charmer rehearses,
> To whom he writes sonnets and copies of verses . . .

> But the Reason of this any Person may guess –
> Then tell me my friend, of these Hermits would you
> Choose to live as the Old or the Modern ones do?
> Answer: Why faith as the Moderns, and I think so would you.

20. LL vol.I p. 94.
21. 19 March 1757, JM.
22. 13 July 1758, JM.
23. Andrew Clark, *The Colleges of Oxford*, 1891.
24. 29 Nov. 1758, JM.
25. Quoted in 'Gilbert White's Fellowship', in *Selborne Magazine*, vol. 25, 1914.

26. LL vol.I pp. 98–108, vol. II pp. 43–8.
27. Survey and Terrier of Selborne Lands, 1793, CP 3/18, MCA.

5 GREEN RETREATS

1. 2 Nov. 1758, GK.
2. 13 April 1759, GK.
3. 13 Jan. 1761, JM.
4. 24 Jan. 1761, GK.
5. Horace Walpole, *Anecdotes of Painting in England*, ed. J. Dallaway, 1828.
6. 21 May 1761, GK.
7. Letter XLVI to Barrington, NHS.
8. Ibid.
9. See A.E.C. Kennedy, *Steven Hales, DD, FRS*, 1929.
10. GW to Marsham, 25 Feb. 1791, LL vol. II p. 230.
11. For a full discussion of changing attitudes towards animals' rights and welfare, see chapter IV 'Compassion for Brute Creation' in Keith Thomas, *Man and the Natural World*, 1983.
12. 9 Oct. 1762, JM.
13. See LL vol. I pp. 129–38.
14. GW to Catharine Battie, 88 HL. The manuscript note contains 15 kisses, inscribed in crucifixes or daggers.
15. 28 July, 1763, GK.
16. LL vol. I p. 135.
17. LL vol. I p. 136.
18. 3 Oct. 1763, JM.
19. Ibid.
20. 7 Dec. 1763, JM.
21. 6 Jan. 1764, JM.
22. TB vol.I p. 501.
23. 24 June, 1765, JM.
24. 'Sir' John Hill, *The British Herbal*, 1755; John Ray, *Synopsis methodica stirpium Britannicarum*, 3rd edition, ed. J.J. Dillenius, 1724; William Hudson, *Flora Anglica*, 1762 (the first English flora to use Linnaean names).
25. Gilbert White, *Flora Selborniensis*, 1766. A facsimile was published by the Selborne Society in 1911.
26. 25 April 1766, JM.
27. 20 Oct. 1767, GK.

6 A MAN OF LETTERS

1. 13 Oct. 1767, JM.

Notes and References

2. Ibid.
3. Ibid.
4. GW to John White, 29 March 1774, LL vol. I p.245.
5. 10 Aug. 1767, TP.
6. Thomas Pennant, *The Literary Life, by Himself*, 1793.
7. Ibid. Pennant was also a great writer to the papers, and was the author of an extraordinary, and rather prurient, note to the *General Evening Post* about the fashion among young ladies for masculine clothes that followed the one for rustic dress (see page 92):

   > Miss Dorothy ... with a great yawn flung her arms over her head, and her legs a yard before her, and informed us, it was dressing time: then pulling her watch out of, I believe, tight leathern breeches, acquainted us, that it was half past two; and returned it to its place with a most officer-like air ... My niece Elizabeth in defence of this new mode, says, that its [the watch's] motions are considerably altered since it has experienced a new situation. No wonder, since it had quitted the temperate for the torrid zone.

8. Thomas Pennant, *A Tour of Scotland*, 1769.
9. Robert Plot, *The Natural History of Oxfordshire*, 1677. A printed sheet of preliminary *Enquiries* was circulated in 1670, as well as being included in the book.
10. W.P. Jones, 'The Vogue of Natural History in England, 1750–1770', in *Annals of Science*, 1937.
11. Letter X to Pennant, NHS.
12. Preface to NJ.
13. Benjamin Stillingfleet, *Miscellaneous tracts, including The Calendar of Flora*, 1755
14. Originally 12 May, 1770, TP, but published as Letter XXVIII (March 1770) to Pennant, NHS. The letter continues with some recollection of the moose while it was still alive:

   > This poor creature had at first a female companion of the same species, which died the spring before. In the same garden was a young stag, or red deer, between whom and this moose it was hoped that there might have been a breed; but their inequality of height must always have been a bar to any commerce of the amorous kind.

15. 30 March 1768, TP.
16. GW to Joseph Banks, 21 April 1768, TB vol. II p. 241.

17. 2 June 1768, JM.
18. 26 July 1768, JM.
19. 28 Feb. 1769, TP.
20. Ronald Blythe, 'An Inherited Perspective', in *From the Headlands*, 1982.
21. 8.Oct. 1768, TP.
22. 28 Feb. 1769, TP. Published as Letter XXIII to Pennant, NHS.
23. 2 Jan. 1769, TP.
24. Letter XXII to Pennant, 2 July 1769, NHS.
25. Letter XXXI to Pennant, 14 Sept. 1770, NHS.
26. Letter XXV to Pennant, 30 Aug. 1769. NHS.
27. 10 Aug. 1769, NJ.
28. 1 Sept. 1769, TP.
29. Daines Barrington, *Miscellanies*, 1781.
30. Ibid.
31. Charles Lamb, 'The Old Benchers of the Inner Temple', in *London Magazine*, 1821.
32. Letter IV to Barrington, 19 Feb. 1770, NHS.
33. Letter V to Barrington, 12 April 1770, NHS.
34. 12 Jan. 1771, TP.
35. 28 Nov. 1768, TP.
36. Ibid.
37. 12 May 1770, TP.
38. GW to John White, 1769–1772, 108–121 HL. See also the discussion of the correspondence in Paul Foster, 'The Gibraltar Correspondence of Gilbert White', in *Notes and Queries*, 1985, ns vol. 32 nos 2–4 (which also include transcriptions of the letters).
39. GW to John White, 6 Nov. 1770, 114 HL.
40. 12 Jan. 1771, TP.
41. 22 Sept. 1771, NJ.
42. GW to John White, 25 Jan. 1771, 115 HL.
43. 19 July 1771, TP.
44. 26 Dec. 1773, JM.
45. 27 Dec. 1770, JM.
46. 11 July 1772, NJ.
47. 22 Aug. 1772, NJ.
48. 2–15 Nov. 1771, NJ.
49. John White to GW, 1 Aug. 1772, 217 HL.
50. 10 Jan 1773, JM.
51. Selborne Parish Register 1773, 3M M 66 PR 4–14; HRO.
52. GW to John White, 2 Aug, 1773, LL vol. I p. 218.
53. GW to John White, 11 Sept. 1773, LL vol. I p. 222.

54. GW to John White, 1 Oct. 1773, LL vol. I p. 227.
55. GW to John White, 2 Nov. 1773, LL vol. I p. 231.
56. Letter XVII to Barrington, NHS.
57. Ibid.

7 'WATCHING NARROWLY'

1. GW to John White, 2 Nov. 1773, LL vol. I p. 233.
2. Gilbert White, 'An Account of the House-Martin, or Martlet', in *Philosophical Trasactions of the Royal Society*, vol. LXIV, part 1, 1774.
3. 15 Feb. 1774, JM.
4. Gilbert White, 'An Account of the House-Swallow, Swift, and Sand-Martin', in *Philosophical Transactions*, vol. LXV, 1775.
5. Preface to Letter XVI to Barrington, NHS.
6. Letter XVI to Barrington, NHS.
7. Letter XVIII to Barrington, NHS.
8. GW to John White, 12 Jan. 1774, LL vol. I p. 238.
9. Letter XXI to Barrington, NHS.
10. GW to John White, 15 July 1774, LL vol. I p. 258.
11. Letter XXI to Barrington, NHS.
12. Daines Barrington, *Miscellanies*, 1781.
13. Letter XL to Pennant, NHS.
14. GW to John White, 29 March 1774, LL vol. I p. 244.
15. GW to John White, 29 April 1774, LL vol. I p. 250.
16. GW to John White, 15 July 1774, LL vol. I p. 258.
17. E.M. Nicholson, introduction to *Selborne*, 1929.
18. 14 Jan. 1774, NJ.
19. 15 Feb. 1774, JM.
20. 'Jack' White to Samuel Barker, 6 April 1774, LL vol. I p. 247.
21. Letter XLV to Barrington, NHS.
22. 15 Feb. 1774, JM.
23. GW to John White, 18 June 1774, LL vol. I p. 255.
24. John White to GW [Aug] 1774, LL vol. I p. 263.
25. Personal communication from Charles Clark. The case concerned, Donaldson vs Beckett (4. Bur. 2408), had come before the Lords early in 1774, and had confirmed that the Copyright Act of 1709 (8. Anne chapter 19) had extinguished, or 'merged' as it was put, the old common law of copyright. This had been based on the assumption that the author of any literary composition and his or her assignees had the sole right of printing and publishing the composition in perpetuity;

The 1709 enactment reduced this to a period of fourteen years after the author's death, with a maximum additional fourteen years if he or she was still alive.

26. GW to John White, 9 March 1775, LL vol. I p. 279.
27. Her best-seller was *Letters on the Improvement of the Mind*, 1772.
28. GW to Anne Barker, 26 Nov. 1774, LL vol. I p. 273.
29. 17 Nov. 1774, JM.
30. 18 March 1775, NJ.
31. 8 July 1775, JM.
32. GW to John White, 12 Aug. 1775, LL vol. I p. 288.
33. Ibid. p. 289.
34. Rotha Clay, *Samuel Hieronymus Grimm*, 1941.
35. See his Commonplace Book in GWM.
36. GW to John White, 30 Jan. 1776. LL vol. I p. 299.
37. GW to John White, 9 Aug. 1776, LL vol. I p. 326.
38. GW to John White, 2 Nov. 1776, LL vol. II p. 4.
39. GW to John White, 11 Sept. 1777, LL vol. II p. 16.
40. GW to John White, 31 Oct. 1777, LL vol. II p. 18.
41. Ibid. p. 18.
42. This introduction, edited by W.H. Mullens, was published as a pamphlet by the Selborne Society in 1913.
43. Anthony Rye, *Gilbert White and his Selborne*, 1970.
44. 14 Jan. 1776, NJ.
45. Letter LXII to Barrington, NHS.
46. 26 March 1776, JM.
47. 16 July 1776, JM.
48. See GW to Sam Barker, 1 Nov. 1776, LL vol. II p. 3.
49. GW to John White, 9 Aug. 1776, LL vol. I p. 326.
50. 30 Nov. 1777, JM.

8 A PARISH RECORD

1. 12 Oct. 1776, NJ.
2. 16 Oct. 1776, NJ.
3. GW to John White, 2 Nov. 1776, LL vol. II p. 6.
4. 19 Aug. 1777, JM.
5. 4 Nov. 1777, NJ.
6. Letter XLII to Barrington, NHS.
7. GW to Sam Barker, 6 May 1790, LL vol. II p. 216.
8. GW to Molly White, 19 Oct. 1778, LL vol. II p. 31.
9. GW to Molly White, 17 April 1779, LL vol. II p. 34.
10. GW to Molly White, 31 Mar. 1780, LL vol. II p. 48.

11. 24 April 1780, DB (partially published as Letter L, NHS).
12. 27 May 1780, NJ.
13. 28 Mar. 1782, NJ.
14. Letter from Timothy, LL vol. II p. 125. There is a delightful book about Timothy – and incidentally one of the most perceptive essays ever written on White – by Sylvia Townsend Warner, called *The Portrait of a Tortoise*, first published in 1946 and re-issued in 1981.
15. GW to Barbara White, 21 Sept. 1780, 93 HL.
16. GW to Molly White, 30 Sept. 1780, LL vol. II p. 55.
17. GW to Molly White, 13 Nov. 1781, LL vol. II p. 75.
18. Molly White to Thomas Holt White 24 Aug. 1779, 241 HL.
19. Court Books, V59, V60, MCA.
20. Selborne Parish Registers (1780) 32 M 66 PR 4–11, HRO. A rough cross made of local yew branches regularly hangs above the choir in Selborne church.
21. See Harry Hopkins, *The Long Affray: the Poaching Wars in Britain*, 1985.
22. 24 April 1780, DB (published partially as Letter XLIX, NHS).
23. Ibid.
24. Letter LV to Barrington, NHS. Current beliefs about the whereabouts of martins when they have ceased returning to the nest to roost are very different. Chris Mead of the British Trust for Ornithology believes that all the evidence points to martins roosting on the wing, like swifts, and that this is their custom in winter too. No night-time assemblies have ever been found in the summer months here; and, despite the ringing of 100,000 martins in this country, only one has ever been recovered from their wintering quarters in Africa, which would be a remarkably low figure if they were in the habit of coming to earth regularly. Gilbert, I am sure, would have been delighted by the idea of short-term 'aerial torpidity'.
25. 24–31 Aug. 1781, NJ.
26. 5 June 1782, NJ.
27. 11 May 1782, NJ.
28. GW to Sam Barker, 3 Nov 1774. LL Vol. I p. 269.
29. John Arthos, *The Language of Natural Description in Eighteenth Century Poetry*, 1949. See also Joseph Warton's 1763 edition of Virgil and John Aikin, *An Essay on the Application of Natural History to Poetry*, 1777.
30. GW to Churton, 4 Jan. 1783, LL vol. II p.89.

31. 2 June 1782, JM.
32. 13 Feb. 1779, JM.
33. 2 June 1782, JM.
34. Henry White's journals, extracts in 'Notes on the Parishes of Fyfield', ed. R. Clutterbuck, n.d.
35. Letter LXV to Barrington, NHS.
36. GW to Molly White, 13 Feb. 1784, LL vol. II p.113.
37. 'On the dark, still, etc', TB, vol. I p. 504.
38. GW to Molly White, 19 April 1784, LL vol. II p.120.
39. GW to Molly White, 17 June 1784, GWM.
40. 6 June 1784, NJ.
41. 1 Sept. 1784, NJ.
42. 16 Oct. 1784, NJ.
43. GW to Anne Barker, 19 Oct. 1784, LL vol. II p.134.
44. Richard Jefferies, preface to Round About A Great Estate, 1880.
45. GW to Anne Barker, 19 Oct. 1784, LL vol. II p.136.
46. Selborne Parish Registers (from 1784), 32 M 66 PR series, HRO.
47. GW to Sam Barker, 17 April 1786, LL vol. II p.157.
48. Selborne Highway Accounts (from 1774) 32 M 66 PS I, HRO.
49. Henry White, see note 34 above.
50. 1 Feb. 1785, NJ.
51. Richard Jefferies, introduction to Selborne, 1887.
52. Letter XXVII to Barrington, NHS.
53. Molly White to GW, 13 Feb. 1783, GWM.
54. Georgiana White, Memorandum Book, 1813, 67 HL.
55. 12 Dec. 1789, NJ.
56. George Sturt, Lucy Bettesworth, 1913.
57. Virginia Woolf, 'White's Selborne', in The Captain's Death Bed, 1950. See also chapter 3 of W.J. Keith, The Rural Tradition, 1974.
58. GW to Molly White, 26 Nov. 1787, LL vol. II p. 172.
59. GW to Molly White, 13 March 1788, LL vol. II p. 181.
60. GW to Sam Barker, 8 Jan. 1788, LL vol. II p. 177.
61. 19 Mar 1788, NJ.
62. GW to Benjamin White, jnr, Feb [1788] LL vol. II p. 177.
63. GW to Churton, 4 Aug, 1788, LL vol. II p. 185.
64. 5 Nov. 1788, NJ.
65. 'To Myself Commencing Author', AS p. 189.
66. 15 Dec. 1788, JM.
67. Henry White's Journal, 1788. Bodleian Library: Misc English Mss. C 154.

68. LL vol. II p. 194.
69. GW to Molly White, 14 Sep. 1791, 149 HL.
70. Montagu to GW, 27 June 1789, LL vol. II p. 203.
71. Marsham to GW, 24 July 1790, TB vol. II p. 246.
72. GW to Marsham, 13 Aug. 1790, TB vol. II p. 249.
73. GW to Marsham, 18 Jan. 1791, TB vol. II p. 258.
74. 7 Sept. 1791 NJ.
75. GW to Marsham, 19 Dec. 1791, TB vol. II p. 272.
76. Marsham to GW, 12 Feb. 1792, TB vol. II p. 276.
77. GW to Marsham, 13 Aug. 1790, TB vol. II p. 251.
78. See also: Arthur Young, *The Example of France: a Warning to Britain*, 1793.
79. GW to Marsham, 2 Jan. 1793, TB vol. II p. 297.
80. GW to Benjamin White, 19 Feb. 1793, LL vol II p. 261.
81. Parish Register, 1789 32 M 66 PR, HRO.
82. James White to GW, 12 Feb. 1793, LL vol. II p. 259.
83. GW to Marsham, 20 March 1792, LL vol. II p. 242.
84. 27 Aug 1792, NJ.
85. 29 May 1793, NJ.
86. GW to Marsham, 15 June 1793, TB vol. II p. 301.
87. LL vol. II p. 271.

EPILOGUE
1. LL vol. II p. 272.
2. Edward Martin, *A Bibliography of Gilbert White*, 1934.
3. See J.L. and B. Hammond, *The Village Labourer*, 1911, and E.J. Hobsbawm and G. Rude, *Captain Swing*, 1969.

INDEX

'Account of the House-Martin, or Martlet' (essay), 138
Addison, Thomas, 53
Aikin, John, 188, 217
animals: 18th-century attitudes to, 83–5, 210
Arthos, John, 188
Auden, W.H., 6
Augustinian Priory, Selborne, 26–8

Baker, Harriot (Anne's cousin), 88, 91
Baker's Hill, Selborne, 52, 56
ballooning, 194–6
Banks, Sir Joseph: and Pennant, 107, 112; GW invites to Selborne, 112; voyage, 115, 134, 196
Barker, Anne (née White; GW's sister): marriage, 20; GW visits at Lyndon, 79; and GW's dislike of winter, 154; at Ringmer, 157; visits Selborne, 174, 189
Barker, Becky (Benjamin White's daughter), 174
Barker, Elizabeth (Anne's daughter), 189
Barker, Jenny (Benjamin White's daughter), 174
Barker, Mary (Anne's daughter), 157, 189
Barker, Sally (Anne's daughter), 157
Barker, Sam (Anne's son): letter from GW on monks, 27; correspondence with GW, 131; and Jack White's letter on landslip, 148; at Ringmer, 157; GW recommends poetry to, 188; and Selborne shortages, 197; transcribes part of Natural History, 203; and death of Henry White, 207
Barker, Thomas (Anne's husband), 20, 44
Barrington, Daines: presents Naturalist's Journal to GW, 109–10, 112, 119; suggests GW write book, 119, 122, 124, 127; character and beliefs, 119–22; correspondence with GW, 121, 127, 134–5, 138, 146, 172, 183, 199, 203–4; Lamb on, 121; and bird hibernation, 144; and Hawkley landslip, 149; and tortoise, 177; 'false letters' in Natural History, 203; Miscellanies, 121
Basingstoke (Hampshire), 34
bats, 108, 127, 193, 198
Battie, Anne (William's daughter), 88, 92, 94
Battie, Catharine (Kitty; William's daughter), 88–94
Battie, Philadelphia (William's daughter), 88, 92, 94

Battie, William, 88
beech trees, 24
bees, 199
Benham, Thomas, 57, 200
Bentham, Edward, 36
Bentham, Jeremy, 85
Berger, Alexander: Calendar, 110
Berriman, John, 61
Berriman, Robert, 175, 182
Bin's Pond, Woolmer Forest, 25
birds: shooting of, 86–7; procured for G.W., 111, 118, 183, 200–1; song and sounds, 116, 132; migration, 116–18, 126; Barrington on altitude of, 120; preservation of specimens, 125; flight movement, 173; see also individual species
bitterns, 147
Black Acts, 182
Black Spring (1771), 126
black-winged stilts, 183
Blackburn (Lancashire), 130, 133
Blake, William, 85
Blanchard, Jean, 193–4
Blunden, Edmund, 10
Blyth, Edward, 18
Blythe, Ronald, 115
Bostal (Hangar path), 179–80
botany: GW develops interest in, 98–102
Bradley (Hampshire), 88
Bradley, Richard: The Gentleman and Gardener's Kalendar, 55
Breckhurst, John, 56
Bristol, 68
Bristow, Dr D., 61, 69, 72
Bunyan, John, 5
Burbey, John, 175, 178, 182, 193, 200, 204, 215
Burbey, Mary, 216
Burney, Charlotte Anne, 41
Burroughs, John, 8
Butcher (attorney), 46
Butler, Richard, 200

Calendar of Flora, A see Garden Kalendar, The
candles, 199–200
Cane, Rev. Basil (Dorothea's husband), 19, 74, 89–90
Cane, Dorothea (née White; GW's aunt), 19
carder beetle, 129
Carpenter, John and Mrs, 57

Index

Index

Index

Index

Index

Index